DESIGNING IN DARK TIMES

DESIGNING IN DARK TIMES/RADICAL THINKERS IN DESIGN
edited by Clive Dilnot and Eduardo Staszowski.

These two series push at the boundaries of contemporary design thinking, responding to the world's current and pressing social, economic, and environmental challenges and crises.

Exploring the interaction of design with critical thought and social research and presenting both modes of thought (models, concepts, arguments) and courses of action (scenarios, strategies, proposals, works), titles engage polemically with the opportunities now presented to rethink what acting in the world and designing might be.

FORTHCOMING TITLES IN THE SERIES

Politics of the Everyday, by Ezio Manzini
Acting in Dark Times: The Urgency of the Possible, by Clive Dilnot
Under Attack! Design Lessons from the Global South, by Zoy Anastassakis and Marcos Martins
Making Trouble: *Design and Material Activism*, by Otto von Busch
Designs to Reshape Humanity: Integrity and Cunning in the Anthropocene, by Ann Light
Biocentric: Designing for all of Life, by Martin Avila
Relationality, by Arturo Escobar, Michal Osterweil, and Kriti Sharma

RADICAL THINKERS IN DESIGN

designing designing, by John Chris Jones
Wild Things: The Material Culture of Everyday Life, by Judy Attfield
Defuturing: A New Design Philosophy, by Tony Fry
Design Noir: *The Secret Life of Electronic Objects*, by Tony Dunne and Fiona Raby
The Disobedience of Design, by Gui Bonsiepe, edited by Lara Penin
Architecture as Cultural Criticism, by Kenneth Frampton, edited by Miodrag Mitrašinović

DESIGNING IN DARK TIMES
AN ARENDTIAN LEXICON

Edited by
Eduardo Staszowski and Virginia Tassinari

With additional contributions by Hannah Arendt,
Richard J. Bernstein, Kenneth Frampton, and
Martha Rosler

BLOOMSBURY VISUAL ARTS
LONDON · NEW YORK · OXFORD · NEW DELHI · SYDNEY

BLOOMSBURY VISUAL ARTS
Bloomsbury Publishing Plc
50 Bedford Square, London, WC1B 3DP, UK
1385 Broadway, New York, NY 10038, USA

BLOOMSBURY, BLOOMSBURY VISUAL ARTS and the Diana logo are trademarks of
Bloomsbury Publishing Plc

First published in Great Britain 2021

Cover design by Andrew LeClair and Chris Wu of Wkshps

A catalogue record for this book is available from the British Library.

A catalog record for this book is available from the Library of Congress.

ISBN: HB: 978-1-3500-7026-4
PB: 978-1-3500-7025-7
eBook: 978-1-3500-7027-1
ePDF: 978-1-3500-7028-8

Series: Designing in Dark Times

Typeset by Newgen KnowledgeWorks Pvt. Ltd., Chennai, India
Printed and bound in Great Britain

To find out more about our authors and books visit www.bloomsbury.com
and sign up for our newsletter.

Contents

Series Foreword:
Designing in Dark Times

Responding to the current and wide-ranging systemic, social, economic, political, and environmental challenges we face, the aim of this new series is to bring together a series of short, polemical texts that address these crises and their inherent possibilities. Understanding that the old division between the theoretical focus of the sciences and the practical stance integral to designing, making, and shaping the world is dissolving, *Designing in Dark Times* explores new ways of acting and knowing concerning the artificial. Identified by a refusal of resignation to what-is and by the equal necessity and urgency of developing new models of the possible, the series works to present both modes of thought (models, concepts, arguments) and courses of action (scenarios, strategies, proposals, works) at all levels from the local and the micro (the situation) to the global and the macro (the universal). The aim is to push the boundaries of both design and thought, to make each more capable of opening genuine possibilities for thinking and acting otherwise and thus of better facing, and facing down, the myriad failures of the present. Rethinking the relation between justice and making, and between material human needs and the means and modes of how these can be realized, *Designing in Dark Times* is conceived as a contribution to the wider necessities of dealing with a vulnerable precarious world; of establishing project not profit as the basis of action; and of building the bases for wide-ranging emancipatory politics. As the world descends into crisis these books seek to offer, in small ways, a counterview. Against the instrumental they use the fact that design is *also* a means of articulating hitherto unforeseen possibilities—for subjects as much as for the world—to show how at base it offers irreplaceable capabilities for thinking and acting well in the artificial. In so doing, they point us toward ways of reversing some of the negative and destructive tendencies threatening to engulf the world.

Preface: On Hannah Arendt
Kenneth Frampton

*Editorial Note: As a way of connecting Hannah Arendt's
thinking in the decades after the publication of* The Human
Condition *(1958) and the issues opened in this volume we have
placed as a preface this brief appreciation of the impact of her
presence and thought by the architectural historian and critic
Kenneth Frampton. Ware Professor of Architecture at Columbia
University since 1973 and author of, among other works,*
Modern Architecture: A Critical History *(1980: 4th ed. 2007; 5th
ed. in preparation),* Studies in Tectonic Culture: The Poetics of
Construction *(1995) and* A Genealogy of Modern Architecture:
Comparative Critical Analysis of Built Form *(2015), Frampton
attended Arendt's lectures at The New School in the years
she was University Professor in Philosophy (1967–75). His
volume of critical essays* Labor, Work and Architecture *(2002)
is dedicated to her memory, while the opening essay of that
volume,* "The Status of Man and Status of His Objects" *(1979),
remains the most extended mediation on what Arendt's thought
offers to architectural thinking and more widely to how we can
think the relationship between persons, politics, and making.*[1]
*The notes below are extracted from a recent interview with
Kenneth Frampton by Thomas McQuillan.*[2]

McQuillan: You suggest in the "Philosophical Excursus" to *A
Genealogy of Modern Architecture* that your critical method
with respect to the analysis of the case studies is based on
your reading of Hannah Arendt's *The Human Condition*, that
is to say, her distinction between "work" and "labor," and the
corresponding character of public and private spaces. How does
Arendt's thesis underlie your view of architecture?

---

1   Frampton's essay on Hannah Arendt is in *Labour, Work and Architecture*
    (London: Phaidon, 2002), 15–42.
2   The interview was conducted in March 2016. The full version is available
    online at *Architectural Histories*, the open access journal of the European
    Architectural History Network (EAHN). https://journal.eahn.org/
    articles/10.5334/ah.231/.

Frampton: I just have to confess that I'll never recover from the thesis of her book. It was a total revelation about many things at once, like the idea of a spatial hierarchy, which maybe I could never articulate before, i.e., the relation between the public and the private, which determines much of the analysis in these case studies. From this I also develop the idea that the subject is formed to some extent by the space and that the "space of appearance" allows the subject to come into being in this sense—the subject—both as a unitary subject but also as a collective, family, group. So that the space itself, the articulation of hierarchy of space, is significant, that the meaning is built in into what the space can induce—not in a behavioristic sense that "this space will produce this behavior"—but in the sense that the space is an availability which may be consummated fully by the being.

Arendt's distinction between the public and the private corresponds to the two definitions of the word "architecture." In the Oxford English Dictionary, these are: (1) "the erection of edifices for human use" and (2) "the action and process of building." Process aligns with Arendt's idea that labor is process, while work can create something that is both memorable and durable. But what's beautiful about this concept is that it opens to different degrees of expression in a work between something that is commemorative or symbolic and other parts, even in the same building, which are much less so, and this makes possible a great range of expression.

McQuillan: I found the sentence where you paraphrase Arendt very beautiful:

> In this regard with respect to memory, the *homo faber* hypothetically creates a world that is not only useful and durable, but also beautiful and memorable, as opposed to the *animal laborans* who in the conviction that life is the highest good, seeks only to lengthen the span of life and make the act of living easier and more comfortable.[3]

---

3   Kenneth Frampton, "Towards a Critical Regionalism: Six Points
    for an Architecture of Resistance," in Hal Foster (ed.), *The Anti-
    Aesthetic: Essays on Postmodern Culture* (Seattle: Bay Press, 1983), 24.

It's incredibly precise with regard to its definition of power as something embedded in the memory. Such precision is fascinating in Arendt, given that in your search for the ontological, you might easily have gone back to Heidegger, whose sentences are often so muddy. Nonetheless, it seems that Arendt's idea of appearance can be traced back to Heidegger's idea of truth as unconcealment.

Frampton: And I think you can trace the same idea in Semper, in his notion of concealing and revealing, which clearly embodies a latent erotic aspect. However, Arendt argues in her final chapter, "The Victory of the *Animal Laborans*," that labor is all-pervasive today and that we consume our houses and cars like fruits of the earth, which will perish if they are not immediately eaten.

McQuillan: You mention that Arendt's work presages the commodification of the environment, and you say that this is of particular consequence for architecture and sustainability inasmuch as it categorically opposes a state of affairs in which the environment is constantly on the verge of being overwhelmed by the proliferation of "unrelated, amortizable free-standing objects."

Frampton: If the sustainability is not cultural, then it remains very fragile. You can't simply depend on a technological fix, a LEED standard or whatever. But durability itself is already a crucial form of sustainability, although it is somehow seen as disconnected. However, there is an aspect to commodification that wants to screen out all of this. As Antoine de Saint-Exupéry beautifully puts it—and I quote him in the front of *Studies in Tectonic Culture*—"We don't ask to be eternal beings. We only ask that things do not lose all their meaning."

Acknowledgments

In this book, our role as editors has been mainly an imprudent act of bringing together a community of designers and scholars of design and related fields who kindly accepted our invitation to respond to concepts and quotations drawn from Hannah Arendt's work and thereby to set up the basis of the lexicon. We would like to thank them here for their courage to engage with Arendt's thought to thinking about "Designing in Dark Times" and for their patience with our editorial process. Without them there would be no lexicon at all, so we give heartfelt thanks to Mariana Amatullo, Ahmed Ansari, Simone Ashby, James Auger, Martín Ávila, Nik Baerten, Jocelyn Bailey, Massimo Bianchini, Thomas Binder, Andrea Botero, Constantin Boym, Jamie Brassett, John A. Bruce, Pablo Calderón Salazar, Carla Cipolla, Chiara Del Gaudio, Elena De Nictolis, Clive Dilnot, Caroline Dionne, Carl DiSalvo, Arturo Escobar, Laura Forlano, Tony Fry, Alastair Fuad-Luke, Lorraine Gamman, Claudia Garduño García, Eric Gordon, Anke Gruendel, Joachim Halse, Julian Hanna, Jamer Hunt, Liesbeth Huybrechts, Christian Iaione, Tim Ingold, Michael Kaethler, Mahmoud Keshavarz, Eva Knutz, Sophie Krier, Outi Kuittinen, Tau U. Lenskjold, Stefano Maffei, Henry Mainsah, Ezio Manzini, Victor Margolin, Thomas Markussen, Sónia Matos, Shannon Mattern, Andrew Morrison, Aleksi Neuvonen, Dimeji Onafuwa, Macushla Robinson, Søren Rosenbak, Andrew Shea, Nidhi Srinivas, Radhika Subramaniam, Maurizio Teli, Mathilda Tham, Adam Thorpe, Cameron Tonkinwise, Otto von Busch, Anne-Marie Willis, Susan Yelavich, and Francesco Zurlo.

In this project we were also fortunate to have the support of the *Designing in Dark Times* book series' Editorial Working Group who supported us in peer-reviewing the contributions, providing us with many precious suggestions and enriching the overall project: Otto von Busch, Clive Dilnot, Caroline Dionne, Anke Gruendel, Victoria Hattam, Andrew LeClair (the designer of the book), Macushla Robinson, and Rashmi Viswanathan.

We would like to acknowledge the help and support of the *Designing in Dark Times* book series' Advisory Board, the Office of Research Support at The New School, and Rebecca Barden and Claire Constable at Bloomsbury who strongly believed in the project and supported it throughout the whole process. We would also like to say a special thanks to Macushla Robinson and Laura Wing, who supported us as managing editors in the different phases of this project.

Special gratitude goes to Martha Rosler for allowing us to reproduce *Reading Hannah Arendt (Politically, for an American in the 21st Century)*; to Richard J. Bernstein and Kenneth Frampton for their agreeing to allow for the republishing of their thoughts on Arendt; and to Jerome Kohn and Schocken Books for allowing us to reproduce Hannah Arendt's 1970 seminar on Imagination.

INTRODUCTION

Eduardo Staszowski and Virginia Tassinari

Part One: Hannah Arendt and Designing in Dark Times

> *But where the danger is, grows the saving power also*
>
> Friedrich Hölderlin

I. Designing in "Dark Times"

> *... history knows many periods of dark times in which the public realm has been obscured and the world become so dubious that people have ceased to ask any more of politics than that it show due consideration for their vital interests.*[1]

Political philosopher Hannah Arendt uses the idea of dark times for describing her contemporaneity: a time where *"the disorder and the hunger, the massacres and the slaughters, the outrage over injustices and the despair"*[2] rule. However, the term "in dark times"—in a broader sense—should not be understood exclusively as a reference to the monstrous atrocities of the twentieth century to which Arendt's writing responds. The evil in question goes beyond catastrophic events. She argues that these

> *are not what constitute the darkness. The darkness is what comes when the open, light spaces between people, the public spaces where people can reveal themselves, are shunned or avoided, the darkness is the hateful attitude toward the public realm, toward politics.*[3]

---

1 Hannah Arendt, *Men in Dark Times* (New York: Harcourt, Brace, [1955] 1993), 11.
2 Arendt, *Men in Dark Times*, viii.
3 Elisabeth Young-Bruehl, *Why Arendt Matters* (New Haven, CT: Yale University Press, 2006), 6.

This is, in many ways, also our own contemporaneity.

We are living in times that remind us in many ways of those described by Arendt more than fifty years ago. The novelist Franz Kafka, much praised by Arendt, describes this darkness using the image of a tunnel, a place where beginnings and ends are unclear, and where humans feel a sense of paralysis. In a situation like this, would it be better to just do nothing, or to act despite doubt? Here Arendt provides us some concrete indications on how to respond to these dark times, in a humble, and yet powerful, way. Refusing the cynical stance, and against the denial of knowledge or understanding of what is at stake, Arendt writes,

> *we have the right to expect some illumination, and that such illumination might well come less from theories and concepts than from the uncertain, flickering, and often weak light that some men and women, in their lives and their works, will kindle under almost all circumstances.*[4]

So, today, we ask, what forms might these illuminations take? If it is better to act—and clearly we must, or face disaster—how do we act? What does *action* mean in this context?

These are timely questions for those who live in dark times. Yet, what possibilities can unfold if these questions are directly addressed to professional designers? How can designers (re) act to dark times? More specifically, what does *action* mean for designing (which is itself already, of course, a mode of acting)? Designing, in the broadest definition of the term, has become indistinguishable from action in general, and professional designers are increasingly engaging in the public realm, exploring new models of action to transform our relationship with governments, cities, organizations, technologies, and natural systems. Can designing (action) be understood not just as praxis but also as thought, as reflective practice? One question for designing is whether designers' actions could today potentially possess this same "flickering" possibility to illuminate the present.

---

4   Young-Bruehl, *Why Arendt Matters*, ix.

Again, we might look to Arendt as a possible guide in this process. What does it mean to consider design's role in times of fear and uncertainty? Can her definition of "dark times" be helpful to understand these possibilities? How might Arendtian perspectives inform the work of designers as they attempt to shape the ways in which we act in the world?

The dark times through which Arendt lived did not stop her from theorizing a possibility for action. Far from being a naive optimist, she nonetheless declared that dark times can *also* be precious moments for developing an "activity of thought,"[5] where the thinking and action are deeply intertwined. This activity of thought is to her an intellectual praxis that individuals can articulate from within situations of despair, which has the potential to open new courses of action: it has a deeply transformative—and therefore political—potential. To her it is in those that seem the most hopeless[6] of times that something like an activity of thought, and therefore also the thinking of new forms of acting, also becomes possible. This is the reason why reading today's world through the lens of Arendt's notion of dark times is not a pessimistic operation. Instead, it brings some hope.

To think, where thought is a political activity, orientated to change, is something one must do with others, in dialogue with others. This is not an intellectually abstract activity but, rather, one that must inevitably lead to action, more specifically, a process that leads to action in the public realm.

Acting politically as well as acting through designing in these times means thus moving in this space of possibilities, where one can experience a freedom and creativity that can never happen in private. For this to take place a space of appearance is required: in other words, a politics. Every individual can find for himself or herself this space of freedom, and yet cannot find it alone. Designers are also granted this possibility. But the

---

5 Hannah Arendt, *Between Past and Future* (London: Penguin Books, 2007), 12.

6 "Only for the sake of the hopeless ones have we been given hope." Walter Benjamin, *Selected Writings vol. 1* (Cambridge: Belknap Press, 1996), 356.

transformative character of the processes and consequences of designing to begin something new can only be fully enacted when our individual understanding of our actions and our words becomes part of a discourse.

If it is true that the capacity to start something new, to begin, to do what is truly unexpected, is for Arendt the freedom that defines us as humans, it is also true that this freedom describes our own space of responsibility. Working on the possible *is* possible but has its own demands. The specific way in which designers can develop their own activities of thought—merging action and speech in their own reflective practices—gives them the potential to react to dark times and to lead to new beginnings. But it also brings responsibility with it. Designing needs to face this potential and undergo a serious reflection, *"an ontological shift that transforms how design is viewed, heard, felt, thought, understood, explained and done."*[7]

In *The Human Condition* Arendt says that dark times emerge from the loss of [public] realms where people can share their views and aspirations, their hope for brighter times. With the disappearance of the public realm, we are confined into a time of mystifications:

> *If it is the function of the public realm to throw light on the affairs of men by providing a space of appearances in which they can show in deed and word, for better and worse, who they are and what they can do, then darkness has come when this light is extinguished by "credibility gaps" and "invisible government," by speech that does not disclose what is but sweeps it under the carpet, by exhortations, moral and otherwise, that, under the pretext of upholding old truths, degrade all truth to meaningless triviality.*[8]

In the public realm, speech and action are for Arendt connected to one another. Speeches on common interests—in which the individuals acknowledge also their own private

---

7   Tony Fry, *A New Design Philosophy: An Introduction to Defuturing* (Sydney: UNSW Press, 1999), 7.

8   Arendt, *Men in Dark Times*, viii.

ones—are directed toward actions in the public, and the latter therefore result from conversations and negotiations on those common interests. When this intimate connection between private and public interests started to be mystified, consequently this understanding of speech and action also started to disappear together with the same public realm.

The disappearance of the public realm has serious consequences: not only does it undermine the possibility of the political, but it also leads to the loss of the completeness of the human condition. This weakening of the public makes such an easy target for totalitarianisms, where individuals—in their loneliness—decide to let the system—represented by authoritarians—control every aspect of their lives.

The idea that an individual can exist separately from other people is another myth: *"... men, not Man, live on the earth and inhabit the world."*[9] The political, as the in-between, the connector between persons, is at the core of the human condition. When the political is in place, we have weapons against the loneliness of individualism—which leads so often to totalitarianism:

> *The world lies between people, and this in-between ...*
> *is today the object of the greatest concern and the most*
> *obvious upheaval in almost all the countries of the globe.*[10]

Yet, this space "in-between" that forms the body politic(s) is little considered. What does it mean to take this in-between seriously, and to take it as the main concern of words and deeds?

For Arendt, to rethink the *in-between* is not only one of the possible tasks that intellectuals should undertake in dark times: it is the necessary (political) task. As she was conscious of the risk of a theoretical reflection that could not also be considered a political action, she preferred to be considered a political thinker rather than a philosopher. Deeply interested in the world she was living in, Arendt could not stand *"the philosophers' resignation*

---

9   Hannah Arendt, *The Human Condition* (Chicago, IL: University of Chicago Press, [1958] 1998), 7.
10 Arendt, *Men in Dark Times*, 4.

to do no more than find a place for themselves in the world, instead of changing the world and making it 'philosophical.'"[11] Her specific attitude toward action and her skepticism toward the dichotomy theory/practice make her particularly interesting for designers today to support them to go beyond the paths of an idea of designing as pure praxis.

This courage of a *"thinking without the banister"*[12] to seek to change the world is much needed in design today. We believe with her that the role and responsibility of the engaged intellectual, the designer, is an active, critical engagement with the world, with the in-between, to combat the erosion of politics, promote hope, and eventually avoid a social disaster, unmasking the many mystifications of our time. It is exactly in moments where—as today—speech loses its political value of connecting people and empowering them toward actions that Arendt theorizes the possibility of something radically new to happen: new beginnings that are not just a projection of our interpretation of the past casted toward the future, but something radically different and transformative toward dark times.

The rearticulation of this in-between seems to us more than ever a key task and responsibility for engaged designers in a time of erosion of politics. We chose to look into Arendt's philosophy in this specific historical moment as we believe it can contribute to question the intellectual, political task of rethinking this in-between.

Arendt's politics also helps us to focus on how concretely designing can be powered by this courage she envisions for intellectuals in dark times, entangling the relationship between actions, words, and artefacts and, in detail, addressing the importance of action and speech for human artifice. Without

11   Hannah Arendt quoted in George Prochnik "The Philosopher in Dark Times," April 12, 2018, *The New York Times.*

12   Hannah Arendt, *Thinking without a Banister: Essays in Understanding 1953–1975* (New York: Schocken, 2018). In a review for the *New York Times* of Arendt's book *Thinking without a Banister,* George Prochnik reminds us of how Arendt was passionate about Marx's famous statement (from *Theses on Feuerbach*) that *"philosophers have only interpreted the world. … The point, however, is to change it."*

action and speech, artifices lose their meanings, and ultimately their reason to be. They become superfluous:

> *Power preserves the public realm and the space of appearance, and as such it is also the lifeblood of the human artifice, which, unless it is the scene of action and speech, of the web of human affairs and relationships and the stories engendered by them, lacks its ultimate raison d'être. Without being talked about by men and without housing them, the world would not be a human artifice but a heap of unrelated things to which each isolated individual was at liberty to add one more object.*[13]

Yet, Arendt also provides an argumentation of how artifices are constitutive of action and speech, and provide them stability, permanence, and relevance:

> *... without the human artifice to house them, human affairs would be as floating .... without action to bring into the play of the world the new beginning of which each man is capable by virtue of being born, "there is no thing under the sun"; without the enduring permanence of a human artifact, there cannot be "any remembrance of things that are to come with those that shall come after.*[14]

Arendt's attention to what makes meaningful artefacts and their potential for the political makes her thought particularly relevant for designers today.

II. Design and Reflection: Creating a Lexicon

It is often claimed that for designers, actions come before thought. This, we argue, is a false understanding of designing. As design theorist Gui Bonsiepe once speculated, a *"design historian in the year 2050 who looks back at the design scenery at the end of the 20th century might be surprised about the*

13 Arendt, *The Human Condition*, 204.
14 Ibid.

binarism between action and contemplation."[15] Against this, he
concluded that

> *I would like to see intellectuality maintained as a virtue
> of design in the next century: readiness and courage to
> put into question the orthodoxies, conventions, traditions,
> agreed-upon canons of design—and not only of design.
> That is not only a verbal enterprise, an enterprise that
> works through the formulation of texts, an enterprise of
> linguistic competence of a critical mind. The designer
> acting as designer, that is, with the tools of his or her
> profession, faces the particular challenge of an operational
> critique. In other words, she or he faces the challenge not
> to remain in critical distance from and above reality, but
> to get involved and intervene in reality through design
> actions that open new or different opportunities for
> action.*[16]

This Lexicon takes up Bonsiepe's challenge. It opens a
discussion on the interplay between design word, concept,
and action. In reconnecting word and action with respect
to design, old divisions between abstract thinking and the
practical stance of designing, making, and shaping the world
dissolve. By extension, the dissolution of artificial boundaries
between thought and action refuses other kinds of unproductive
bifurcations, for example, the conventional separation between
design and social theory or those even more fundamental
separations between subject and object, artifice and nature. It
also opens up new possibilities to rearticulate the relationship
between design and philosophy and thought in general, where
design can find in philosophy and thought tools for reshaping
and strengthening its thinking from within—and through which,
conversely, philosophy and thought can be triggered to be a real
action of thought, to become interventions and affirmations and
not merely contemplative critique (which today can no longer

15 Gui Bonsiepe, *Interface—An Approach to Design* (Maastricht: Jan Van
    Eyck Academy, 1997), 153.
16 Bonsiepe, *Interface—An Approach to Design*, 153.

speak power to truth because power has dispensed with truth and hence with critique).

Much has been said about the growing relevance of designing for society, and in detail of its ability to address complex problems and inform new possibilities. This is something both theorists and practitioners have been thinking through in a variety of different ways and from a variety of different motivations. As design's influence and agency increases, so must designer's responsibility increase to confront the inherent political and philosophical questions raised by their work and the world in which they live. This means that a deeper understanding of the meanings and consequences of their actions is crucial:

> *Fundamentally we act to de-future because we do not*
> *understand how the values, knowledges, worlds, and*
> *things we create go on designing after we have designed*
> *and made them.*[17]

There is in designing today often a tendency to not pay much attention into ways in which it articulates its own inventions: a "loss" or lack of words, a too simple assumption that the "work" (whatever form it may take, tangible or intangible, processual or systemic) can "speak for itself." We know that in actuality it cannot, or far less than its creators assume. Works require a compossibility of work, reflection, speech, and discourse—and above all today, and especially politically and socially, the ability to translate the works' invention into its implications for wider models of acting.

This lack of attention goes along together with a reliance on given language, which is today often corrupted, up to the point of losing significance. In their introduction to *The Dialectic of Enlightenment*, the philosophers Theodor W. Adorno and Max Horkheimer argue that language has undergone a commodification process, which has impoverished it to the point to make it unreliable. We need some skepticism towards everyday language if we want to scratch under the surface:

---

17   Fry, *A New Design Philosophy: An Introduction to Defuturing*, 12.

> *If public life has reached a state in which thought is*
> *being turned inescapably into a commodity and language*
> *into celebration of the commodity, the attempt to trace*
> *the sources of this degradation must refuse obedience to*
> *the current linguistic and intellectual demands before*
> *it is rendered entirely futile by the consequence of those*
> *demands for world history.*[18]

Adorno not only criticizes the distortion of language in Western contemporary societies but also sees a fundamental problem in language as such. In *Minima Moralia*, he says,

> *any possible knowledge must not only be first wrested from*
> *what is, if it shall hold good, but is also marked, for this*
> *very reason, by the same distortion and indigence which*
> *it seeks to escape.*[19]

We agree with him that every knowledge is marked by fallibility. Yet, we also acknowledge that we need to be confronted with the necessity to understand, to use words to infuse our actions, so that they can have a reflective quality. To question the current use of words we encounter every day in our profession as designers and as citizens—such as the ones we propose in this Lexicon—is then a necessary task that yet cannot be considered done once and forever, but rather needs continuous reframing and problematization. Of course, such a project is necessarily imperfect; it can never be fully realized as such. And yet, as we take up this challenge we are convinced that designers need to take up seriously their being intellectuals, and therefore also take seriously the words used to infuse their reflective actions. Therefore, we need both to question and expand the language we use; to push forward a more critical and conscious use of words. Arendt was aware of the power of words, which for her are deeply connected with actions and artefacts. To have a world that can be inhabited; in other words,

18   Theodor Wiesengrund Adorno and Max Horkheimer, *Dialectic of Enlightenment* (London: Verso, [1947] 1974), xv.
19   Theodor Wiesengrund Adorno, "Finale," in *Minima Moralia* (London: Verso, 1978), 247.

to have a politics, we need these three elements—language, actions, and artefacts— working in conjunction.

Where this links more closely to designing than we usually think is that actions in the world have essentially a dialogic nature. They are as infused by words as words are by actions. Designing actions, where words and deeds naturally tend to merge, have a specific capability or *"virtue"*[20] for (re)acting in dark times—in that the merging or dialogical play opened in designing allows reflection on the human condition to penetrate into actions and artefacts just as it allows actions and artefacts to have greater resonance (and ideally greater support) for human conditions.

In dark times, real actions are only the ones that have a specific political meaning. Arendt teaches us that to be fully political, an action needs to find its origin in a discussion in which meanings are shared. Deeds are inextricably connected to words. In order to value and articulate actions and for these to be political in the Arendtian sense, one must explore words infusing them and providing them with their political meaning, making out of these words a discourse, a shared discussion. If this is true, then to rethink the political character of actions and words—and their interconnectedness—is a relevant and timely task for design.

Arendt speaks of dark times as a space of possibility, populated by individuals able to find again the political character of their words and actions. She does not theorize new systems but tells the story of how individuals can shed even a weak light by their way of being in the world—and therefore also speak and act (politically).

I have always believed that, no matter how abstract our theories may sound or how consistent our arguments may appear, there are incidents and stories behind them which at least for ourselves, contain in a nutshell the full meaning of whatever we have to say. Thought itself—to the extent that it is more than a technical, logical operation which electronic machines may be better equipped to

20 Bonsiepe, *Interface—An Approach to Design*, 152.

perform than the human brain—are out of the actuality of
incidents and incidents of living experience must remain
its guideposts by which thinking oars, or into the depths
to which it descends.[21]

This attention to the stories of one's own living experience
in Arendt's philosophy has guided us also methodologically
in editing this Lexicon: instead of theorizing what Arendt's
philosophy can represent for designers today, we decided to
collect different voices—stories, "*incidents*"—of design scholars
and practitioners represented by their own actions and words
in our times. As in the case of the *Men in Dark Times*, we don't
know if our "*illuminations*" are the trembling lights of a candle
or that of the blazing sun. Yet, we agree with Arendt that this
seems somehow secondary, as only the future will be able to
judge on this. The most important thing for us is the attempt
to act from within these dark times and to acknowledge this
moment and our own responsibility. This Lexicon testifies to
these many attempts, different illuminations in dialogue with
each other, forming together an organic, nonsystematic, and
inevitably nonconclusive discourse.

Part Two: The Organization of the Lexicon

There are two major reasons that urged us to edit this Lexicon.
The first is that it is perhaps not a coincidence that in this
moment in history, in times of fear and uncertainty, marked
by complex environmental, economic, social, and political
challenges, designers who are engaging in the public realm
are now increasingly tangling with concepts like citizenship,
equality, human rights, humanity, and public realm that are
remarkably close to the language used more than fifty years ago
by the political philosopher Hannah Arendt, while articulating
ways to react to her "*dark times.*"[22] Less important here are
the keywords per se, but the (re)introduction to key themes in

---

21 Arendt, *Thinking without a Banister: Essays in Understanding*
    1953–1975, 200–1.
22 Arendt, *Men in Dark Times*, 11.

Arendt's work that resonate with our contemporary problems and the potential to carry her work in new directions, especially in relation to designing and acting in the world today.

The second reason to look at and to think at the words enforcing our reflective design practices is to rescue them from their loss of meaning. In his essay on politics and language, the novelist George Orwell wrote the following: *"But if thought corrupts language, language can also corrupt thought."*[23]

What could be the effects of language on our ability to think design and to translate this thought into reflective practices? If we accept that design is in part a rhetorical practice and that design work, as a product of persuasion, is always open to debate and disagreement, then it follows that designing is also determined by an agenda and subjected to political ramifications. Is the only answer to risks of co-optation to continuously reject existing words and invent new ones, running the risk that they might quickly undergo the same destiny of those words whose meaning has been corrupted and eroded by their use and abuse? A viable alternative, so that we do not end up in a babel where it is no longer possible to understand each other, is to find a way to provide some criticality to those words that are key for design discourse and practice, without simply rejecting them when their meanings have been eroded by their use and abuse.

The Lexicon is an experimental project to this end, an attempt to create building blocks for a more developed discourse around designing that illuminates rather than obscures and opens a greater horizon of possibilities for engaging with our times. In its simplest form the book uses the exploration of fifty or so terms derived from Arendt's body of work to try to begin shaping a vocabulary among a global field of practitioners and scholars, both in and beyond design, interested in the key ethical, sociocultural, and political issues of our day. Focusing especially on terms bearing on the question of how we should act (both subjectively and objectively), the Lexicon challenges designers to find new ways to *(re)*

---

23 George Orwell, *Politics and the English Language* (London: Penguin Modern Classics, 2013), 137.

act to dark times, where reflective design practices ought to be considered "activities of thought" from which new and unexpected beginnings can take place.[24]

As editors, we decided to work with design scholars and practitioners who are engaged through their work with some of the words that are key in Arendt's philosophy.

The ways in which they were dealing with those concepts did not necessarily have to overlap with Arendt's interpretation. In fact, we wanted to open a dialogue between Arendt and those scholars and practitioners, rather than analyzing if and how her concepts were actually explicitly present in their work. After a close examination of Arendt's work and of some of her major scholars, we selected keywords and passages of her writing that were, in our opinion, relevant for starting a conversation and asked the designers to enter in dialogue with Arendt's interpretation of those concepts that are also relevant for their own work.

In this itinerary, we saw Arendt's quotations as starting points for thought.[25] In so doing we adopted her own idea of quotation that she summarizes while talking of Walter Benjamin's use of quotations:

---

24   Arendt herself is instructive here: "to act, in its most general sense, means to take an initiative, to begin ..., to set something into motion ... the fact that man is capable of action means that the unexpected can be expected from him, that he is able to perform what is infinitely improbable." Arendt, *The Human Condition*, 178.

25   Marie Luise Knott, in her comments on quotation in her book *Unlearning with Hannah Arendt*, gets close to our intent:

> Benjamin's quotations, according to Arendt, prove nothing. They have no need to document an analysis or interpretation of the world, no need to shore up a logical argument. Quotations are voices the author introduces into the space of a text, voices that can encounter one another in continually new ways in the here and now of writing just as they do in the here and now of reading. They repeatedly illuminate one another in different ways within the space of the text. The impoverished world of today, where the act of thinking is under collapse, has need of "thought fragments" from the past, voices that the author brings into the space of the text and allows to associate with one another ... [creating] a multilayered and polyphonic plurality.

Marie Luise Knott, *Unlearning with Hannah Arendt* (New York: Other Press, 2015), 95.

> *Quotations in my works are like robbers by the roadside*
> *who make an armed attack and relieve an idler of his*
> *convictions. (Schriften I, 571) This discovery of the modern*
> *function of quotations, according to Benjamin, who*
> *exemplified it by Karl Kraus, was born out of despair—not*
> *the despair of a past that refuses "to throw its light on the*
> *future" and lets the human mind "wander in darkness" as*
> *in Tocqueville, but out of the despair of the present.*[26]

Quotations from Arendt have been used here therefore not as an authoritative reference to her philosophy—which, as indicated by many scholars, has blind spots that naturally need to undergo a serious critique—but rather as prompts, ways to shake the use of words in thinking and practicing design today. In this sense the Lexicon might be considered as a kind of *Wunderkammer*, a collection where every piece is like a prismatic rock stone that shows different facets to the living experience of the different contributors.

In concrete terms, in each instance, we asked contributors to "adopt" one of Arendt's political and philosophical concepts that can be considered as key for contemporary design (and, in first instance, for their own work) and to write a short essay (generally under 1500 words) with an eye toward exploring its implication for understanding what it is for them to design in these dark times. Each of them was invited to choose their own register (academic, speculative, informal, etc.) and, starting from their own point of view, their own story/incidents and push Arendt's language, to define new terms, identify possible futures, and suggest new courses of action.

We also decided not to ask Arendt's scholars to work on these words, as we believe that a real dialogue between these pieces of a collections—these words and quotes—and designers was not to be filtered: these words needed to resonate in their own living experiences. The result is a work that sometimes misses the qualities of a strict philosophical analysis, and yet it had to pay this price for being a real dialogue, which is, as in

---

[26] Hannah Arendt, "Introduction: Walter Benjamin: 1892–1940," in Benjamin, *Illuminations* (New York: Harcourt, 1968), 38–9.

real life, made of different registers. This variety of voices is, we believe, the strength of this project.

What all the contributors of this Lexicon share in common is the conviction that it is worth to critically explore Arendt's perspectives as this might help designers to understand concepts than can inform their acting in the world, to enable the renewal of public life, and support designers to make sense of the profound issues of our times and reflect on how intellectually, and therefore politically, to take action. Again, this is an ambitious and risky proposition. In which ways this dialogue will, as Arendt says, translate into future courses of action is still to be further explored, as part of the *Designing in Dark Times* book series.

The terms selected for the Lexicon do not pretend to be comprehensive, nor do they make any claim to represent all or even most of the essential terms for today. But neither are they arbitrary. They emerge both from Arendt's concerns and interests and from what is of concern today. Despite the more than fifty years in separation, there is less difference here than it might be imagined. In any case, it is sometimes the slight gap between Arendt's times and ours that allows her terms to cast fresh light on current conditions.

Considered broadly, the terms fall into five (necessarily overlapping) groups or clusters:

(i)   The first consists of terms that encompass basic human capacities and conditions. Beginning from the most fundamental—MORTALITY and NATALITY, the second of which especially has particular meaning for Arendt—they address and explore capacities such as COURAGE, CREATIVITY, FREEDOM, IMAGINATION, PLAY, SPEECH, SPONTANEITY, THOUGHT (and its opposite, THOUGHTLESSNESS) as well as subjective conditions that are never simply subjective (such as PRIVATE REALM and SOLITUDE).

(ii) A second group takes up terms that explore how these capacities and conditions are externalized, for example, expressively in stories and through history, but also how they engender ways of being in the world—*VITA*

CONTEMPLATIVA, VITA ACTIVA, ANIMAL RATIONALE—and in engaging with it—as understanding (COMPREHENSION in Arendt's particular sense of this term), but also through establishing BEGINNINGS, through creating and working through the IN-BETWEEN, and all that which connects persons to the wider political world.

(iii) These terms link closely to a third cluster of concepts based around the social and political worlds, particularly in the sense of what is common—COMMON GOOD, COMMON INTERESTS, COMMON WORLD—and what is public—THE PUBLIC—and what flows from the creation of what is common and what belongs to this realm: questions of CITIZENSHIP, DEMOCRACY, EQUALITY, HUMANITY, HUMAN RIGHTS, THE IN-BETWEEN, PLURALITY, TOGETHERNESS, but also of how this is manifest, on the one side in political life, as ACTIVISM (*VITA ACTIVA*) and on the other in and through institutions: the inescapable enigmas of BUREAUCRACY, LAW, and POWER.

(iv) The fourth group of words in the Lexicon deal more directly with questions of LABOR and work: as mentalities (INSTRUMENTALITY, OBJECTIVITY), as modes of acting in and on the world (FABRICATION, LABOR, METABOLISM, TECHNOLOGY), and as the creation of ontologies or modes of being-human (*ANIMAL LABORANS*, ANTHROPOCENTRISM, *HOMO FABER*).

(v) Finally, stemming from the last two are terms that shade into more dystopian moments: ALIENATION and REIFICATION in relation to making; but also the negative side of politics—BUREAUCRACY, LAW, and POWER in their worst moments; IMPERIALISM AND TOTALITARIANISM in general; each with the concomitant evils that arise in their wake: THOUGHTLESSNESS, VIOLENCE, SUPERFLUITY, the creation of the PARIAH (today the refugee), and the institutionalization of EVIL.[27]

---

27 Although we have grouped the terms here in ways that already show their connections and linkages, we have decided to present them alphabetically. The reason is similar to that which Raymond Williams gave in *Keywords*,

As a whole, these groups of terms make no claims either to being comprehensive (even in terms of Arendt) or to exclusivity as the necessary terms for today. Regarding Arendt's thought, there are "missing" terms. Some of these are contingent (authors withdrawing from the project and the like), others the product of relative arbitrariness that any selection, limited not least by number and volume size, will involve. But this is not a dictionary. The contributions, to repeat the point, are essays, not definitions. They are explorations of some key terms in Arendt's thought terms that have resonance both in her thought and to our times and—this is the wager of the volume—to designing as it increasingly engages with the wider world. As was noted earlier, not only does language require constant rescue but we need to constantly think—and indeed to *critically (re)imagine*—the terms we use.

Moreover, in the book we have not encouraged but certainly are happy with degrees of overlap on how key concepts are explained. Some might find repetitive, especially if the book were to be read from cover to cover as a text with a beginning, middle, and end. But a Lexicon is never intended to be read in this way. It is a text to be referred to, and to be explored. The structure of the work lends itself to both approaches.

As for exclusivity as to key terms for today, no claims are made since on the contrary, other Lexicons are both imaginable and required. Today in particular—and we hope this will be part of a future project of the series—we need a Lexicon of designing that looks at non-Western, non-given concepts of designing and acting. Arendt's work is firmly within, and is both enabled by and limited by, the Greek–German philosophical tradition. As the Arendtian democratic discourse comes from a certain tradition, we are well aware that, for example issues around coloniality and diversity, have not been adequately addressed. After all, there is also a form of colonialism inherent in organizing the Lexicon—what the Indian social scientist Ashis Nandy calls the domination of "developed, assertive language(s) of

which is that the problem with grouping terms is that while they suggest or establish one set of connections they do so by often "suppressing another" in Raymond Williams, *Keywords* (London: Croom Helm, 1976), 22. We have made as much use of cross-referencing as we can and especially paid attention to unexpected linkages. But no single mode of organization can satisfy all requirements.

dialogue."[28] While recognizing this difficulty, within the limits of this project, we were not able to solve the problem, only note the paradox produced here. An urgency for now is to create wider vocabularies of terms or concepts that can bring new energy as well as can unsettle dominant epistemologies—almost by definition these will need to largely come from outside the Western tradition: that can articulate other truths concerning how we think, make, and act in the world. In concrete terms, a possible project within this book series is to work on opening up other kinds of Lexicons, using concepts and categories drawn from diverse traditions and communities.

This is all the more the case in that, even if we are convinced that Arendt's philosophy can still significantly speak to our dark times and provoke new thinking and acting in designing, we also want to sincerely acknowledge the limitations of her thinking and take distance from some of her positions that are still deeply imbued by a Western-centric, colonial mindset. This is certainly the case when it comes to the subject of anti-Black racism, as, for instance, in her "Reflections on Little Rock" (1959), in which she showed a fundamental inability to fully understand the intricate discourse on anti-African American racism, its origins, and its dramatic implications in her contemporary American context. Furthermore, her reasonings concerning African cultures, languages, and literatures—as expressed in *The Origin of Totalitarianisms* (1951) and *On Violence* (1970)—are deeply unacceptable and indeed surprising for a thinker who experienced first-hand the absurdity of any form of racism.

The dark times in which we are living now are also times in which dramatically enough many human beings are still deprived of their human condition and more than ever require us to keep a radical distance from such positions. As editors, we are aware of this and explicitly wish to stress distance ourselves from the way in which Arendt addressed those issues.[29] First and foremost as

28 Ashis Nandy, *Traditions, Tyrannies and Utopias: Essays in the Politics of Awareness* (New Delhi: Oxford University Press, 1987), 14–15. Quoted in Arturo Escobar, *Designs for the Pluriverse* (Durham: Duke University Press, 2018), 100.

29 Also, we want to explicitly acknowledge that "the woman question in Arendt" is problematic and deserves a more punctual articulation, which

humans—and second as designers—we need to seriously address colonialism and racism and its consequences, both for Western philosophy as well as in designing, in order to better shape our responsibility in giving form to the world to come.

Finally, we should note four particular contributions to the volume. The first is that the entry on IMAGINATION is by Arendt herself. The short text we reproduce comes from Jerome Kohn's recent editing of some of Arendt's essays (*Thinking without a Bannister: Essays in Understanding, 1953–1975*).[30] It was written for a seminar she gave on Kant's theory of imagination in 1970 at The New School in New York. It feels doubly appropriate to include an entry by Arendt, especially on a theme that, while often downplayed in professional philosophy, is far more than merely subjective import in the context of thinking designing in dark times.

The second contribution forms the preface to the volume. This is by Kenneth Frampton, Ware Professor of Architecture at Columbia University, one of the world's foremost historians and critics of modern architecture. In the 1970s he attended Arendt's lectures at The New School in New York, where her thinking had a major impact on his outlook. The brief extract from a 2016 interview with Frampton where he speaks on her impact of her thought is both a testament to her influence and provides a bridge between Arendt's teaching in New York in the 1970s and critical reflection on architecture and design today.

The third and very significant addition is a series of artists pages by Martha Rosler. The work consists of a typographic rendering of thirteen of the large-scale transparent hanging Mylar panels of quotations from Hannah Arendt's political writings. Created for the 2006 exhibit *Hannah Arendt Denkraum/Hannah Arendt Thinking Space* held in Berlin on the centenary of Arendt's birth, and thought under the rubric of "At the present moment, thinking is greatly to be desired," "*Reading Hannah Arendt (Politically, for an American in the 21st Century)*" is Martha Rosler's response to the continuing challenge of Arendt's thought to how we need to think politics today.

yet goes beyond the scope of this book. On this matter, we would like to point the reader toward the work of scholars such as those collected, for example, in Bonnie Honig (ed.), *Feminist Interpretation of Hannah Arendt* (University Park: The Penn State University Press, 1995).

30   Hannah Arendt, *Thinking without a Bannister: Essays in Understanding 1953–1975* (New York: Schocken, 2018).

Finally, the afterword to the book is a short reflective piece on the import and relevance of Arendt's thought today by Richard J. Bernstein, professor of philosophy at The New School in New York. Bernstein knew Arendt and has written extensively on her.[31] His essay is a reminder—if such is needed—of her import to contemporary political and philosophical thought as a whole. He does this most powerfully perhaps when, in the conclusion to his recent book on Arendt, he offers a quotation from her and its gloss which can act here both as the conclusion of this introduction and the opening to the Lexicon as whole. The quotation from Arendt comes from the beginning of *The Origin of Totalitarianism*. It is on comprehending the world:

> *Comprehension does not mean denying the outrageous, deducing the unprecedented from precedents, or explaining phenomena by such analogies and generalizations that the impact of reality and the shock of experience are no longer felt. It means, rather, examining and bearing consciously the burden our century has placed on us—neither denying its existence nor submitting meekly to its weight. Comprehension, in short, means the unpremeditated, attentive facing up to, and resisting of, reality—whatever it might be.*[32]

And here is Bernstein's concluding gloss that defines precisely the relevance and necessity of comprehending for our times, not least for designing:

> The task she set herself is now our task—to bear the burden of our century and neither to deny its existence nor submit meekly to its weight. Arendt should be read today because she was so perceptive in comprehending the dangers that still confront us and warned us about becoming indifferent or cynical. She urged us to take responsibility for our political destinies. She taught us that we have the capacity to act in concert, to initiate, to begin, to strive to make freedom a worldly reality. "Beginning, before it becomes a

31 Most recently, Richard J. Bernstein, *Why Read Hannah Arendt Now?* (Cambridge, MA: Polity Press, 2018).
32 Hannah Arendt, *The Origins of Totalitarianism* (New York: Harvest Books, [1951] 1979), viii. Quoted in Bernstein, *Why Read Hannah Arendt Now?*, 120–1.

historical event, is the supreme capacity of man: politically it is identical with man's freedom."[33]

Appendix: Works by Hannah Arendt drawn on for this volume

The majority of the originating quotations for the Lexicon entries were drawn from the following books:

The Origins of Totalitarianism (New York: Harcourt Brace, [1951] 1979)
The Human Condition (Chicago: University of Chicago Press, [1958] 1998)
Between Past and Future (London: Penguin Books, [1961] 2007)
On Revolution (New York: Viking Press, 1963)
Men in Dark Times (New York: Harcourt Brace, [1968] 1993)
On Violence (New York: Harcourt Brace, 1970)

There are additional references to:

Eichmann in Jerusalem: A Report on the Banality of Evil (London: Penguin, [1963] 1994)
"A Special Supplement: Reflections on Violence," *New York Review of Books* (February 27, 1969)
The Life of the Mind: Volume Two, Willing (New York: Harcourt Brace Jovanovich, 1979)
Lectures on Kant's Political Philosophy (Chicago: University of Chicago Press, 1992)
Essays in Understanding, 1930–1954: Formation, Exile, and Totalitarianism, ed. Jerome Kohn (New York: Harcourt Brace, 1994)
"Philosophy and Politics," *Social Research*, vol. 71, no. 3 (2004)
"Truth and Politics," in Jose Medina and David Wood (eds.), *Truth: Engagements across Philosophical Traditions* (Oxford: Blackwell, 2010)
The Last Interview and Other Conversations (Brooklyn, NY: Melville House, 2013)
Thinking without a Banister: Essays in Understanding 1953–1975, edited by Jerome Kohn (New York: Schocken, 2018)

33 Bernstein, *Why Read Hannah Arendt Now?*, 479.

ACTION
ACTIVISM
ALIENATION
ANIMAL LABORANS
ANIMAL RATIONALE
ANTHROPOCENTRISM

ACTION

Action is the process of doing something to accomplish a purpose, especially when dealing with a problem or difficulty. For Arendt, the general human capacity for action encompasses also a capacity for creation: not only to reproduce what is given but to reimagine and rework the given—including the political: "To act, implies taking an initiative and setting something into motion."[1]

The intentional attempts at transforming the world in which one is living has become a disciplinary cornerstone of design practice, entailing a professionalization of creative action, specifically through the verbal and material articulation of propositions of alternatives to status quo. Creating proposals for, and sometimes bringing into socio-material existence, things that do otherwise not exist is what we can call design action.

Design action works through a hopeful "if," setting things into motion by asking evocative questions: what if we understood the issue in this way; what if we arranged our efforts in that way; what other futures might we envision if we challenge and unpack some of the contingencies that hold current reality in place?

It is no coincidence that these phrases entail a "we" since no design action (and no political action) is accomplished in isolation. As it is for politics, collaboration is a condition for design, not a preference. In Arendt's words, "To be isolated is to be deprived of the capacity to act."[2] This means that the "if" is never intended for an individual's loss from others: in other words, it always has a political implication.

1   Hannah Arendt, *The Human Condition* (Chicago, IL: University of Chicago Press, [1958] 1998), 176–7.
2   Arendt, *The Human Condition*, 188.

Design Reframing by Visiting

When faced with situations of high complexity and uncertainty, i.e., so-called wicked problems,[3] design offers a capacity for action through reframing of the problematic issue. By inventing new analytical frames for understanding and appreciating the issue at hand, new openings for meaningful action arises, what Schön calls naming and framing.[4]

Challenging the current understanding of an issue, as it is often encapsulated in given design briefs, is common to conceptually inventive design practice. In this, design practitioners routinely seek to transcend the limits of their own habitual ways of seeing the world. Arendt called this "to train one's imagination to go visiting,"[5] trying to see an event from another vantage point, from an unfamiliar lifeworld.

Donna Haraway has developed Arendt's notion of "visiting" into what she calls "response-ability": a practice of curiosity that insists on welcoming the responses of those one engages with: "to venture off the beaten path to meet unexpected, non-natal kin, and to strike up conversations, to pose and respond to interesting questions, to propose together something unanticipated, to take up the unasked-for obligations of having met."[6] This is what Haraway calls cultivating response-ability.

This line of thinking supports a notion of Design Action as a propositional and iterative dialogue with the Other. This emphasizes the collaborative aspect of common design events: the studio crit, reviews, workshops, prototyping, field trials, and user testing, but it also points to two other different levels of dialogue: on the one side, designers acting with others, often from different fields; on the other side, designers as

---

3 Horst W. J. Rittel and Melvin M. Webber, "Dilemmas in a General Theory of Planning," *Policy Sciences* vol. 4, no. 2 (1973): 155–69.
4 Donald Schön, *Educating the Reflective Practitioner* (San Francisco, CA: Jossey-Bass, 1987), 33.
5 Hannah Arendt, *Lectures on Kant's Political Philosophy* (Chicago, IL: University of Chicago Press, 1992), 43.
6 Donna Haraway, *Staying with the Trouble: Making Kin in the Chthulucene* (Durham: Duke University Press, 2016), 130. Haraway argues for the necessity of cross-species collaboration on a damaged earth, while pointing toward philosophical potentials of more livable futures.

enabling actions of others with others (citizens, for instance). This might suggest design action as both "design action" and design *for* action.

Design Action Is Enabling

In the wake of modernity, all too often design has been referred to as a noun denoting an outcome, which presupposes a heroic designer's capacity to act and thus cause novel outcomes.

This figure may have seemed comforting, but as Arendt has it, "the popular belief in a 'strong man' who, isolated against others, owes his strength to his being alone is either sheer superstition … or it is conscious despair of all action, political and non-political."[7]

The capacity for action is not a given. Accounts of humanitarian crises and suffering—such as that by Michael Jackson from postwar Sierra Leone—have time after time shown action as an ongoing existential struggle of humans "working to transform the world into which one is thrown, into a world one has a hand in making."[8] War, enforced migration, imposed social change, racist or sexual humiliation, debilitating illness, unemployment, and depletion and pollution of natural resources, or lack of recognition, bereavement all disable the capacity for acting. If one's habitus is destroyed, then capacities for acting, building, and speaking are invalidated and may lead to loss of confidence, satisfaction, and enjoyment of life.[9]

Action in this sense is not a capacity that is given, but a "privilege" that can be negated. Our times call for another, humbler image of design action than that of the strong man. In this image, a designer's agency is not the immanent prerequisite for great design outcomes; rather, the propositional and iterative dialogue itself is polite enough to enable the agency of both

7   Arendt, *The Human Condition*, 188.
8   Michael Jackson, *Existential Anthropology: Events, Exigencies and Effects* (Oxford: Berghahn Books, 2005). In this collection of essays Jackson recounts empirically multiple atrocities in which human beings find themselves and theorizes their struggle to create viable forms of social life.
9   Ibid., xxii.

designer and others. Design action must aspire to behavior that is respectful and considerate of not only desires within but also of vulnerabilities of others.

Overly Wishful Design Thinking

In successful design processes time is experienced as a future we have, as a space of opportunity yet to be explored. Some of the optimism from the twentieth century's design successes is seen in the distilment of design process into the five steps of design thinking omnipresent in today's business world. It bluntly promises competitive advantage and future profit: "by using design thinking, you make decisions based on what future customers really want."[10]

While the global successes of design thinking—and the application of the mighty "How Might We …?" question to more and more domains of human life—are beyond dispute, the uncritical application of design optimism is becoming increasingly untenable in light of the complexities of contemporary issues of disproportionate wealth distribution, environmental deprivation and pollution, and engrained colonialism.

Faced with seemingly insurmountable challenges of global crises, design communities are challenged to avoid falling into despair and resignation. In moments of existential crisis, time is no longer experienced as a future one has, but as an oppressive lack of a future, often mixed with a vague longing for a past. The experience of an increasing gap between wishful thinking of better worlds and what seems possible to realize in the given circumstances is overwhelming.

To illustrate, let's juxtapose the optimistic attitude of the "How Might We …?" question with some examples of pressing issues (forgive the overt attempt at absurdity). How might we:

10 IDEO, accessed November 24, 2018, https://www.ideo.com/pages/designthinking.

- Optimize the service experience of being laid off?
- Create smooth onboarding experiences of refugees at Mediterranean beaches?
- Optimize the customer journey of food stamp applicants?
- Deliver plastic removal services to ocean mammals?
- Compensate citizens who feel betrayed by politicians of their country?

The short answer is that we don't and we shouldn't. But deploying the rhetoric of current design trends in the context of systemic crises might help accentuate the central question here: What constitutes meaningful design action in times of crisis?

Meaningful Action in Dark Times?

The classic design disciplines as we know them—industrial, graphic, interior, fashion, and furniture design—are under increasing pressure from contemporary societal issues. Climate changes, disproportionate distribution of wealth, lack of faith in political institutions, and ethnic animosities throughout the world are increasingly forcing us to think differently about design's role in society. Can Arendt's idea of action help us here?

With Arendt's "On Humanity in Dark Times," we may take inspiration to see in this a moment of possibility to question fundamental social and political structures. For example, the exhibition "Climactic: Post Normal Design" is a case in point, presenting alternative models for design that broaden human capacity to understand and intervene in accelerated social and environmental crises.[11] The overwhelming scale and complexity of these issues cannot be adequately addressed by any single discipline, let alone any discipline that insists on staying within a singular medium, scale, or mode of production.

While design as we knew it from the times of seemingly unlimited industrial growth is increasingly seen as part of the problem rather than its solution, there are new generations of designers who refuse to work in the shadow of conventional

11   Katherine Moline, Ahmed Ansari and Deepa Butoliya, "Climactic: Post Normal Design" (Miller Gallery, Carnegie Mellon University, 2016), 1–4.

patterns of production and consumption. Designers are increasingly addressing truly wicked problems in healthcare, migration, environment, public policy, community building, and general livability.

Faced with issues of uncertainty, it brings hope when designers abandon the role of grand auteur, and instead go politely visiting, insist on the open-ended, extend design collaborations to animals, and slow things down by embracing the idiotic.[12] They give hope that design holds a potentially more able, yet humble role, despite the daunting global challenges.

If we support the new generation of designers, not only in employing solid craftsmanship and technology skills but also to collaborate, empathize, and bring design capacities to the whole of society, they may take on roles of responsible designers with the ability to help collaboratively shape the conditions for human existence.

Like any other area, design suffers in times of crisis, but thinking with Arendt nurtures our ability of finding a new sense of relevance for design that critically includes human and nonhuman concerns of emotional, intellectual, cultural, sociological, and political well-being. Meaningful action in dark times is one that critically engages with possible futures.

Joachim Halse

See also
COMMON WORLD, FREEDOM, NATALITY, SPONTANEITY, TOGETHERNESS

---

12 Examples cited in Thomas Binder et al., "Democratic Design Experiments: Between Parliament and Laboratory," *CoDesign* vol. 11, nos 3–4 (2015): 152–65.

ACTIVISM

> Activism, moreover, seemed to provide new answers to the
> old and troublesome question, "Who am I?" which always
> appears with redoubled persistence in times of crisis. If
> society insisted, "You are what you appear to be," postwar
> activism replied: "You are what you have done."
>
> Hannah Arendt, *The Origins of Totalitarianism*[1]

The passage above from Arendt's *The Origins of Totalitarianism*
is preceded by a paragraph where she notes that the "pronounced
activism of totalitarian movements" attracts those who are
trapped in certain societal conditions where their own sense of
identity, like that of the First World War "front generation," leads
to alienation and fatality. It is a cogent reminder that activism is
positive or negative according to one's ideological orientation,
and that recruits to activism, at least initially, are often found
among minorities, the marginalized, the Other, and radical
visionaries.

Her preface for the first edition of *Totalinarianism* is
dated the summer of 1950, with subsequent prefaces added in
1966 and 1967 during the turbulent social revolutions of the
1960s. "Dark times" might perfectly describe the international
events of 1968, including: The short-lived Prague Spring in
Czechoslovakia later subdued by Warsaw Pact troops; the Viet
Cong attack on the U.S. Embassy in Saigon; anti-Vietnam War
demonstrations in London; the assassination of Martin Luther
King Jr. in Memphis, Tennessee; the student riots in Paris; a
coup d'état in Iraq elevating Saddam Hussein to vice chairman
of the Revolutionary Council; and Richard Nixon becoming
president of the United States. Arendt's article entitled "On
Humanity in Dark Times: Thoughts about Lessing," originally

---

1   Hannah Arendt, *The Origins of Totalitarianism* (New York: Harvest
     Books, [1951] 1979), 331.

published in 1968² based upon her 1959 acceptance address
for the Lessing Prize of the Free City of Hamburg, reflected
the times:

> the world and the people who inhabit it are not the same.
> *The world lies between people.* … (My italics)

She argued that a retreat from the public realm by
individuals, especially in turbulent times, leads to a loss of "the
specific and usually the irreplaceable in-between" that needs
to form between individuals and their fellow humans. In this
condition that she calls "inner emigration," there will be a loss
of humanness and a rejection of reality. This, clearly, allows
others to dominate the public realm not, necessarily, for the
benefit of all. What is required, to reunite citizens, is dialogue of
citizens through a *polis* as an act of political friendship through
philanthropia, "love of man," as acts of sharing the world with
others.

Her pronunciations about the public realm in the 1960s were
correct and false. It simply depended upon where you stood in
the world and what happened next. Citizens did animate their
polis, enforce greater democratic measures in civil and political
life. Yet, these societal gains in democracy were often subverted
by rising neoliberal or conservative forces (Nixon in the United
States, Thatcher in the UK), or taken away violently (the Pinochet
junta in 1973 in Chile), or eroded by the increasing influence of
transnational companies, especially in petroleum, agriculture,
pharmaceuticals, ICT, and arms. Consequently, futurists like Alvin
Toffler in his seminal book *Future Shock*³ saw an urgent need for
small, local plebiscites to create futures together.

Fast forwarding through postmodernity⁴ and liquid
modernity⁵ to our emergent (post-)human condition, where

---

2   Hannah Arendt, "On Humanity in Dark Times: Thoughts about Lessing,"
    trans. Clara and Richard Winston, in Hannah Arendt, *Men in Dark Times*
    (New York: Harcourt, Brace, [1955] 1993), 3–31. Copyright by Hannah
    Arendt 1968, renewed 1996 by Lottie Kohler.
3   Alvin Toffler, *Future Shock* (London: Pan Books, 1971), 431.
4   Jean-François Lyotard, *The Postmodern Condition. A Report
    on Knowledge*, trans. Geoff Bannington and Brian Massumi
    (Minnesota: University of Minnesota Press, [1979] 1984).
5   Zygmunt Bauman, *Liquid Modernity* (Cambridge, MA: Polity Press, 2000).

would Arendt see the public realm today? She would certainly
have to review her conception of modernity.[6] However, the
tenets of her theory of action as a mode of human togetherness,
participatory democracy, freedom, and plurality through *acts
of disclosure*[7] in the public realm still apply. *Where* we can
disclose ourselves and our agency has undergone seismic shifts,
even in relatively recent times. With 4.5 billion people having
access to the Internet today it is, in effect, a perfect artificial
intelligence (AI) machine for ambitions in the public realm
be they neoliberal, totalitarian, or other ideology. Jonathan
Albright, assistant professor of communications at Elon
University, North Carolina, who studied the targets of 300 fake
news sites on U.S. media, shows how easy it is to broadcast
falsities.[8]

What kind of activism do our human, posthuman, and other-
than-human conditions call for to deal with our contingent
realities? Given the ubiquitous presence of designed things and
systems, including AI systems that are designing themselves, and
other designed forms of mechanical, electronic, and biological
life, are dystopian posthuman futures already upon us?[9] The
scene seems primed for design-led activists[10] to challenge the

---

6   Passerin d'Entrèves (2016) characterizes her conception of modernity
     as being based upon the key features of world alienation (loss of
     intersubjectivity constituted world of experience and action), earth
     alienation (science and technology exploring space, extending our
     biological lives), the rise of the social (everything is seen as accumulation
     of capital and social wealth), and the values of labor prioritizing *animal
     laborans* over *homo faber* or [hu-]man as *zoon politikon*. Passerin
     d'Entrèves, "Hannah Arendt," *The Stanford Encyclopedia of Philosophy*,
     Winter 2016 Edition, Edward N. Zalta, ed. https://plato.stanford.edu/
     archives/win2016/entries/arendt/.

7   Disclosure as action, speech, or deeds reveals the identity of the individual,
     the agent.

8   See a description of Albright's work at "Google, Democracy and the Truth
     about Internet Search," by Carole Cadwalladr, December 4, 2016, *The
     Guardian*, online, https://www.theguardian.com/technology/2016/dec/04/
     google-democracy-truth-internet-search-facebook, accessed March
     22, 2017.

9   Beatriz Colomina and Mark Wigley, *Are We Human? Notes on an
     Archaeology of Design* (Zurich: Lars Müller, 2016).

10   Alastair Fuad-Luke, *Design Activism: Beautiful Strangeness for a
     Sustainable World* (London: Earthscan, 2009), 27.

"distribution of the sensible"[11] through provoking new modes of thought, perception, action, and production while simultaneously generating substantive, intensive new "images of thought."[12] This can be achieved by: applying design interventions as a form of activist inquiry for "placeholder concepts," open-ended objects and breaching experiments,[13] seeing design processes as a means for anticipatory democracy,[14] and enabling codesigned narratives[15] with aesthetic acts of disruption[16] and design f(r)ictions[17] to open up the public space to participation. These discursive, dialogic, and disruptive design practices can manifest as a collective remaking of the world. Naturally, this remaking depends upon one's ideological or conceptual starting point. From a sustainability perspective, we might prefer Félix Guattari's ecosophical approach—a tridos of mental, social, and

11 Jacques Rancière, *The Politics of Aesthetics: The Distribution of the Sensible*, Gabriel Rockhill (ed. and trans.) (London: Bloomsbury, [2000] 2004).

12 Petra Hroch, "Sustainable Design Activism: Affirmative Politics and Fruitful Futures," in Betti Marenko and Jamie Brasset (eds.), *Deleuze and Design* (Edinburgh: Edinburgh University Press, 2015), 223, and 226–9.

13 Joachim Halse and Laura Boffi, "Design Interventions as a Form of Inquiry," in Rachel Charlotte Smith et al. (ed.), *Design Anthropological Futures: Exploring Emergence, Intervention and Formation* (London: Bloomsbury, 2016), 89–103.

14 Fuad-Luke, *Design Activism: Beautiful Strangeness for a Sustainable World*, 196–200.

15 Virginia Tassinari, Francesca Pireddda, and Elisa Bertolotti, "Storytelling in Design for Social Innovation and Politics: A Reading through the Lenses of Hannah Arendt," *The Design Journal* vol. 20: sup. 1: S3486–s3495.

16 Thomas Markussen, "The Disruptive Aesthetics of Design Activism: Enacting Design between Art and Politics," *Design Issues* vol. 29, no. 1 (2013): 38–50.

17 The concept of f(r)ictions was originally generated by Monida Gaspar Mallol and then further developed by Alastair Fuad-Luke. See, for example, Gaspar Mallol, "F(r)ictions. Design as a Cultural Form of Dissent." Paper presented at *Design Activism and Social Change* conference, Design History Society, Barcelona, September 2011. Available at http://www.historiadeldisseny.org/congres/pdf/38%20 Gaspar%20Mallol,%20Monica%20FRICTIONS%20DESIGN%20AS%20 CULTURAL%20FORM%20OF%20DISSENT.pdf; and Alastair Fuad-Luke, "Fictions, Frictions and Functions: Design as Capability, Adaptability and Transition," in Elisa Bertolotti, Heather Daam, Francesca Piredda, and Virginia (eds.), *The Pearl Diver: Designers as Storyteller* (Milan: DESIS Network Association – Dipartimento di Design, Politecnico di Milano, 2016), 90–5.

environmental ecologies—to confront what he called Integrated World Capitalism (IWC).[18] Today, we could redefine IWC as "Integrated World Monopolism (IWM)," as 1 percent of humans have accumulated half of all capitalist financial wealth. They extend their power through AI combined with vast networks and physical infrastructure, wage suppression, and fluid movement of financial capital. Here is a slippery economic totalitarianism that we, with the connivance of governments, keep in power. To confront IWM, design activism needs to make tangible new biolocal, bioregional social imaginaries and economies through thoughts and deeds. Designers should seek collaborations with citizens, professionals, and activists seeking similar transformations or, as Arendt would say, they can disclose [their agency] together to build alternatives for inhabiting the in-between.

Building alternatives in-between has the merit of disturbing existing systems while catalyzing or potentializing the existence of emergent systems. New connections, relations, and social actions coalesce to disclose the world differently. The ability of design (and designers) in bringing (different) people together to codefine possibilities, cofind problems, coframe challenges, and cocreate new modes of action lies in participatory processes and tangible aesthetic experiences that create difference. As Markus Miessen notes, "participation becomes a form of critical engagement," especially when it includes those outside of "pre-established power relations of expertise."[19] How the designer engages with and facilitates other actors and stakeholders is a tactical decision dependent on situational and contextual factors but may involve both consensus and dissensus through balancing agreement, agonism, and/or antagonism, which confers freedoms beyond certain constraints inherent in social design commissioned from existing power structures.[20]

18   Félix Guattari, *The Three Ecologies*, Ian Pindar and Paul Sutton (trans.) (London: Bloomsbury, [1989] 2000).

19   Markus Miessen, "Crossbench Praxis as a Mode of Criticality," in Yana Milev (ed.), *D.A. A Transdisciplinary Handbook of Design Anthropology* (Frankfurt: Peter Lang, 2013), 1238–51.

20   Alastair Fuad-Luke, "Design Activism's Teleological Freedoms as a Means to Transform Our Habitus," in Fuad-Luke, Anja-Lisa Hirscher, and Moebus

Frictions hold the potential of generating productive difference[21] and it is within the ongoing creation and production of difference that constitutes, for philosophers Deleuze and Guattari, an intensive resistance, the "new" that counters neoliberal capitalism's tendency to eliminate difference.[22] Elimination of difference is also the ambition of totalitarian regimes, nationalists, fascists, and extremists who demonize the Other. For designers to stand tall in these gathering Dark Times it is necessary that they take the role of nonaligned social brokers[23] or noninstitutionalized free agents.[24] Stepping into the in-between requires some courage, but inspiring examples of emergent design practices dealing with critical sociopolitical, economic, and ecological issues seem to be on the rise. For example, concerning the contentious issue of migration into Europe, diverse modes of design practice are being deployed to raise public awareness, correct misinformation or propaganda, generate skill and job opportunities, provide productive means for integration and, most importantly, dignity for the migrants and local citizens.[25] Many of these design projects confirm Arendt's observation that the "world lies between people," but we should also be careful not to be blinkered by our anthropocentricity as the other-than-human world is undergoing significant suffering and change primarily due to *our* activities. Dark Times stalk other critters. We are a long way from Donna Haraway's vision

(eds.), *Agents of Alternatives: Re-designing Our Realities* (Berlin: AoA, 2015), 280–95.

21 Miessen, "Crossbench Praxis as a Mode of Criticality," 1242.
22 Hroch, "Sustainable Design Activism: Affirmative Politics and Fruitful Futures," 222.
23 Fuad-Luke, *Design Activism: Beautiful Strangeness for a Sustainable World*, xxi.
24 Miessen, "Crossbench Praxis as a Mode of Criticality," 1243.
25 Design for Migration, a project by Matteo Moretti, is gathering projects in Italy and elsewhere in Europe that illustrate diverse design approaches and practices dealing with migrant issues, see http://www. designformigration.com. See also other work involving visual data journalism to correct misperceptions—Matteo Moretti, "Reporting the 'Invasion:' Perception and Reality of Chinese Migrants in Bolzano, Italy," in Tom Felle, John Mair, and Damian Ratcliffe (eds.), *Data Journalism: Inside the Global Future* (New York: Abrams Image, Imprint of Harry N. Abrams, 2015).

of multispecies symbiosis, sympoiesis, and symanimagenesis.[26] Taking micro-steps locally with people is where the production of difference incubates. Whether that difference is healthy for societies and other-than-humans depends, in no small part, on the ideological seed from which it grows, as Arendt duly observed. *Our* Dark Times certainly require us to engage, once again, with philanthropia while simultaneously engaging with *biophilia*. It is time to extend our love to other living things whose condition is already critical.

Alastair Fuad-Luke

See also
ACTION, *ANIMAL LABORANS*,
ANTHROPOCENTRISM, BEGINNINGS,
CITIZENSHIP, IN-BETWEEN, PLURALITY,
SUPERFLUITY, *VITA ACTIVA*

---

26 Donna Haraway, *Staying with the Trouble: Making Kin in the Chthulucene* (Durham: Duke University Press, 2016), 98.

ALIENATION

Design furnishes the world. At its best, it helps us make sense of our environment by shaping it back to us, whether it be a suspension bridge, a healthcare service, or an app for staying in touch with our loved ones. However, in addition to, or better, precisely through all these material things, design also furnishes our imaginaries, relentlessly showing us how things could be different (as opposed to a given) as one of its unique offerings to the world.

When discussing imaginaries in a Western context, an important distinction is necessary. In this day and age it seems straightforward to relegate imagination to the domain of our individual dreams and desires. In Arendt's terms this private space, decisively cultivated by capitalism, is characterized by a relentless metabolistic process of consumption and laboring. In this never-ending ebb and flow, there is only so much space for imagination to begin with. Arendt theorizes that in a harmonic human condition, imagination used to be connected to the public sphere.[1] She also describes how since the mutilation of the human condition, where the public realm ceased to play a key role in individuals' life, imagination has been relegated to the private sphere. This led to a mutilated idea of imagination, as it excludes the public. Further, capitalism has largely succeeded in superseding with an individualized inventory of tamed consumerist desires and aspirations: in other words, how this shrinking of imagination translates in capitalistic societies. Here, the degree to which our lives could be different is measured by the degree to which we are able to consume ourselves into slighter brighter futures. Thus, when Arendt defines alienation

---

1   In *The Human Condition*, Arendt also provides an example of how in ancient Greece imagination used to be fostered: namely, the theater. This used to be a tool to open up the public imagination, where individuals could learn how to be "heroes," being citizens taking their own responsibilities in the public realm, by means of their speeches and deeds. Hannah Arendt, *The Human Condition* (Chicago, IL: University of Chicago Press, [1958] 1998).

as "the atrophy of the space of appearance and the withering of common sense," she goes on to note that this is "carried to a much greater extreme in the case of a laboring society than in the case of a society of producers," the figure Arendt refers to as Homo Laborans, the fabricator of things in the world, comprising both the making of work and the cyclicality of labor. Of course, imaginaries should extend way beyond this particularly claustrophobic space of capitalist aspirations. Notably, they are able to cut across individuals and act as nourishment for our public discourse, with its collective dreaming and future making: how could things be radically different for "us," i.e., for all human and nonhuman living things in the world?

Much is at stake, as the question of alienation from the world is essentially a question of nothing less than "humanness" itself. As we withdraw from the public realm and the continuous discourse with our fellow humans that uniquely unfolds in the space, we are effectively making the world a little bit more inhuman, as we step out from a well-balanced human condition. This withdrawal is one characteristic of what Arendt refers to as "dark times." However, a further precision is needed. In recent years, much has been said about the way that statements such as "save the world," "heal the earth," etc., in a way betray the situation that we are in. The world, as Arendt rightly reminds us, is inherently inhuman. It only becomes human to us through our passionate and insistent chatter about it.

Let us return to the question of how things could be radically different for "us" and unpack this notion of "us" a bit further. Every year we are told how an increasingly small group of billionaires own as much as half of the world's population. For 2017 Oxfam reported that this number was eight. The extreme income gap is of course only one way of describing a world where the basic notion of commonality is eroding on several different fronts. Another point relates to "filter bubbles,"[2] a term that refers to the way in which our experienced realities are increasingly customized (in particular through the algorithms shaping our digital experiences) to become frictionless

2   Eli Pariser, *Filter Bubbles: What the Internet Is Hiding from You* (New York: Penguin Press, 2011).

bubble-wrapped echo chambers of unchallenged consensus. In fact, when Arendt remarks that "[a] noticeable decrease in common sense in any given community and a noticeable increase in superstition and gullibility are therefore almost infallible signs of alienation from the world," it is hard to not think of the wildfire of conspiracy theories and fake news currently deteriorating political discourse on social media.

Survivalism, the active preparation for the impending collapse of civilization, while being a phenomenon with a long history, certainly has not lost momentum through the fear mongering and collective sense of panic that social media offers. The rising popularity of survivalism is perhaps mostly evident in the case of the aforementioned superrich. In the New Yorker article "Doomsday Prep for the Super-Rich," Evan Osnos extensively traces the survivalist reasoning and strategies among the world's 1 percent, concluding: "Fear of disaster is healthy if it spurs action to prevent it. But élite survivalism is not a step toward prevention; it is an act of withdrawal." Here, at the pinnacle of capitalism, the sense of imagination has shrunken to a luxurious private escape plan from this world. In a sense, when faced with a structure such as the Survival Condo Project, an Atlas Missile Silo turned into fifteen stories of luxury condos deep down in the Kansas desert, it is as if you are witnessing the ultimate alienation from the world, carefully brought into existence through design. When some of the most able individuals by the measures of our contemporary Western society start to bring their escape plans into worldly existence, getting ready to literally disappear from the face of earth, we have to start considering the degree to which this deep mistrust in the future of humanity in effect is producing a self-fulfilling prophecy of the complete erosion of the public realm. Consequently, is there any other way to look at structures such as the Survival Condo Project as exquisite, invisible tombstones of our collective imaginary and public discourse? Is there an alternative way to those survival strategies that are again only connected to the private sphere and do not really touch upon the collectivity?

Returning to the 99 percent others, what about a public image of surviving beyond survivalism, inclusive of the many different "us"? Arendt discusses and problematizes "inner emigration"[3] as a way of coping with living through dark times, drawing on the example of life under the Hitler regime in Nazi Germany. The term covers a sort of reflective escapism, a withdrawal that is yet acutely tied to an awareness of the world that is (momentarily) escaped. Arendt's definition, though clearly concerning the peculiar conditions in the Third Reich between 1933 and 1945, has resonance for today:

> As its very name suggests, the "inner emigration" was a curiously ambiguous phenomenon. It signified on the one hand that there were persons inside Germany who behaved as if they no longer belonged to the country, who felt like emigrants; and on the other hand it indicated that they had not in reality emigrated, but had withdrawn to an interior realm, into the invisibility of thinking and feeling. It would be a mistake to imagine that this form of exile, a withdrawal from the world into an interior realm, existed only in Germany, just as it would be a mistake to imagine that such emigration came to an end with the end of the Third Reich. But in that darkest of times, inside and outside Germany the temptation was particularly strong, in the face of a seemingly unendurable reality, to shift from the world and its public space to an interior life, or else simply to ignore that world in favor of an imaginary world "as it ought to be" or as it once upon a time had been.[4]

Design knows well how to produce luxury condos of eternal bliss, just as it knows how to make the apocalypse into a dizzying spectacle. In this sense "utopia" and "dystopia" are tired, overused tools in its toolbox. We are currently seeing the public realm increasingly being eroded, and governments around the world turning dangerously fascist. Therefore, we urgently need to pay more attention to the shifting middle ground between utopia and dystopia[5]—the gray zone spanning between them—as

---

3   Hannah Arendt, "On Humanity in Dark Times: Thoughts about Lessing," in *Men in Dark Times* (New York: Harcourt, Brace, 1955), 3–31.

4   Arendt, "On Humanity in Dark Times: Thoughts about Lessing," 19.

5   The insistence on the binary of utopia and dystopia is often stopping the public imaginary, and what lies in the gray zone between the two is

exemplified through this task of designing for "inner emigration" here and now.

While this might pose a provocative task for design, it is by no means intended to contradict design's role in continuously nurturing public discourse, e.g., through its activist, empathic, and critical capabilities. It is simply a way of recognizing the very large group of people who are already or very soon will be living through what Arendt refers to as a "seemingly unendurable reality."[6] When do we recognize that this point has been reached, and what does design have to offer to today's "inner emigrants" already living through dark times? How will it help bring them back into the world, by empowering them to action?

Søren Rosenbak

See also
METABOLISM, MORTALITY, PRIVATE REALM, REIFICATION

actually what can empower the public imaginary, and therefore empower conversations/actions.

6   Arendt, *Men in Dark Times*, 19.

ANIMAL LABORANS

Donkeywork: A Eulogy

The Donkeyman lies in the 1939–1945 Berlin War Cemetery
near the Grunewald forest. The cemetery is in the shadow of
Teufelsberg, the mountain built from the postwar rubble of the
city, on which the U.S. National Security Agency established a
listening station during the Cold War to conduct surveillance of
the east. These days, there is little to be heard near the devil's
mountain but the barking of a dog on a walk in the woods; those
long dead are troubled by no more than birdsong and a passing
car. In the cemetery, a towering cross of sacrifice oversees row
upon row of uniform headstones for the men buried, almost
uniformly it would seem, at 22 or 23 years of age.

Like most such cemeteries maintained by the Commonwealth
Graves Commission in Europe, North Africa, and Asia, this
one too inters the fallen not only from the UK but also from its
dominions and former colonies. Standing together at one end are
the gravestones of compatriots from countries that were at that
time yet-to-become. Munawar Ali, Donkeyman was from one of
these future nations, a merchant marine involuntarily drafted into
the war when his ship, the S. S. Devon, was attacked by a German
commerce raider.[1] The men were taken prisoner and the ship
sunk but not before the largely Indian crew was separated from
the Europeans and put back to work on another ship. This crew
was later to end up in a war camp in Germany, particularly poorly
treated. If we are to find permanence in his life, it would appear
to be only in the way such a death is recuperated, in the tranquil
green of this cemetery, into a narrative of wartime honor and
glory in a land in which if alive today, he could not be assured of
a welcome.

---

1   "2008 Log Entries," BIship, accessed November 24, 2018, https://
     www.biship.com (for all those with an interest in British India Steam
     Navigation).

A donkeyman was so called because he was responsible for a donkey engine on board the ship. The steam donkey on ship or shore was a small engine used as a winch to load and unload cargo and was auxiliary to other engines. Originally used on sailing ships, its use extended to timber operations where large, heavy logs had to be transported downstream to mills. Nested within this curious nomenclature, pulling its weight behind engine and man, we find the donkey itself, a signifier of the vast retinue of draft animals—bullocks, horses, camels, yaks, and mules—that we have yoked to our purposes since the very beginning. By any yardstick, this is a peculiar category: the beast of burden; one defined solely by its capacity to undergird the fertile exchanges of another's enterprise. In Hannah Arendt's tripartite division of the active life—labor, work, and action—this would fall under labor, that which confronts the foundational necessities of life and being. She termed it *animal laborans*, which in antiquity was performed by the enslaved, whether men, women, or what she refers to as "tame" animals, thus freeing others to participate in *action* which is the public realm of political life. The assumptions and tensions inherent in these hierarchies are entrenched and pervasive. Beasts of burden, no less than the donkeyman and the young perishable men beside him, are routinely drafted to bear the burden of decisions not of their making.

On a summer's day in 2005, as four burros grazed in a field, John Berger found himself transfixed by their legs.[2] He marveled at the surety concentrated in their slender bones. These are legs for crossing mountains, carrying unimaginable loads on slim joints that belie their strength—in contrast to them, he says, the legs of horses look hysterical. The imprints of animal bodies lie buried in every action through which we humans have tried to mold the inheritance of our planet into our own worlds: there are hoofprints in the black furrows of ploughed earth, in the sunlit roofs, walls, towers, and spires of our cities, in the weight of loads carried to market, in the film of coal dust brought up from the bowels of the earth, in the panniers of sloshing water drawn

---

2 John Berger, "Ten Dispatches About Place," *Orion Magazine*, July/August 2007, https://orionmagazine.org/article/ten-dispatches-about-place/.

and carried on roads that themselves often follow the lead of animal tracks. In some terrain such as jungles, high mountains, or sandy deserts, only animals can safely traverse. Beasts of burden haul provisions; draw carts; raise water from wells; lug cargo, agricultural produce, and baggage; tow artillery and supplies, enabling human mobility, migration, conquest, construction, and creation.

This is donkeywork, the backbreaking, repetitive routine labor usually dismissed as drudgery. Indeed, who wants to do donkeywork when one's mind could be freed for higher things? For Arendt, the labor of sustenance alone produces a life unable to harness meaning—worldless, in fact. Worlds are shared environments—of objects, structures, relationships, and frameworks—brought into being through human artifice, activity, and ingenuity. These worlds, according to Arendt, are produced by *work*, the intermediate activity in her conception of the *vita activa*—not by labor. Distinct from both the necessities of labor and the freedom of political action, work brings into being around us a stable, enduring world of objects, craft, architecture, and institutions. The labor that sustains them remains necessarily subterranean, the lives of donkeys as much as donkeymen ever replaceable.

Women in Kenya, recognizing shared lifeworlds of bearing—both burdens and children—are not so quick to disparage such labor. Asked about her donkey, one woman says, *If my baby could speak, she would tell her life as the child of a donkey.* The income that she and the donkey generate together feeds and clothes her family. Perhaps it is no surprise that such a care worker would recognize the animal as a fellow being, a partner, even a parent. *Basically, the donkey is like me*, she says, *but to plainly put it, the donkey is me.*[3]

Capitalist consumerism tends to push all activity toward donkeywork. To Arendt, the distinctions between labor and work had receded in contemporary society. No longer is there a separation between the needs of the body and the skills of the

3   Kendra Coulter, *Animals, Work and the Promise of Interspecies Solidarity* (New York: Palgrave Macmillan, 2016), 124.

hand. Work has become labor, atomized and broken up in such a way that it no longer creates a durable world of objects and meaning but a cycle of endless consumption. In the face of such a senseless and futile existence, we might respond by looking for generative spaces in which work might still flourish. It is tempting to try to infuse into a society of consumption, obsolescence, and waste, the skill, pleasure, knowledge, and interaction inherent in craft, even at a small scale. But even as forethought, rigor and care for the worlds thus created converge in such interventions, they inevitably restore the distinction between labor and work. As making remains inextricably linked to market processes, to chains of supply and demand, every creative act is predicated on labor that frequently happens out of view, on the steady grinding of lives whose existence scarcely rises to the level of notice and whose departure is barely noted as tragedy.

Is the life of an ass tragic, asked Friedrich Nietzsche, when it perishes under a burden it is neither able to bear nor able to shake off?[4] Yet every day, unbearable burdens are borne by human and nonhuman alike across the planet. Hiding in plain sight are lives whose fragility and persistence would otherwise seem unimaginable. In a time marked by the effects of rampant profit making, exploitation, xenophobia, resource extraction, and ecological devastation, there is a growing urgency to address lives made vulnerable on a planet rendered precarious. Dare I suggest that there could be something of value in attending to donkeywork? I don't mean the busywork that people are subjected to under the sign of making a living nor even courage and fortitude in the face of indescribable hardship, although that is surely inspiring. No, I'm thinking of the sheer capacity to withstand—to find, against all odds, the strength to bear the burden and to permit—even to foster—the growth of permanence, stability, beauty, and courage on one's own back.

It isn't easy to accord the lives of donkeys and donkeymen, let alone donkeywork, the narrative illumination to which Arendt said we have a right in dark times. Such light provides

---

4   Friedrich Nietzsche, "Twilight of the Idols," in Walter Kaufman (ed. and trans.), *The Portable Nietzsche* (New York: Penguin, 1954), 468.

no great life lessons. But glance at the shade: the sixteen legs of the burros under the tree. Looking at them, Berger says he feels a substratum of what he can only describe as gratitude. Perhaps that is one place to begin at this time: with a modicum of gratitude for those who involuntarily but actually carry the weight of the world.

Radhika Subramaniam

See also
FABRICATION, *HOMO FABER*,
INSTRUMENTALITY, STORIES, VIOLENCE

ANIMAL RATIONALE

> If it were true that man is an *animal rationale* in the sense
> in which the modern age understood the term, namely, an
> animal species which differs from other animals in that
> it is endowed with superior brain power, then the newly
> invented electronic machines, which ... are so spectacularly
> more "intelligent" than human beings, would indeed be
> *homunculi*. As it is, they are, like all machines, mere
> substitutes and artificial improvers of human labor power,
> following the time-honoured device of all division of labor
> power to break down every operation into its simplest
> constituent motions ... All that the giant computers prove is
> that the modern age was wrong to believe with Hobbes that
> rationality, in the sense of "reckoning with consequences,"
> is the highest and most human of man's capacities, and
> that the life and labor philosophers, Marx or Bergson or
> Nietzsche, were right to see in this type of intelligence
> ... a mere function of the life process itself ... Obviously,
> this brain power and the compelling logical processes
> it generates are not capable of erecting a world, are as
> worldless as the compulsory processes of life, labor and
> consumption.
>
> Hannah Arendt, The Human Condition[1]

For political reasons,[2] Hannah Arendt insists on the speciesist
claim that humans are ontologically distinct from animals. The
title *"animal rationale"* says that we (for what other species is

---

[1] Hannah Arendt, *The Human Condition* (Chicago, IL: University of
Chicago Press, [1958] 1998), 171–2.

[2] Arendt's claims are very deliberately unscientific ones. They are political
demands that we humans commit ourselves to ways of being in the world
that are distinct from what we understand to be the being of animals.
Arendt's speciesism is a self-fulfilling prophecy, a performative speech act
in the name of creating and sustaining a space and time for humans to be
postanimal. For the counterstrategy, reasserting scientific findings about
animals (in this case, their play) in order to defend human being from

reading this?) are still animals, but animals with the power of rationality, a capacity that allows us to contain and even control our animality. The animal that can rationalize its urges and its relation to its environments is the animal that can make itself be not-animal. The capacity to speak and reason means that we humans can give an account of what we are doing and why, which means that we are also able to imagine other preferable ways of doing what we are doing. In other words, the *rationale* that differentiates the animals that we are from all other animals is the power to design, the capacity to design ourselves into preferable environments and activities, which is to say, the capacity to design ourselves into humans.

The distinction between humans and animals, however, is not unproblematic for Arendt. For Arendt, animality is characterized by the unceasing labor of living, whereas post-animality manifests as action. Action is the key differentiator of the human from all other forms of life because the results of action have no utility for living. They are metaphysical—ideas, affects, events—and so surpass the timeframe of a life, even the life of their authors. Nevertheless, they are so distinct from the project of living that Actions also do not seek to be eternal, living forever; instead, they are ephemeral, or better effervescent, shining out beyond a lifetime, but then still in the end withdrawing to make way for other Actions.[3] Actions are therefore acts that create meaningfulness for a while; they may be works of art that speak powerfully to a set of people; they may be political ventures that people collectively commit to; they may be hard-won understandings of the natural world or historical societies or new human capacities.

If we are animals, even though we have capacities to be more than animals, we also are subject to the unceasing labor of sustaining our existence. It is one thing to commit to the possibilities of *vita activa*, a life dedicated to action; it is another to have the capacity to break out of the cycle of survival in order

instrumentalism, see David Graeber, "What's the Point If We Can't Have Fun?" *Baffler* no. 24 (January 2014).

3   For a critical elucidation of Arendt's philosophy in relation to mortality, see Chapter 2 of Thomas Tierney Thomas, *The Value of Convenience: A Genealogy of Technical Culture* (Albany, NY: SUNY Press, 1993).

to exercise this distinctly human way of life. Arendt's *The Human Condition* situates its argument in the societies of Ancient Greece and Rome, which only had domains of action because of slavery. Arendt presumably is not extoling slavery as means justified by its ends—the *polis* and its poetry, theatre, art, and philosophy—but rather indicating that animality is the condition of being enslaved to servicing survival, and that action requires being distinct from that enslavement.

The way to break free of the labor of bare life that may not require enslaving fellow humans as laboring animals is Work. Work produces artefacts that allow the labor of living to be done more effectively, affording surplus time that can be given over to action. Work's artefacts, being more or less permanent, can constitute domains that hold the never-ending variation of life at bay, freeing those who dwell in these new artificial environments for political and creative Actions. In Arendt's argument, for humans to be authentically human, dedicated to Actions that have nothing to do with the mere living of all other creatures, humans must first have the capacity to be *homo faber*.

As with *animal rationale*, the term *homo faber* claims that the capacity to make artefacts is itself a differentiator of some animals, especially humans, from others. This is because there is nothing inherently natural about making. To feel an urge, such as might come with being hungry or cold for instance, but then, rather than deal with that situation directly, deciding to expend energy on the imaginative and so risky task of fabricating a tool that may or may not help deal with that situation in the future, is quite a detour away from what is most immediately apparent. To do that imaginative work—which we should call by its proper name, design—involves not only controlling a present urge but being able to see things in the world not as they are, or more accurately as what they afford with respect to pressing urges, but as what else they might be. A tree is not a tree, but a potential plank to be cut straight from the trunk and then bent about some braces to make up the hull of a ship to sail to the other side of the planet to get ores that can be smelted into weapons to conquer other parts of the world to satiate an empire's hunger. To make things is to be distinct from how the world presently appears; to design a new world out of the things of the existing world is to be already removed from the pressing concerns of the immediate world, to be already dwelling in those other imaginary worlds. This means that artefacts enable what is properly human—the capacity for action—not merely because they allow labor to be done more effectively but because they are manifesting the way in which the animals-that-can-make have already broken out of only experiencing the world in terms how it affords survival.[4]

However, although Work is a condition of Humans attaining a capacity for action, it itself is not a mode of action according to Arendt, which means that it maintains aspects of animality. The workshops of artisans are private spaces, which for Arendt always means spaces of privation, separated off from the public realm of action. This is why manufacturing happens mostly in silence. Artefacts are imagined in a gesture that bears no relation to the nature of animalistic existence, but then the production process is guided by those designs so that the act of making is reduced to one of reproduction, a smaller version of mass production that returns humans to processes of dehumanizingly repetitive labor. Even the unnatural gesture of designing an artefact tends to be structured around a utilitarian version of the human: "if one makes man the measure of all things for use, it is man the user and instrumentalizer, and not man the speaker and doer or man the thinker, to whom the world is being related."[5]

This way Work frees humans for Actions while also reenslaving them to labor, is apparent at the other end of the history of making. Arendt was writing as computation was beginning to impact production with the first promises of artificial intelligence (AI). Digital artefacts may still be fundamentally material, but the digital environments they enable—what we today call "social media"—can seem to promise spaces for metaphysical action. Arendt is scathing of this suggestion, insisting, for example, that quantitative acceleration of calculation can never compare to the qualitative shift entailed

4   I am paraphrasing Martin Heidegger's account of animality as being bound in an environment in which only that which affords urge satiation shows up. Heidegger describes this "ringed in" form of existence in his 1929–30 Seminar, *Fundamental Concepts of Metaphysics: World, Finitude, Solitude* (Bloomington: Indiana University Press, 1995).
5   Arendt, *The Human Condition*, 158.

by the concept of multiplication. Machination, especially of "learning," crowds out conceptual insight.

The phrase *animal rationale* is therefore very accurate: humans may be the animals capable of rationality, but that is because rationality is still animalistic, failing to attain any world-building qualities; to characterize humans as *animal rationale* is to admit that such creatures, no matter how quickly they can calculate what is preferable out of a myriad of options, are not yet any kind of "homo" capable of creating preferable options in the first place. AI is an intensification of human animality, which is why its outcomes, when they are not just exponentializations of productivism, feel so poor-in-world.[6]

Animal Rationale therefore signals that humans are, to some extent, already ruptured from a world made up of only what affords survival. Because of that rupture, we humans can make things, things that take care to some extent of our living, affording us a capacity for action, for the creation of meaningfulness, for disclosing new worlds.[7] But that same capacity, when focused only on improving living, conveniently increasing the logistical speed of living, reenslaves us to an animalistic bare life.

Cameron Tonkinwise

See also
IN-BETWEEN, SUPERFLUITY, TECHNOLOGY, THOUGHTLESSNESS, *VITA ACTIVA*

---

6   "Poor-in-world" is Martin Heidegger's definition of animal being, as opposed to the "world-building" of Dasein: Heidegger, *Fundamental Concepts of Metaphysics*.

7   Charles Spinosa, Fernando Flores, and Hubert L. Dreyfus, *Disclosing New Worlds: Entrepreneurship, Democratic Action, and the Cultivation of Solidarity* (Cambridge, MA: MIT Press, 1999).

ANTHROPOCENTRISM

> The only way out of the dilemma of meaninglessness in
> all strictly utilitarian philosophy is to turn away from
> the objective world of use things and fall back upon the
> subjectivity of use itself. Only in a strictly anthropocentric
> world, where the user, that is, man himself, becomes the
> ultimate end which puts a stop to the unending chain of
> ends and means, can utility as such acquire the dignity of
> meaningfulness. Yet the tragedy is that in the moment *homo
> faber* seems to have found fulfilment in terms of his own
> activity, he begins to degrade the world of things, the end
> and end product of his own mind and hands; if man the
> user is the highest end, "the measure of all things," then not
> only nature, treated by *homo faber* as the almost "worthless
> material" upon which to work, but the "valuable" things
> themselves have become mere means, losing thereby their
> own intrinsic "value."
>
> Hannah Arendt, *The Human Condition*[1]

Nothing seems more irrefutable than the case which can be made
against the anthropocentric. The reason is obvious. Is it not
anthropocentrism not the least of the attitudes that have helped
bring about the situation in which we now find ourselves, a
world in which our own species survival, let alone that of others,
cannot be assured?[2] In the light of this is it not an obscenity in
continuing to regard human beings as recipients of a God-given
right to dominance over all other living things?[3] In any case,

1 Hannah Arendt, *The Human Condition* (Chicago, IL: University of
   Chicago Press, [1958] 1998), 155.
2 It is a measure of our anthropocentrism that we currently consider the
   crises of global warming/climate change to be of greater consequence than
   the loss of biodiversity and the extinction of species. The former may be
   managed, albeit with enormous difficulty. The latter is irreversible.
3 *King James Bible (1611)*: Genesis, chapter I, v. 26–28:

   26 And God said, Let us make man in our image, after our
   likeness: and let them have dominion over the fish of the sea,

what are we to make of the fact that for those who still claim
this right it seems that it is precisely this view of the world (and
all that it implies for action) that erodes the capacity to manage,
well, relations, even with respect to their own affairs, let alone
those of the wider social and natural world—which continues to
sink further into the likelihood of extreme (multiple) crises. If
social and ecological catastrophe attends the anthropocentric,
if it grows out its logic, it is because in forcing centrality, in
making man, in the classic formulation, "the measure of all
things" it excludes every relation of reciprocity. This is most
obvious in the case of nature. Placed as service it has no other
role save as the "almost worthless material" on which extraction
works. Whether as matter or system it can *only* be dominated
or denied—or the object of a sentiment. But what applies to
nature applies today to every other element in the situation.
Today, profit, which is the only reason for the perpetuation of
domination, will happily sell the entire world. But profit is no less
anthropocentric. It too participates in what anthropocentrism
solidifies: the declaration of an absolute difference that denies
the real incommensurabilities at work in relations—the
nonabsolute differences that can only, in the end, be negotiated
with. Like capitalism, the anthropocentric makes it impossible to
engage, let alone to resolve, the social and natural crises we face.
On these grounds (and more) the anthropocentric (and all that
today under different guises enacts a similar logic—especially
technological reasoning, data, and artificial intelligence) is that
from which we need to free ourselves. It is through which we
cannot think (or act) our way out of the complex impasse in
which we find ourselves. To put it bluntly, it must be deleted from
thought.

Why then, given this, in the lines given above, do we
find Arendt asserting—strongly—the necessity of "a strictly
anthropocentric world?"

> and over the fowl of the air, and over the cattle, and over all
> the earth, and over every creeping thing that creepeth upon the
> earth. 27 So God created man in his own image, in the image
> of God created he him; male and female created he them. 28
> And God blessed them, and God said unto them, Be fruitful,
> and multiply, and replenish the earth, and subdue it: and have
> dominion over every living thing that moveth upon the earth.

The answers to this are complex and inherently ambiguous. They point to the difficulties of how we "overcome" the legacies we inherit. The immediate hinge, for Arendt, is the question of "Ends and means," which are not merely a matter of words: they translate the anthropocentric division between man (ends) and all other living (and nonliving) things (means) into the realm of action. The "unending chain" of this *non*-relation is what enacts in reality the theological division. But the very fact that action in the world is abstractedly split in this way means that all that is not a subject, that is determined as a mere thing, or as "means," is *essentially* devalued. The world becomes "meaningless"—which is to say that meaning is sought only in profit—that which, in the absence of project, "tells us what to do." The dominance of profit in turn perpetuates—ever more radically in the scale of things, both natural and human—the split. How then to escape this trap? One answer is to declare the opposite: "antihumanism," "biocentrism," and to pursue these with moral and political fervor. The problem is that these are "answers" to a condition that no longer exists. For Arendt, the consequences of the anthropocentric gave rise to an existential, but not yet a substantive crisis (one that could, c.1958, scarcely be glimpsed in the forms we now encounter it). But today the anthropocentric is inescapable. At the level of global impacts of economic life and under the generalized condition of the artificial (today it is no longer nature but the artificial that constitutes the horizon, medium and prime condition of existence of the world) the anthropocentric is no longer that which seeks its theological justification by attributing to God what man desires. It is rather that which is enacted on a daily basis by actions in the world. Today we *live* the anthropocentric. We are anthropocentric in every one of our consequential acts. No mere mental "stepping out" of this condition dissipates its force. "Antihumanism," "biocentrism," and so forth are merely means of seeking to displace this actuality. Much of our unhappiness is as a consequence of refusing to acknowledge this fact.

But this brings us to a paradox. The anthropocentric is a major source of crisis. Yet there is no other than the anthropocentric (to pretend otherwise is delusional). But this means that, unless we accept disaster, the only way out of the anthropocentric (out of crisis) is *through* the anthropocentric. As Arendt so cleverly puts it, it is only through adopting a *strictly* anthropocentric perspective that we might overcome the nihilism that has been created. "Strictly" means here to acknowledge and take the consequences of the anthropocentric. For us that means accepting the responsibility of being/acting/world-making in inevitably and inescapably anthropocentric ways. To be strict concerning the anthropocentricism of all that we do in the world is to accept our *absolute* dependency, first on that which we make (our crises, and those of nature, are crises, in the widest historical sense, of "manufacture") and second on everything (meaning every living thing and every natural system) that constitutes the context of our making. But this in turn means, and here the anthropocentric itself begins to twist, both accepting this condition and understanding that it is only through *how*, that is, through the manner, the modes, of how we manifest the anthropocentric in the world that we can learn to go beyond the historical limits of the anthropocentric. We can accept these dependencies and turn them to long-term advantage once we understand that in its daily concrete negotiations with the *real* incommensurabilities of persons and nature, the artificial does not *only* repeat and enshrine the anthropocentric in the traditional sense, it also, both in instances and in deeper potential, enacts, or shows us how to enact, the overcoming of the means–ends division—how to break, in other words, with the mechanisms that maintain "unending chain" of the original anthropocentric split. In these moments, which are, once we understand them, the conditions and possibilities of the artificial itself, the means–end separation dissolves. What at present defutures—and radically so—turns: means become ends, ends conversely means; that is, the means to what is not defuturing. Half a century ago, even beyond her own arguments, Arendt pointed us in this direction, out of a condition that has ruled, disastrously, for half-a-millennia. Thus the paradox she understood and that we must face: that only the "strictly anthropocentric" can save us from the consequences of the anthropocentric.

Clive Dilnot

See also
BEGINNINGS, COMMON INTERESTS,
INSTRUMENTALISM, OBJECTIVITY,
TOGETHERNESS

BEGINNINGS
BOURGEOIS
BUREAUCRACY

BEGINNINGS

"*With the creation of man, the principle of beginning came into the world itself …,*" Arendt wrote in *The Human Condition.*[1] Each human is born into this world as a unique being, distinguishing himself/herself from equals through speech and action. "*It is in the nature of beginning that something new is started which cannot be expected from whatever may have happened before,*" Arendt continued.[2] It is because man is capable of action that he is capable of unexpected novelty. A little later, she circumscribes this novelty as follows: "*the new … always appears in the guise of a miracle.*"[3] As such, Arendt's notion of new beginnings is intimately linked to the miracle of birth, hence deeply human.

Later, the English physicist and science fiction writer Arthur C. Clarke utilized a similar vocabulary when he wrote: "*Any sufficiently advanced technology is indistinguishable from magic,*" thereby extending the miracle, the magic of "the new" beyond man to technologies.[4] In Arendt's view, each individual's novelty is intimately linked to their "birth" among equals. This makes one wonder whether in the case of such advanced technologies we could also extend her notion of this deeper "web of human relationships"? Who is equal to whom? What would the web of relationships between humans and technologies entail?

It is a world pregnant with such Clarke-like magic and Arendt-like miraculous "novelty" on the brink of which we might find ourselves today: one in which novelty-generating actions might no longer be a human privilege. When artificially intelligent "things" can autonomously act within the surroundings they coinhabit with their human counterparts and when they are sufficiently advanced as to be able to reflect on their

1   Hannah Arendt, *The Human Condition* (Chicago, IL: University of Chicago Press, [1958] 1998), 177.
2   Arendt, *The Human Condition*, 177.
3   Ibid., 178.
4   Arthur C. Clarke, *Profiles of the Future: An Inquiry into the Limits of the Possible* (Popular Library, [1962] 1973).

condition and the world and engage in dialogue about it with
us, a new dimension of relationships is opened up to us. At
that point we are no longer talking linear, goal-directed robotic
laborers incapable of action, in Arendt's sense, but we might
technologically create or uphold a situation in which also these
technological *"doers of deeds"* are simultaneously *"speakers of
words,"*[5] each developing a unique personal identity in a world
among humans.

Decades ago designer John Chris Jones saw a need for the
role and focus of designers in the future to shift from simply
seeking solutions to a deeper exploration and more profound
understanding and definition of the problems or problem spaces.[6]
Jones emphasized that to come to new ideas one needs to take
away the foundations of the old ones. As such, as "doers of
deeds" and "speakers of words" one can imagine future teams,
consisting of humans and artificial intelligences, to be engaged
in a design process fundamentally driven by debate, one in
which they challenge each other's views and understandings
of the problem at hand as a way to nurture the coevolution of
their ideas. What propels this helix-like motion of coevolution
is the human–nonhuman interdependency, anchored in a search
for mutual understanding and intellectual challenge. Ideally, in
this setting human and nonhuman designers would question
their underlying viewpoints and frameworks, rather than just
their design decisions. After all, it is only by unearthing and
challenging the assumptions underlying our current systems and
conditions that we can come to new understandings and new
beginnings.

In this reframing of design as a debate, a dialogue between
human and nonhuman intelligences, its deeply social and even
political dimensions come to the fore, this time just not solely
between human beings. By confronting one another with
different viewpoints—even those of an artificial intelligence—we
may grow our understanding not only of the problem at hand
but also of ourselves, our "nature," our humanity. Nonhuman
or no-longer-(entirely)-human intelligences may help humans

5   Arendt, *The Human Condition*, 178–9.
6   John Chris Jones, *Design Methods* (New York: John Wiley, [1970] 1992).

to perceive their world and actions in a different light as much as in return humans may help them to keep their actions sound and humane, to safeguard the quality and breadth of our mutual interdependence. This could be one way of framing our interdependence.

Although the world described above might not be fully here yet, and although the challenge of how to position ourselves when designing these artificially intelligent systems is not even a new challenge, the rapid technological advancement makes it one we can no longer ignore or postpone. As designers, we need to ask ourselves: How do we wish for such relationships, actions, and interactions to shape the futures we will coinhabit? How do we design what it is that binds and balances the human and the nonhuman? How do we make sure enough voices are heard, how do we ensure plurality, living as unique beings among equals? How do we design for common "*inter-ests*," as Hannah Arendt would say? In light of the complexity of some of the challenges we face as humanity, it is likely we will need the help of artificial intelligences increasingly over the coming decades, not just within the context of the likes of climate change and space travel but also with respect to interhuman issues of politics, governance, human rights, peacekeeping, wealth distribution, etc. One could argue that the very notion of interdependence and symbiosis could be established as a common interest that would drive and guide the actions of both humans and artificial intelligences. How to shape these relationships are important design choices for us to make.

While many fear the advent and proliferation of nonhuman intelligences, one ought not to forget it is inherently human to seek extension of our capabilities through the technologies and tools that we create. We owe it to ourselves, to humanity, and its surrounding world of nature and ideas, to engage in a collective imagination—a making of new *common sense* between human and nonhuman agents, to use an Arendtian term—of benevolent future outcomes for this new world to unfold while we are creating it. These guiding images, these guiding debates—through and with our technological creations—carry the potential of taking us humans and our full ecosystem of relationships within this world to new heights. We should do so not out of techno-optimism but out of our belief in human imagination and inventiveness and the realization that without it we might head toward even darker times. The designing *of* and *as* a dialogue between human and nonhuman agents has the potential to fuel the continuous changes of perspective necessitated by a changing, complex world, the imagination of alternatives which—once uttered—can materialize (into) new things.

Nik Baerten

See also
ANIMAL RATIONALE, FREEDOM,
INSTRUMENTALITY, PLAY, TECHNOLOGY

BOURGEOIS

How we assess, valorize, and justify knowledge is a powerful mechanism instrumentalized by the bourgeois to exert an indelible influence on society. Hannah Arendt makes a clear distinction between the *responsible* citoyen who is "concerned with public affairs as the affairs of all," heavily invested in the public realm, and that of the private and isolated bourgeois who "judges and uses all public institutions by the yardstick of his private interests."[1] The bourgeois irresponsibly wield what Foucault refers to as power-knowledge, by controlling what is considered valid knowledge, its means of verification, and by determining the relationship between the knower and the known, ultimately defining who can be a "knower." The Western tradition of design, intertwined with the logic of post-enlightenment reason and born from the capitalist mode of production, is an important purveyor of this epistemological marginalization.[2] Design has and continues to be a set of practices, a disciplinary orientation and a mode of thinking that acts in support of a specifically modern structure of power—sustaining bourgeois and colonial pursuits.[3] This text confronts the bourgeois design epistemology vis-à-vis theories of coloniality and design practices from the global south.

Knowledge has been, and continues to be, one of the core tools for sustaining and reproducing coloniality—the continuing structures and cultures of colonialism in the modern capitalist system. This can be seen in the dominance of scientific rigor (veracity), analytical gaze (relationship between knower and known), and the authority of English language and "Western" academic institutions (knower). Yet it is essential, in order to make any meaningful commentary on this respect, that we

---

1 Hannah Arendt, *The Origins of Totalitarianism* (New York: Harvest Books, [1951] 1979), 336.
2 Tony Fry, *Design History Australia: A Source Text in Methods and Resources* (Sydney: Hale & Iremonger, 1988).
3 Mathew Norman Kiem, *The Coloniality of Design* (PhD Diss., Western Sydney University, 2017).

recognize the global epistemicide that has occurred at the hands of bourgeois epistemology.[4]

The bourgeois epistemology decouples the subject from its epistemic location, rendering it universalist and totalizing. This can be traced back to Descartes; his famous *ego-cogito* struck a wedge between mind and nature, deifying the mind without situating its thoughts in the *fallen* world. With this, the particular of the local is obliterated by an abstract universalism, empowering the "ego-politics of knowledge" over the "geopolitics of knowledge," which, Roman Grosfoguel explains, "has allowed Western man (the gendered term is intentionally used here) to represent his knowledge as the only one capable of achieving a universal consciousness, and to dismiss non-Western knowledge as particularistic and, thus, unable to achieve universality."[5] Such a decoupling befits modernist and colonial exploits, establishing dominance through the dismissal of situated knowledge.

Design, Coloniality, and Knowledge

While design epistemology is still nascent, it must be challenged, prodded, and provoked to wrench it free from the sociocultural trajectory from whence it emerged, and aiming to open up new possibilities for emancipatory transformations. A key starting point is the question, "from *where* does the subject, in this case the designer, speak?" from which ethnic, cultural, gender, sexual, or class *location*? "I am where I think" is a basic epistemic premise to delegitimize claims of an only universal epistemology; it geo-historicizes and biographically locates knowledge.[6] Unlike the bourgeois abstraction of knowledge, which is exercised with impunity, grounding knowledge implies modes of knowing-in-action and can therefore be held responsible and accountable.

---

4   Boaventura de Sousa Santos, *Epistemologies of the South: Justice against Epistemicide* (New York: Routledge, 2015), 1.

5   Ramon Grosfoguel, "The Epistemic Decolonial Turn: Beyond Political Economy Paradigms," in Walter D., Mignolo and Arturo Escobar (ed.), *Globalization and the Decolonial Option* (New York: Routledge, 2013), 68.

6   Walter Mignolo, *The Darker Side of Western Modernity: Global Futures, Decolonial Options* (Durham: Duke University Press, 2011), 81.

The Western design tradition emphasizes a universalism rooted in the requirements of market expansion and with it the distension of the modernist/colonial world system.[7] A detaching of design from the particulars of aesthetics, semantics, and user interaction served the logistical and economic demands of mass production and cultural domination. Ikea, for example, is active in thirty-eight countries and is becoming a global standard for design objects, influencing notions of value, quality, form, aesthetics, and so forth. Ikea promotes the agenda that one design fits all, regardless of the context—across countries as diverse as China, Saudi Arabia, and India.

Calderón and Gutiérrez remind us that in many languages, including Chinese, Arabic, and Hindi (as well as scores of indigenous ones) there is not an etymological trace of the word "design" (with its European roots).[8] They point out that there are terms referring to "forms of prefiguring artefacts that could be considered equivalent to practices of what in the west is considered design."[9] The bourgeois epistemology makes invisible broad swathes of design practices, rendered, at best, as oddities or obscurities. Such is the case of the kaleidoscopically colored *Cholets*, built by new urban dwellers from indigenous communities of El Alto, Bolivia, or the annual reconstruction of the elaborate Q'iswa Chaka rope bridge by the Quechua indigenous community of the Quehue district in Peru. These practices, along with a myriad of others, certainly do not require recognition as design to be validated in their own worlds; however, it would be immensely enriching to design practice and discourse to flatten the epistemological (and praxis) hierarchies, therefore enabling such practices to inform other design practices and not be invisibilized by, for instance, Ikea's cultural universalism.

To recognize epistemic locations is to realize that design cannot be the same in suburban United States as in the slums of Delhi,

---

7   Arturo Escobar, *Autonomía y Diseño: la Realización de lo Comunal* *Autonomy and Design: The Realization of the Communal* (Buenos Aires: Tinta Limón, 2017).

8   Pablo Calderón Salazar and Alfredo Gutiérrez Borrero, "Letters South of (Nordic) Design," *7th NORDES Proceedings, Oslo, Norway, June 15–17.* (2017).

9   Salazar and Borrero, "Letters South of (Nordic) Design," 5.

or in the rural Spanish communities as in the new urban settings of El Alto in Bolivia. Situated epistemologies present critical alternatives to the dominant bourgeois epistemology by providing an *ecology of knowledge*, as de Sousa explains.[10] Such an ecology does not refute scientific rationalism but challenges its dominance by portraying it as one of many possible ways of knowing. It serves not the interests of the bourgeois but those of the public realm, increasing the number of participating voices and perspectives. Arendt emphasizes the importance of thinking "representatively," to be able to think from another's position or standpoint in order to expand our worldview and ultimately arrive at more valid political judgments. For this, she stresses the need for a "multiplication of perspectives" in order to show a particular issue "from all sides, in every possible perspective, until it is flooded and made transparent by the full light of human comprehension."[11]

Our argument is therefore geared at challenging the incumbent bourgeois epistemology in general and in design, in particular, yet without proposing a *better* epistemology. Instead, we would argue for the need of an array of situated epistemologies as standpoints from which to responsibly expand relational practices, such as in design. Shared public discourse is enlarged by this ecology, supporting participative citizen action to combat the obscuring of the public realm. *The dark times* of the bourgeois epistemology have left us blind to a world of astonishing design practices; as Alfredo Gutiérrez and Pablo Calderón aptly put it, "designs with other names have always been present in many subaltern cultures; we have simply been educated to not see them."[12]

Michael Kaethler and Pablo Calderón Salazar

See also
CITIZENSHIP, IMPERIALISM, PLURALITY

10 Boaventura de Sousa Santos, *Epistemologies of the South.*
11 Hannah Arendt, "Truth and Politics," in Jose Medina and David Wood (eds.), *Truth: Engagements across Philosophical Traditions* (Oxford: Blackwell, 2010), 303.
12 Salazar and Borrero, "Letters South of (Nordic) Design," 4.

BUREAUCRACY

The greater the bureaucratization of public life, the greater will be the attraction of violence. In a fully developed bureaucracy there is nobody left with whom one could argue, to whom one could present grievances, on whom the pressures of power could be exerted. Bureaucracy is the form of government in which everybody is deprived of political freedom, of the power to act; for the rule by Nobody is not no-rule, and where all are equally powerless we have a tyranny without a tyrant.

Hannah Arendt, "A Special Supplement: Reflections on Violence"[1]

Thus proclaimed Hannah Arendt in 1969. Since then, it's only gotten worse. While the bureaus that begat bureaucracy might now be beset with fewer carbon copies and Rolodexes than they were in Arendt's time, those workstations still harbor plenty of virtual warrens into which a client can get lost: the ethereal labyrinths of automated telephone attendants; the websites either so deceptively slick or so woefully disorienting that they become black holes of intelligence; the customer support agents perpetually "busy with other callers"; the contact pages through which we file our inquiries or complaints to No One in Particular, and then wait for No One to not respond. Then there are the algorithms that anonymously and inscrutably determine when we become persons of interest, subject to additional scrutiny or extreme vetting; or the neural nets enlisted to identify particular agents and predict behaviors, and whose own methods of autodidacticism defy human comprehension. Who's to blame when the algorithm denies your insurance claim? Where's the tyrant in the Cloud?

1   Hannah Arendt, "A Special Supplement: Reflections on Violence,"
     New York Review of Books (February 27, 1969), http://www.nybooks.com/
     articles/1969/02/27/a-special-supplement-reflections-on-violence/.

Sublimating bureaucracy in the faceless machine only further obfuscates governance and diminishes accountability. Yet the solution is not banishing bureaucracy. As Peter Aucoin proposes, bureaucracy is actually essential to good government, because good government requires "organizational designs that promote democratic direction, control and accountability."[2] Bureaucracy, designed well, can serve these ends.

"Bureaucracy" and "good design": these are two concepts that rarely meet in either thought or practice. Yet architects, activists, and archivists have long sought to design knowledge infrastructures and governance structures—cataloguing systems, professional organizations, treaties, international standards—that promote good global governance. Granted, some of those "best laid plans" ultimately veered more toward aesthetic and ideological authoritarianism than toward democracy. But Futurism and Modernism and other -*isms* have, we hope, taught us that designs for "political freedom" tend to emerge not from elitist, auteurist edicts but through collective, representative negotiation—through public processes that are designed to allow for a little agonism and disarray.

How can the "power of the desk," the etymological root of bureaucracy, promote the "power to act," the power to appear before one another, which Arendt entreats us to do?[3] How do we transform bureaucracy's Nobodies into Somebodies who *can* appear and act—and who can interrogate the desk, the metaphorical administrative apparatus, that sits between them and shapes their agency and interactions?

Maybe design can help. Even the World Bank thinks so. In 2017 they launched a new Bureaucracy Lab with the expectation that design can transform policy, public sector organizations, and officials' motivations for action.[4] Three years earlier, the U.S.

2   Peter Aucoin, "The Design of Public Organizations for the 21st Century: Why Bureaucracy Will Survive in Public Management," *Canadian Public Administration* vol. 40, no. 2 (1997): 291.
3   Hannah Arendt, *The Human Condition* (Chicago, IL: University of Chicago Press, [1958] 1998).
4   World Bank. "Innovating Bureaucracy," November 8–9, 2017, Washington, DC, http://www.worldbank.org/en/events/2017/10/16/ innovating-bureaucracy#1.

Government opened 18F, an agency inside the General Services Administration dedicated to transforming the government's digital service delivery and tech product development.[5] They salvaged Healthcare.gov, the disastrous first-generation website behind the Affordable Care Act; developed the College Scorecard, featuring data on college costs, graduation rates, graduate debt, and so forth; created an interactive website featuring FBI crime data; built Federalist, a platform that allows other government agencies to build websites easily and in compliance with federal requirements; and created login.gov, an identity management portal that allows for a single sign-on across government websites. "We effect change," they proudly proclaim, "by practicing user-centered development, testing to validate hypotheses, shipping often, and deploying products in the open."

All well and good. Who *wouldn't* want an IRS website that minimizes the pain of tax-filing? Who wouldn't prefer a single, all-access, secure password to dozens of discrete codes? Still, I wonder if the platformization of governance, the score-carding and dash-boarding of performance, might be reifying technocratic measurements and commercial values. Do such designed efficiencies at the interface leave the underlying bureaucratic methods unchecked? Does the convenience of a scorecard preclude us from asking whether measurable, graph-able, mappable data offer a valid and sufficient assessment of the value of our public institutions and services? With whom do we argue about the statistics underlying such visualizations? To whom do we present our grievances regarding declining public support for higher education, stats-driven criminal justice, and mass incarceration—all visible in the shadows of these visualizations?

Design has to intervene *behind* the interface, too. Rather than merely making bureaucracy efficient and seamless—or, at the very least, tolerable—designers should marshal their skills and resources to make bureaucracy and its underlying ideologies intelligible and reform actionable. Consider Jenny Hung's *01 magazine*, which strives to deobfuscate the visa application process; and the Center for Urban Pedagogy's various guides that introduce street vendors to their legal rights and restrictions,

---

5   18f, accessed August 8, 2018, https://18f.gsa.gov/.

and that steer recent immigrants through the healthcare system.[6] Consider, too, the Center for Spatial Research's Million Dollar Blocks visualization, which maps the underlying political economy—the "city-prison migration flow"—underlying New York's criminal justice system.[7] Let's also acknowledge the tools designed by myriad digital activists, from Tactical Tech to the Electronic Frontier Foundation, that foreground issues of algorithmic bias and data mining. Let's think, too, about how design can transform patrons' experiences and understandings of government services and civic institutions—how the architecture and interior design of a library, a public housing lobby, or a courtroom can cultivate civic subjectivities. "The objects, procedures, and customs of the court," Anna Altman observes, "all serve to remind us that we are at the mercy of the law …. What if justice was performed in a space that not only afforded respect and agency to everybody involved, from the judge on down to defendants, but treated each person as an equal member of the community?"[8] What if we designed bureaucratic systems and spaces that allow us to appear before one another, to question and challenge the bureaucratic apparatus, to argue productively, to exercise our power to act?

Shannon Mattern

See also
ACTIVISM, LAW, REIFICATION, SPONTANEITY,
SUPERFLUITY

---

6   o1 Magazine, accessed August 8, 2018, http://www.o1mag.com/.
7   Center for Spatial Research, "Million Dollar Blocks," accessed August 8, 2018, http://c4sr.columbia.edu/projects/million-dollar-blocks.
8   Anna Altman (2018) "The People's Court," *Urban Omnibus* (January 10, 2018), https://urbanomnibus.net/2018/01/the-peoples-court/.

CITIZENSHIP
COMMON GOOD
COMMON INTERESTS
COMMON WORLD
COMPREHENSION
COURAGE
CREATIVITY

CITIZENSHIP

To discuss citizenship from Arendt's politics and philosophy means to understand first and foremost not necessarily what citizenship means, entails, provides, or makes, but the lack thereof. As a Jewish refugee with a deprived German citizenship, which left her without a state for eighteen years, Arendt understands the condition of statelessness as central to citizenship. In truth, unlike many design initiatives that take the status of the citizen for granted, Arendt would rather think about citizenship based on the lived experiences of noncitizens, those whose lack of belonging to a state due to their exclusion from a national community results in lacking the rights that citizenship provides, including human rights:

> The fundamental deprivation of human rights is manifested first and above all in the deprivation of a place in the world which makes opinions significant and actions effective. Something much more fundamental than freedom and justice, which are rights of citizens, is at stake when belonging to the community into which one is born is no longer a matter of course and not belonging no longer a matter of choice, or when one is placed in a situation where, unless he commits a crime, his treatment by others does not depend on what he does or does not do. This extremity, and nothing else, is the situation of people deprived of human rights. They are deprived, not of the right to freedom, but of the right to action; not of the right to think whatever they please, but of the right of opinion.[1]

Without *having a place in the world*, Arendt argues that politics that is performed through acting in the plurality of the world is not imaginable. "To have a place in the world means that each singular individual, who is different from other individuals, has a site from which to form a distinctive opinion on a common,

1   Hannah Arendt, *The Origins of Totalitarianism* (New York: Harvest Books, [1951] 1979), 296.

shared world."[2] This tangible world is the world made by the plurality of different human beings, the artifice, the materialized realm. However, such a world is not necessarily egalitarian. It becomes egalitarian by organization and struggle. Thus, to be a citizen for Arendt means (i) to have a place in the shared, common world and (ii) to be able to appear in such a world through imagining and forming opinions as well as participating in the processes of testing and judging hers and her peers' opinions.

What are the material practices generated by state and nonstate actors that result in the *loss of a place* in the world? How does this loss hide behind different techniques and designs, in what ways is it generated through objects and technologies, and fashioned by innovation and progress? These questions would help us to think how designing has been, and still is, complicit in the destruction of the ability to have a place in the world for many, producing the displaced and stateless populations worldwide while providing and securing a place for many others. This is done in a world where citizenship, nationalized by different nation-states, operates through various material and specific design practices such as passports, biometrics, and visa regimes. In such a world, citizenship is frequently protected, advertised, and reproduced by cultural productions and institutions as something authentic, pure, and homogenous, which others have to assimilate to or otherwise be expelled from. Furthermore, in such a world access to material resources and infrastructures is strictly regulated and thus uneven. Consequently as seen by states and supported by many citizens, the access in order to remain exclusive requires protection through fortification of territories and criminalization of irregular migrants and all those who flee to seek asylum and refuge by various violent material means of detention, encampment, and deportation.

Moreover, what are the material conditions for *having a place* in the world? If the world Arendt talks about is the shared, common, tangible, made world, what are those concrete objects,

---

2   Richard Bernstein, "Hannah Arendt on the Stateless," *Parallax* vol. 11, no. 1 (2005): 56.

systems, services, and practices that provide and secure such places in the world? How can these places be imagined, thought, and configured through materials and materialities at hand? How are they made, designed, and mobilized? Who has the agency and ability to imagine, prototype, and produce these places? This might sound abstract but will appear real, situated, and concrete if one pays attention to the amount of labor, struggle, organization, and creativity behind the political projects that undocumented migrants, illegalized border transgressors, and stateless refugees have mobilized. Their struggle reminds us that citizenship is nothing pure, authentic, and transcendental. It is made and can thus be unmade and remade at any moment. They teach us that citizenship as practiced today does not automatically bring justice or equality. Hence, we urgently need to expand and work harder for another concept of citizenship beyond the one that is tied to nationalized welfare states. This entails processes of collective imagination for articulating new relations to the state, individuals, and various rights[3] beyond the current liberal European notion of citizenship that is built upon a constructed image of a homogenous people imagined as ethnically pure, singular, and united; produced and sustained historically through racial segregation, forced and slave labor, and land confiscation—upon exclusion of many to include a deserving few based on their gender, race, or class. In this time of the rerise of neofascism, when nationality and race are secured as the ground for membership, it is important to reject the notion of citizenship as identical with nationality in order to be able to imagine new openings. In other words, "one can no longer be a bystander"[4] while witnessing the increasing loss of the ability to have a place in the world for those who are born outside of citizenship or are pushed toward its margins and thrown out of it in the name of the nation and its welfare.

As designers engage more and more with how citizenship can be practiced, imagined, and negotiated, Arendt reminds us

3   Engin F. Isin and Greg M. Nielsen, eds., *Acts of Citizenship* (London: Zed Books, 2008).

4   Hannah Arendt, *Essays in Understanding, 1930–1954: Formation, Exile, and Totalitarianism* (New York: Harvest Books, [1951] 1979), 4–5.

that we may think of how the condition of statelessness is the very constitution of our current conception of citizenship. Before turning to citizens, we may want, just like Arendt, to first question citizenship and its exclusionary mechanisms and then think of how designing can engage in resisting the loss of a place in the world and supporting the political struggles of undocumented migrants and stateless refugees worldwide who try to make a place in the world.

Mahmoud Keshavarz

See also
COMPREHENSION, EVIL, PARIAH

COMMON GOOD

> When Robespierre declared that "everything which is necessary to maintain life must be common good and only the surplus can be recognized as private property," he was not only reversing premodern political theory, which held that it was precisely the citizens' surplus in time and goods that must be given and shared in common; he was, again in his own words, finally subjecting revolutionary government to "the most sacred of all laws, the welfare of the people, the most irrefragable of all titles, necessity."
>
> Hannah Arendt, *On Revolution*[1]

When we invoke the words "common good," we intimate that our futures are bound and that our collective survival must compel us to think differently about how we live together. Such an invocation should also inspire us to see specific resources we might have once assumed to be held privately as belonging to everyone and are consequently essential to our collective welfare. Common good reorients us from what Arturo Escobar calls the patriarchal capitalist modernity,[2] toward a more maternalistic mode of existence that privileges collective needs over individual wants.

A shift of this magnitude necessitates that resource allocation requires a profound commitment to collective expertise. For example, when designers work for the common good, they make room for other voices, which implies that an acknowledgment of their limitations grants agency to "nonexpert" participants and ensures that as Hannah Arendt writes, "everything which is necessary to maintain life must be common good."

Design for common good reveals a different type of politics, that is, one that not just favors the making (of) things but also making (with) things. When designers commit to this mode of

1   Hannah Arendt, *On Revolution* (New York: Viking Press, 1963), 60.
2   Arturo Escobar, *Designs for the Pluriverse: Radical Interdependence, Autonomy, and the Making of Worlds* (Durham: Duke University Press, 2018).

working, they participate in a larger ecosystem where they are constantly negotiating with other problem owners. They no longer work in silos and they no longer make paternalistic decisions that are not often beneficial to the collective. We might be able to understand the politics of designing for the common good from overlapping vantage points relating to what exactly is the focus of negotiation, the participants, and where and how such participation might occur. The above mode of questioning allows us to critically situate the role of *the designing commoner*—one who works from within the problem, as a participant within a broader ecosystem that includes nonhuman entities.

Not Just Surplus

Regarding what is being negotiated, designers working with artefacts combine with such artefacts to "make explicit the protocols of design."[3] In so doing, their combined agency opens up spaces for rethinking, reframing, and re-engaging with resource management, resulting in a different approach to resource sharing. Pelle Ehn describes this shift as design moving beyond projects (or use before use) to collective engagement (or design before design). However, collective engagements do not exclusively relate to surplus resources, especially when the limits that determine surplus are blurred. For example, the limits of private ownership of nonrivalrous goods (or goods whose consumption does not result in their depletion, such as software code or data) are difficult to ascertain.

In his book *Here Comes Everybody,* Clay Shirky posits that excess contributions of nonrivalrous goods happen via social exchange and other social mechanisms. Shirky draws from Ronald Coase's theory that contributors of surplus resources would be able to operate under what is called the Coasean floor where transactional costs and managerial interference are lowered.[4] Shirky concludes that such social exchanges that lower

3 Pelle Ehn, "Participation in Design Things," in *Proceedings of the Tenth Anniversary Conference on Participatory Design 2008* (Indianapolis: Indiana University, 2008), 92–101.
4 Clay Shirky, *Here Comes Everybody: How Change Happens When People Come Together* (London: Penguin UK, 2009).

transaction costs often occur without external governance. But as Arendt indicated in the introductory quote, it is not just the surplus that should be held in common but the welfare of all should be prioritized over private property, and that such welfare is negotiated in the public realm.

A Revolutionary Form of Governance

Regarding where the negotiation occurs, Hannah Arendt identifies the *polis*, or public realm, as the place where concerns are negotiated and where collective agency is exercised.[5] This public realm of collective negotiation is distinct from private life. For one, the public is an artificial institution relating to the Greek *isonomy*, that is, equality of civic or political rights that precedes and is independent of the State. Also, the *polis* guarantees that such a form of equality is earned in association with others. According to Arendt, equality must primarily exist in the political realm, since it is through negotiation with peers in the *polis*, as the Greeks contend, that equality is birthed. The *polis*, therefore, stands as a political sphere where freedom is mutually ensured.[6]

Collective Welfare as Necessity

Regarding how the negotiations happen, we can look at commons as a way that communities have historically built rules and norms around resource sharing. When, for example, a group of fishers in the Niger Delta form structures around the enforcement of fishing routes, they necessitate governance of resources by the resource users themselves. Even in design, several texts document how designers explore collective modes of engaging with others through making and collectively exploring problems, often through artefacts. From Carl DiSalvo's construction of the publics, to Erling Björgvinsson, Pelle Ehn, and Per-Anders Hillgren's agonistic participation in design, and others, designers continue to embrace the politics of working

5   Arendt, *On Revolution*, 31.
6   Ibid., 32.

together. DiSalvo characterizes the publics as not preexisting but instead constructed through issues, relating to the realization of the current state and the anticipation of the future implications of these issues.[7] In other words, when publics do not exist around an issue, it means that the issue was neither identified nor was it adequately articulated. Also, different publics may arise from the same issue.[8] For example, a renter-activist group that primarily serves the needs of minority renters such as the Community Alliance for Tenants based in Portland, Oregon, may respond differently to the injustice of exponential rental price increases than a majority-white Portland Tenants United in the same city.

In contrast, agonistic participatory design emphasizes collaboration by participants over consensus building and "Thinging" and infrastructuring as opposed to projects.[9] The concept of "Things," or "Thinging," has etymological origins in ancient Nordic and Germanic languages, and originally describes assemblies, or gatherings around rituals, and particularly places where disputes are publicly aired. According to Björgvinsson et al., Things are not derived from human interactions alone, but they also describe sociomaterial "collectives of humans and non-humans" where "matters of concerns" are addressed. Agonistic participation does not assume consensus and rational conflict resolution as its core goals. Instead, the "politics of the passionate disputes" present a flat hierarchy for engaging participants.[10]

Common good acknowledges the combined expertise of humans and nonhumans (with unique expertise) to form a new collective agency—one that enables us to "recommon" certain privatized resources as belonging to the commons. As shared earlier, the path to negotiation with our world from a long-term problem-solving perspective requires a reconstituting of our

7   Carl DiSalvo, "Design and the Construction of Publics," *Design Issues* vol. 25, no. 1 (2009): 48–63.
8   DiSalvo, "Design and the Construction of Publics," 50.
9   Erling Björgvinsson, Pelle Ehn, and Per-Anders Hillgren, "Agonistic Participatory Design: Working with Marginalised Social Movements," *CoDesign* vol. 8, nos 2–3 (2012): 127–44.
10 Björgvinsson, Ehn, and Hillgren, "Agonistic Participatory Design: Working with Marginalised Social Movements," 42.

collective livelihood to one that consistently considers the needs of the "other," from understanding what is being negotiated, to determining who the participants are, identifying where such negotiation occurs, and how such negotiation happens. The ancient West African Adinkra symbol *Sankofa* tells us that we must look to the past to determine where we are going. In the same vein, the Anthropocene age causes us to see the expansion of design's profile to that of confronting the way we have engaged with our world, and asking us essential questions about our shared future existence. The realities of this age show us that we can no longer sustain a selfish path since our actions increasingly bear direct consequences on others. Working in this mode emphasizes mutual dependence that implies common good and causes us to engage with "companion species" by sharing vital resources with a long-term posture.

Dimeji Onafuwa

See also
ANTHROPOCENTRISM, DEMOCRACY,
TOGETHERNESS

COMMON INTERESTS

What does it mean to design for "common interests"? Arendt uses this concept to define what lies between us (*"inter-est"*) or the rather intangible *"web of human relationships."*[1] She calls people involved with common interests "heroes." She states that in the ancient Greek period citizens were involved in debating common interests in the *agora*. However, people in the Roman period focused increasingly on their private interests and lost interest in being heroes, which led to the idea of representative democracy and the delegation of decision-making on common interests to a selected group of people.[2] Today, people still lack interest in what lies in-between them: organizations and individuals mainly focus on their private needs. This is what Arendt calls "dark times of the public realm": "History knows many periods of dark times in which the public realm has been obscured and the world became so dubious that people have ceased to ask any more of politics than that it shows due consideration for their vital interests and personal liberty."[3] However, she sees these dark times as an opportunity to do things differently, an idea that we are going to further develop by introducing the question what role designers can play in activating actors' recognition of and engagement in what they (can) have in common ("common interests") in times when the public realm is obscured.

Based on my experience in a case study "WegenWerken (RoadWorks)," which aimed to investigate the role of slow roads in the transformations to more sustainable cities, I argue that this role is dependent on designers' capabilities to articulate and mediate what lies in-between the complexity of—often invisible

---

1   Hannah Arendt, *The Human Condition* (Chicago, IL: University of
    Chicago Press, [1958] 1998), 182–3.
2   Arendt, *The Human Condition*, 136.
3   Ibid., 11.

and conflicting—actors and voices.[4] In detail, I investigated in this project how designers can materialize this mediation process between designers, public and private organizations, citizens, and policy on common interests by looking at the theory of Joanna Drucker on "interfaces." She defines interfaces as mediating environments, "critical zones" where people engage in interpretative activities, based on cues that they encounter on their path.[5] The project investigated a difference between horizontal interfaces that were designed to engage participants in debates across spatial scales and societal domains and vertical interfaces that were created to attract people who are part of local organizations and neighborhoods in concrete actions.

The project explored how designers could mediate the engagement in common interests by cocreating horizontal "favourable enabling ecosystems"[6] for debates between the participants. The common interests that were the subject of this study were soft connections or roads that are used for nonmotorized vehicles in the city of Genk. This city developed over a century from a series of small agricultural settlements into an industrial city of coal mines, structured as a grid of "citées" or mining sites with parts and neighborhoods that are not clearly connected to each other and the center. The involved actors codesigned an interface that took the form of a mental map that could engage people in a critical debate on the importance of soft connections, which are currently undervalued in linking presently disconnected areas on the microscale of the neighborhood and the macroscale of the city and the region. This interface challenged people's image of a car-focused city and activated people to express their diverse views on soft connections as common interests.

---

4   Liesbeth Huybrechts, Henric Benesch, and Jon Geib, "Institutioning: Participatory Design, Co-Design and the Public Realm," *CoDesign* vol. 13, no. 3 (August 2017): 145–7.

5   Johanna Drucker, "Humanities Approaches to Interface Theory," *Culture Machine* vol. 12 (2011): 10.

6   Ezio Manzini and Francesca Rizzo, "Small Projects/Large Changes: Participatory Design as an Open Participated Process," *CoDesign* vol. 7, nos. 3–4 (September 2011): 199–200.

On a vertical level, the project translated these debates in actions in the field[7] via the codesign of six urban interfaces in the city space on particular soft connections. One of the interfaces reconnects the hospital site to the city via soft connections. While the hospital was tightly embedded in the neighborhoods or "citées" during the period of the coalmines, it is now spatially disconnected. As a result, certain socioeconomic groups experience the hospital as difficult to access. As soft connections play an important role in including a diversity of groups in the city, the designers mapped together with residents, policy makers, and students which soft connections were already used to walk, run, or bike between the hospital site, the surrounding neighborhoods, and nature sites. Close to the hospital site, they collaboratively designed and built an urban interface—a wooden crossroad—where most of these soft connections cross, in order to invite people to walk or bike between these sites.

This essay demonstrated the importance of designing for common interests (in the described case soft connections' role in making more sustainable cities) in today's dark times of the public realm. However, it also showed that this is not a simple task. Because of their inherent unclear ownership and responsibilities, common interests are often a blind spot and little interesting for citizens, organizations, and financial investors. It was only after two years of intensive design work on these interfaces that the involved actors made the step from being slightly interested in the project to taking the responsibility to translate these interests into concrete spatial planning decisions. This experience revealed the limits of the question how designers can play a role in activating people's engagement in common interests. In dark times of the public realm, design's challenge is not only designing interfaces that mediate people's engagement with "common interests" but also invite them—as has also been stressed by Arendt—to make

7   Liesbeth Huybrechts, Virginia Tassinari, Barbara Roosen, and Theodora Constantinescu, "Work, Labor and Action. The Role of Participatory Design in (Re)Activating the Political Dimension of Work," *Proceedings of ACM Participatory Design Conference* vol. 1 (August 2018).

the step to take actions in relation to these interests. To enable people to be heroes in Arendt's sense, designers thus need to question how to build people's capabilities to collaboratively engage in *and* act on something beyond their own private interests.

Liesbeth Huybrechts

See also
ACTIVISM, BUREAUCRACY, *VITA ACTIVA*

COMMON WORLD

> The *common world* is what we enter when we are born and
> what we leave behind when we die. It transcends our life-
> span into past and future alike; it was there before we came
> and will outlast our brief sojourn in it. It is what we have
> in common not only with those who live with us, but also
> with those who were here before and with those who will
> come after us. But such a common world can survive the
> coming and going of the generations only to the extent that
> it appears in public. It is the publicity of the public realm
> which can absorb and make shine through the centuries
> whatever men may want to save from the natural ruin
> of time.
>
> Hannah Arendt, *The Human Condition*[1]

What has changed since Arendt wrote this? In a sense,
everything: today we are no longer dealing only with the familiar
ebb and flow of human conflict, but have fundamentally altered
the physical environment—turning it to something irreversibly
artificial and indelibly marked by our existence. At the same time
our perception of the world is rapidly changing too, reflecting this
and other facets of our new reality.

What, then, is to be done? How do we design for the
"common world" of the future, taking into account the ecological
constraints humanity has imposed, intentionally or not, upon
itself? How can we set new coordinates in the hope of creating
a more balanced world? We approached these questions by
first breaking "common" into seven of its component parts;
the resulting fragments reflect the increasing complexity of
our epoch.

---

1 Hannah Arendt, *The Human Condition* (Chicago, IL: University of
   Chicago Press, [1958] 1998), 55.

Commons

Everything, in reality, is held in common, but we live in an illusion—a harmful illusion—of individuality, artificial borders, the illusion of the bubble, the micro-environment, isolated from others, and the consequences of our actions. Marketing encourages this solipsistic selfishness, playing on the ego and the desire for status, which is directly at odds with the idea of shared resources. We must find ethical alternatives to the dominant model of platform capitalism that is rapidly diminishing and depleting—selling off cheaply, subdividing, ring-fencing, confining us to their world—the common natural, cultural, and intellectual resources that in truth belong to us all. We must find a way to preserve and repair, in Wendell Berry's words, "the world that we have set on fire."[2]

Common Time

The condition in which some of us live—and have lived for decades—is undeniably a luxurious one. This luxury is largely a consequence of advances made in the nineteenth century as the practice of burning coal shifted from being a domestic act to an industrial one. The mastering of electricity, generated from the burning of fossil fuels, finally gave humans control over nature—free from time, from the elements, the seasons, and the weather. This is of course an illusion. A piece of coal provides a very impressive eight kilowatt hours of energy per kilogram. But the coal takes hundreds of millions of years to form. This almost unimaginable quantity of time—this shared time, planetary time—is consumed at the flick of a switch, or at the press of a button: all dissipated, all devoured in an instant, all reduced to artificial human time, bringing this sublime gift to an ignoble end.

Common Space

A space where both humans and nonhumans participate in what Bruno Latour has termed "The Parliament of Things."[3]

---

2   Wendell Berry, *The World-Ending Fire: The Essential Wendell Berry* (London: Allen Lane, 2017).

3   Bruno Latour, *We Have Never Been Modern* (Cambridge, MA: Harvard University Press, 1993).

A "common space" confers agency to both nature and society, both life and death intertwine, humans and nonhumans. The concept can be best understood by reading *The Biosphere*, the book by Russian geochemist and mineralogist Vladimir I. Vernadsky that first uses the term in an ecological context.[4] As with John Steinbeck's poetic description of the tidal pool in *Sea of Cortez*—"barnacle and rock, rock and earth, earth and tree, tree and rain and air"[5]—a concept such as the biosphere takes into account both life and death as "powerful cosmic forces" where an "organism circulates its atoms through the biosphere over and over again."[6]

Common Good

A "Common Good" requires attention to scientific and technical solutions as much as ethical ones. Reflecting on "The Tragedy of the Commons,"[7] American ecologist and philosopher Garret Hardin quotes engineer Jerome Wiesner and physicist Herbert York—namely, their concern for the arms race that marked the 1960s. In their conclusion, they declare that such a "dilemma has no technical solution."[8] Hardin expands on this idea by stressing the importance of understanding progress as a change "in techniques of the natural sciences" as much as "changes in human values or ideas of morality."

Common Land

In "Open Spaces of the Future,"[9] social reformer Octavia Hill advocates for the equitable use of open spaces in the city of

---

4   Kevin Desmond, "Vladimir Ivanovich Vernadsky," *Planet Savers: 301 Extraordinary Environmentalists* (London: Routledge, 2008), 62–3; Vladimir Ivanovich Vernadsky, *The Biosphere* (New York: Springer, [1926] 1998).
5   John Steinbeck, *Sea of Cortez: A Leisurely Journal of Travel and Research* (New York: Viking, 1941).
6   Steinbeck, *Sea of Cortez: A Leisurely Journal of Travel and Research.*
7   Garrett Hardin, "The Tragedy of the Commons," *Science* vol. 162, no. 3859 (1968): 1243–8.
8   Hardin, "The Tragedy of the Commons," 1243–8.
9   Octavia Hill, "The Open Spaces of the Future," *Nineteenth Century* vol. xlvi (1899): 26–35.

London. Access to public natural environments is as pressing today as it was in Hill's time. However, space has never been so contested. Often the locus of "social marginalization," the planning of public and accessible open spaces is central to a higher quality of life in urban environments.[10] Advocating for open space is not only pressing for those who lack access to natural habitats—and who could most benefit from the advantages that these accrue—but also as a way of ensuring the geodiversity of our cities.

Common Market

How to build a truly common market, one that balances the idealism of dissolving national borders with resistance to the ravages of neoliberal capitalism? How can we make a market for the common good, rather than submitting to rule by the 1 percent or the 0.1 percent? The hypermarkets that colonized first the suburban landscape and now the virtual sphere have debased the term "market"—a word that once denoted a practical space of community exchange as well as a social hub. Let's create an *uncommon* market for the everyday—a local, seasonal market, not "common" in the sense of the same, centralized, uniform, standardized across places and cultures, but "uncommon" in the sense of diverse, decentralized, distributed, eclectic, *unexpected*.

Common Sense

Common sense is not what it used to be. The new common sense is digital, data driven: the collective unconscious, the hive mind, the Twittersphere, and so on, different, but not necessarily wiser. Then there are the once common skills increasingly being lost to automation. The more we buy into such technological dreams, the more we seem to lose touch with local knowledge, basic skills, and a relationship with the world around us. Back in the 1970s, Italian designer Enzi Mari sought to democratize furniture

---

10   Jordan W. Smith and Myron Floyd, "The Urban Growth Machine, Central Place Theory and Access to Open Space," *City, Culture and Society* vol. 4 (2013): 87–98.

construction with a DIY approach called "*autoprogettazione.*"[11]
The challenge is to bring back this type of common sense and
common skill, to encourage people to get involved—to actively
start building the future they want, with or without technology—
to avoid being exiled, in Jean Baudrillard's terms, "to the
irresponsibility of a mere spectator."[12]

**James Auger, Sónia Matos,
Julian Hanna, and Simone Ashby**

See also
DEMOCRACY, FABRICATION, IN-BETWEEN

11   Enzo Mari, *Autoprogettazione?* (Milan: Edizioni Corraini, 2008).
12   Jean Baudrillard, *The System of Objects* (London: Verso, 1996).

COMPREHENSION

> Comprehension does not mean denying the outrageous,
> deducing the unprecedented from precedents, or explaining
> phenomena by such analogies and generalizations that the
> impact of reality and the shock of experience are no longer
> felt. It means rather examining and bearing consciously
> the burden our century has placed on us—neither
> denying its existence nor submitting meekly to its weight.
> Comprehension, in short, means the unpremeditated,
> attentive facing up to, and resisting of reality—whatever it
> may be.
>
> Hannah Arendt, *The Origins of Totalitarianism*[1]

I

Published exactly halfway through the previous century,
Arendt's injunction has scarcely lost its force. Ours is hardly
a less "outrageous," less "unprecedented" moment. Nor, of
course, do we escape the parallel demand to "examine and bear
consciously" the weight of our own century. But the lesson that
Arendt offers here goes deeper. That which in common-place
speech is simply a form of understanding, without weight,
without direction, is here turned upon its head. In the context
of "Dark Times" comprehension does not remain neutral.
Comprehension (thought) cannot be disengaged from the
crises we face. Explanation—even, especially, to ourselves—
can no longer be "explaining away." It cannot be a matter of
cushioning experience, nor of evading what we already know
is actually the case. None of this should be possible in our
context Arendt insists, because comprehension is not neutral,
not disengaged; it is the means, the *only* means as she puts it,
for the "unpremeditated, attentive facing up to and resisting of

1   Hannah Arendt, *The Origins of Totalitarianism* (New York: Harvest
Books, [1951] 1979), viii.

reality." Without comprehension in this sense *all* attempts at understanding, of "telling it like is" and therefore of resisting to what is happening are gone.

II

Given the dangers of our time, so multiple that this in itself paralyzes thought and action we have to think this more deeply than we might have at first imagined. As with Arendt in 1950, coming out of a half century of European mass death,[2] the nature of our real is so extreme, so *difficult* that we require a means of facing and being able to deal with (in shorthand) the "unprecedented" and "outrageous"—that which, for us, no less than for Arendt threatens defuturing.

"Comprehension" is Arendt's way of facing reality. It is both more and less than understanding. Less, because in situations of acute urgency the neutrality of pure understanding is not available. More, because "attentive" to what-is (in its implications) and engaging what-is historically unprecedented, it is both a "facing up to" of reality *and* the source of resistance to that real. If this pushes beyond where Arendt herself wished to go (judgment was in many ways her boundary) nonetheless "comprehension" (as she herself defines it) holds these two moments together. As the philosopher Badiou rather beautifully describes it in the prologue to his book on politics, resistance occurs in a two-step process: one "tells it [the situation] like-it-is" and then draws the practical consequences from the situation. The "declaration of what the situation is" becomes for the resistor "personally, the bearer for the possibility for action," the "foundation for the examination of practical possibilities."[3]

2   And the more or less half-millennium of the violence that marked European colonization, which then for Europe became a kind of "infernal return," one that today, as defuturing, is being reexported to the global south.

3   See Alain Badiou's *Metapolitics* (London: Verso, 2005), pages 1–9, especially 7–8. A crucial sentence is the following: "Those who did not resist, if we leave aside the clique of conscious collaborators, were quite

III

Now it might be supposed that comprehension, let alone the act of "telling it like-it-is" (to oneself as much as to another) belongs par excellence to language. This is true, but it would be a mistake to see it as only so. Comprehension, especially in Arendt's sense, is always the comprehension of the specific circumstances and *configurations* of history. Her *Origins of Totalitarianism* is precisely this—epitomized most strongly in the great essay on the European construction of Imperialism that takes up the center of the book. The entry into "the subject matter of history itself" is a need to "address the specific configurations of history." This move moves naturally as it were, to the necessity to "write" history in order to explicate it (in its trajectories, in its implications).[4] It will be objected immediately that artists and designers do not "write" history—and therefore that their work cannot reflectively *comprehend* the way Arendt (or even Adorno) intends. But this is to miss the term "configuration" in the earlier sentence—and to fail to reflect in what ways that artists may, in their configurations, make parallels (not at all necessarily literal) between the configurations and events—the sequences—of history, and the configurations, events, and sequences which they establish.

"Comprehension" in other words, in Arendt's strong reflective sense, does not lie outside of art and design. One key to the means whereby comprehension is effected in these realms is offered in Gadamer's *Truth and Method*, in the title to one of its sections: "Transformation into Structure and Total Mediation."[5] By "transformation" Gadamer means that, in art, what is taken from life and from representation is through comprehension, reconfigured into a structure (a "total mediation") that potentially reveals a new understanding of what-is. In other

---

simply those who did not want to tell the situation like it was, not even to themselves."

4   On this see Adorno's lectures *History and Freedom*, ed. Rolf Tiedemann (Cambridge, MA: Polity Press, 2006), especially 39–41.

5   Hans-Georg Gadamer, *Truth and Method* (New York: Continuum, 1974), 110–19.

words, comprehension working the acts of "transformation into structure and total mediation" of what is taken from the situation is capable of rendering that which both presents and goes beyond the given limits of the situation. Such acts of transformation and mediation, Gadamer maintains, "produce and brings to light what is otherwise ... hidden and withdrawn."[6] The "joy of recognition" that happens in encounters with such works is that recognizing "*more* than is already familiar."[7]

Clearly, far more could be said here, nor does space allow the demonstration of the case. Yet examples of precisely this—of the comprehension of that which urgently requires *presented understanding*—come immediately to mind. I think of Margaret Bourke-White's seizing of a situation in the Ohio River Valley in 1937 and turning this into an acute comprehension of the racial and economic divisions of Depression America.[8] Or, of Marion Post Wolcott inserting herself into a triangle of race relations in a street encounter in North Carolina and in so doing comprehending, in a single complex gesture, the racial and gender structures of "Jim Crow" politics just before the Second World War ("Advertisement on the side of a drug store window," Wendell, North Carolina, 1939). Most dramatically, if we agree that there is still much lacking about the public understanding of the Holocaust and above all the question of *how* what happened could have happened, then for me the strongest statement on this problem, the one that undertakes a genuinely political comprehension of "what happened," is not a text but a memorial. *Orte des Erinnerns—Denkmal im Bayerischen Viertel/Places of Remembrance—Memorial in the Bavarian Quarter* (1993)[9] is a

6 Gadamer insists on the relation of such presentations to truth: 'this transformation is a transformation into the true" (ibid., 112). He adds: "operative in artistic presentation is recognition, which has the character of the genuine knowledge of essence: and sense Plato considers all knowledge of essence to be recognition, this is the ground of Aristotle's remark that poetry is more philosophical than history" (ibid., 114).
7 Ibid., 112–13.
8 "The American Way Photos From the Great Ohio River Flood 1937," *TIME*, accessed November 24, 2018, http://time.com/3879426/the-american-way-photos-from-the-great-ohio-river-flood-of-1937/.
9 "Orte des Erinnerns—Denkmal im Bayerischen Viertel/Places of Remembrance—Memorial in the Bavarian Quarter (1993)," accessed November 24, 2018, http://www.stih-schnock.de/remembrance.html.

memorial; "to the perpetrators" as its originators insist, or more precisely to the legal edicts of exclusion and denial that, between 1933 and 1942 gradually created the Jewish population of Berlin as nonpersons and thus enabled their transportation and murder.[10] Arendt herself had at one point lived in the Bavarian Quarter. It seems suitable that the sharpest comprehension, that which least denies the outrageous, refuses precedents, analogies, and generalizations and is most determined to ensure that both the shock of experience *and its thought* (by the perpetrators, no less than today those who encounter the memorial) should, if by partial coincidence, address the understanding of the circumstances of her own attempted destruction.

See also
ANIMAL RATIONALE, *VITA ACTIVA, VITA CONTEMPLATIVA*

---

10   An exercise, we should always remember, that was able to be conducted with as less fuss that one might today take a cheap holiday flight. The question of the politics that *enabled* the Holocaust is here.

COURAGE

To leave the household, originally in order to embark upon
some adventure and glorious enterprise and later simply to
devote one's life to the affairs of the city, demanded courage
because only in the household was one primarily concerned
with one's own life and survival. Whoever entered the
political realm had first to be ready to risk his life, and too
great a love for life obstructed freedom, was a sure sign of
slavishness. Courage therefore became the political virtue
par excellence, and only those men who possessed it could
be admitted to a fellowship that was political in content and
purpose and thereby transcended the mere togetherness
imposed on all—slaves, barbarians, and Greeks alike—
through the urgencies of life.

Hannah Arendt, *The Human Condition*[1]

I

To venture forth, out of the seeming safety of domestic seclusion,
into the swirling and diverse needs and demands of public space
and culture presents us with a paradox of participation. Be
assured enough oneself to stride boldly into the agora of shared
interests and the challenges of uncommonality, yet be open to the
vagaries of deliberative democratic processes and the contests
of perception and action. Fellows we all are, gendered and
hued, tethered and freed by belief, infused with experience and
only ever partly assured of our insights and their location in the
dynamics and negotiations through which fellowship is realized.

For the extraordinary scholar of twentieth-century delights
and horrors, Hannah Arendt, courage must have been an urgent
ever-present need, a state of necessity, an unavoidable stance,
being and body and mind entwined in principled analysis. Likely

[1]   Hannah Arendt, *The Human Condition* (Chicago, IL: University of
       Chicago Press, [1958] 1998), 36.

too, courage would have been a life force for her own cognitive and spirited survival.

Design products and processes, services and interactions are implicated in our own wanton drive for addition—for gain, for advantage—a mass movement undeclared, parts not seen in the wholes, an armada of sinking ships in an age of climate change. Their discourses of achievement necessarily self-praiseworthy lest advancement and need be upturned by questions of sustainability status, temporary solutions espoused.

Hannah Arendt woke up suddenly and thought once again about the etymology of courage, its enactments and its peppered sense and reference relations sprinkled across philosophy and political and cultural theory. The heroics of bravery, pronouncements of valor, from Plato and endurance, Aquinas's ideas of allaying fears and the practice of mercy. She may have thought again of the importance of the person in the plural, antidotes to the purple prose of bruised times. The courage to be and to become, *the courage to make is for design now plural,* accountable to diverse interests, impact instead of engagement, influence not dominance design's watchwords of the day.

And so brushing hair from her forehead and reaching for a cigarette, Hannah Arendt looks across the room and sees there a fluttering text on the window ledge of her Riverside Drive apartment in Manhattan. Blown into her domestic space. Between past and future. A design poetics. An illustration of a wondrous creature, sighted on a "voyage of discovery."

She reads this double act of language thinking, a discursive design, her world now moved into an extended public realm shaped and spoken to face design in dark times. A voice beyond assimilation, a trans-species hybrid citizen voice from an imagined marketplace of ideas. An offering to reconsider, an act of promising, of how we might think of ourselves together for and through the future. A birthing, or natality. A call and a voicing of diversity in civil space, a possible space to be and become.

II

Call me Zivila if you wish. Zivila Octopa. Zivila after Civil. Octopa for my many shaped self in an age of postdeterminism.

A posthuman alternative. That giant creature of the seas in
the Old Icelandic saga now less a tumultuous monster of
destruction, rather a slippery choreographing creation of today's
tomorrow.

A civil creature, an octopomorphic agent, that's me. An
amphibious conjurer of conjecture. A tentacular tendency my
ever-swirling fictioning form. Without a leg to stand on, but eight
to propel me forward and backward, up and down. To slither, to
swim, and to crawl.

But I have eight legs to stand on, you see. I have become
amphibious. My already elaborate choreographic capacities and
my crafty intelligence have been enhanced by human error. I'm
a new public product, species not singularity, more than residue
of the Anthropocene. For I'm a trans-species thinking thing. My
body and mind and world views motionally altered.

Plastic microparticles, sedimented in my Shiva-like form so
that I am able to walk, to run, to spit. And recently I have learned
to jump, to leap forward in space and time, nothing so literal
as those linear design functionalists of the twentieth century,
propulsion my new plasticity.

I've absorbed human stem cells adrift in effluent. Now I am
a regenerative mesh of cells and command structures: a public
product, built by chance more than intention. I dissemble,
but in a care-ful way, camouflage myself to survive, among
the horrors yet still unseen, survival our shared goal. I have
taken the decoy strategies of my ink clouds and turned them
into articulations in print, on screen, and on the sands. Silicon
critical writing I like to think, crystalline in its complexities,
words my new love, grasping for dictionaries, lexicographically
novelistic.

The public, spread around the circumpolar north where
I live, read me as a cipher of climate change, not merely a design
fiction. One of many now, I am of land and sea, of water and
ice, of rock and shifting sand. Moving always in space and time,
a floating, diving, landing, running figure. Pace. A persona of
potential we see only fleetingly, beyond the bows and the littorals
and liminal spaces of the now.

Courageous design inquiry offers an alternative to the
symbolic systems and circulated logics of givens. A beyond and

between space, a presence across perception and reflection, shape shifting, passing through passages of confinement. To navigate and to chart, to suggest and to propose, an active life of choreographic restlessness.

A new tense is mine, ours. The future present. Through courageous design we become together the future present.[2]

Andrew Morrison

See also
CREATIVITY, FREEDOM, PLAY, SPEECH, SPONTANEITY

2   This text is an outcome of a project called *Amphibious Trilogies* (http://amphibious.khio.no/), funded by The Norwegian Artistic Research Programme (NARP), and led by Prof Amanda Steggell, Oslo National Academy of the Arts (KhiO). The project investigates an extended choreography centered on islands, ponds, and passages. My main focus is on climate change, arctic passages, design futures, and design poetics, building on work for the *Future North* research project into Arctic landscapes.

CREATIVITY

For respect for human dignity implies the recognition of my
fellow-men or our fellow-nations as subjects, as builders of
worlds or co-builders of a common world.

Hannah Arendt, *The Origins of Totalitarianism*[1]

Refugees are possibly the most creative people. Forced to
move by any number of pressures—military, social, political,
economic—they make perilous journeys to places safer than
those of their origin, which may nevertheless be fraught with
danger. Anthropologist Arjun Appadurai states that as refugees
move through shifting contexts they "can never afford to let
their imaginations rest too long, even if they wished to."[2] The
requirement for refugees to "build worlds" in response to the
destruction of their homes—places that have constituted their
worlds for years—highlights both their closeness to and their
distance from those into whose worlds refugees now impact.
We all need to build worlds, but for some this imaginative
requirement is more pressing. This is a moment of heightened
importance for the many senses of dignity, subjectification, and
anticipation that Hannah Arendt had already noted.

While imagination may not be a fashionable concept these
days, the impact of Appadurai's words on our times should not
be diminished. In being subjectively resilient and creatively
productive, Appadurai's refugees must also be alert to danger as
they create new lives. For Arendt, refugees[3] occupy an important
place in twentieth-century politics and ethics, and while current
concerns about refugees relate to different historical forces than
hers, they are still people displaced by conflict; as such, refugees
are reckoned to become an increasingly affective condition in our

1   Hannah Arendt, *The Origins of Totalitarianism* (New York: Harvest
     Books, [1951] 1979), 458.
2   Arjun Appadurai, "Disjuncture and Difference in the Global Cultural
     Economy," in M. G. Durham and D. M. Kellner (ed.), *Media and Cultural
     Studies: Keyworks* (Oxford: Blackwell, 2001), 32.
3   Arendt, *The Origins of Totalitarianism*, 458.

times.[4] For us, as for Arendt, refugees test our attitudes to life and creativity.

Creative Futures

"No ideology which aims at the explanation of all historical events of the past and at mapping out the course of all events of the future can bear the unpredictability which springs from the fact that men are creative, that they can bring forward something so new that nobody ever foresaw it."[5] There is something of Friedrich Nietzsche's critique of history in this passage from Arendt. In "On the Uses and Disadvantages of History for Life," he writes,

> If the historical drive does not also contain a drive to construct, if the purpose of destroying and clearing is not to allow a future already alive in anticipation to raise its house on the ground thus liberated, if justice alone prevails, then the instinct for creation will be enfeebled and discouraged.[6]

The notion that a critically anticipatory urge should be a key aspect of historical practice is powerful in both thinkers. For while anticipation can be regarded as creative—insofar as it brings an attitude to plausible futures in order to develop imaginative responses to the present[7]—it does so as an act of opening-up, not of totalization. Anticipatory futures encourage creative possibilities. Anticipation then works in knotting past, present, and future into a complex network of creative acts while refraining from predicting, foretelling, and organizing any of these into well-defined wholes. Arendt goes further than Nietzsche in recognizing the importance of uncertainty, of

---

4   Refugee Rights Data Project (2017), "Top Five Facts. Human Rights for Displaced People in Europe." Available from: http://refugeerights.org. uk/wp-content/uploads/2017/09/RRDP_Top5Facts.pdf (accessed March 24, 2018).

5   Arendt, *The Origins of Totalitarianism*, 458.

6   Friedrich Nietzsche, *Untimely Meditations*, ed. Breazeale and trans. R. J. Hollingdale (Cambridge: Cambridge University Press, 1997), 95.

7   Theodore Zamenopoulos and Katerina Alexiou, "Towards an Anticipatory View of Design," *Design Studies* vol. 28 (2007): 411–36; Roberto Poli, "The Many Aspects of Anticipation," *Foresight* vol. 12, no. 3 (2010): 7–17.

unpredictability, in its relations to complexity and how it has influenced creative thought and practice in contemporaneity.[8]

Creative Dignity

An important consequence of Arendt's words is that we can creatively construct anticipatory futures in order to build current worlds as dynamic, nondetermined, and active interventions into complex, often dangerous, environments. Which mirrors Appadurai's exhortation for refugees not to let their imaginations rest. This is a critical consequence when accounting for the importance of creativity in designing. For even when we are successful in our creative endeavors, we should not rest. A restless imagination is a precondition for creative future production.

But Arendt takes us further than this, bringing to the fore ethical and political concerns to complement the processual or attitudinal ones already mentioned. It is not sufficient for complex, anticipatory, imaginative creativity to operate as solitary practice. Arendt highlights the necessity to align such creativity to the codevelopment of the dignity of fellow-men, as she considers the dimension of action (and, with it, the political) as a precondition for creativity.

Discussing the paradox from which Arendt departs in Chapter Nine of *The Origins of Totalitarianism*: "The Decline of the Nation-State and the End of the Rights of Man," Italian philosopher Giorgio Agamben writes,

> the very figure who should have embodied the rights of man par excellence—the refugee—signals instead the concept's radical crisis.[9]

Agamben's thought here can be illuminating for us, as his understanding of the idea of refugee intensifies political, social,

---

8 Katerina Alexiou, and Theodore Zamenopoulo, "Design as a Social Process: A Complex Systems Perspective," *Futures* vol. 40, no. 6 (2008): 586–95; Jamie Brassett, "Poised & Complex. The Becoming Each Other of Philosophy, Design and Innovation," in Betti Marenko and Jamie Brassett (eds.), *Deleuze and Design* Deleuze Connections Series (Edinburgh: Edinburgh University Press, 2015), 31–57.

9 Giorgio Agamben, *Homo Sacer. Sovereign Power and Bare Life*, trans. D. Heller-Roazen (Stanford, CA: Stanford University Press, 1998), 126.

ethical, cultural, and economic discourses and drives them beyond any particular circumstance of refugee or indigenous person. This also can be said of creativity. The extreme circumstances that refugees have often to endure squeezes almost to exhaustion their creative potential while underlining the political, social, ethical, cultural, and economic conditions that accentuate their conditions. Refugees, pushed to the situation of losing their human rights, are compelled to political action and to be creative in their actions. Furthermore, the mere fact that refugees exist must "concern"[10] all creative practice. Because even though creativity—and any practice, industry, or attitude that it permeates—can be used to separate and antagonize, it can also strengthen relations between seemingly isolated existences through opening them up to others, living and nonliving alike.

> For respect for human dignity implies the recognition of my fellow-men or our fellow-nations as subjects, as builders of worlds or co-builders of a common world.[11]

While the many uncertainties refugees prompt highlight political, economic, social, and design concerns for all of us to act upon, they also sharpen both our recognition of and response to dignity and provide examples of the potentials for

---

"Crisis" is an interesting word for Agamben to use here. It is etymologically linked to "critical" (in both senses of making judgment and being life-threatening), which in complexity theory has important connections to creativity (see note 7 above). John O'Reilly and I discuss it further in terms of philosophy and design; see: Jamie Brassett and John O'Reilly, "Collisions, Design and the Swerve," in Pieter Vermaas and Stéphane Vial (eds.), *Advancements in Philosophy of Design* "Design Research Foundations" Series (Berlin: Springer, 2018), 71–98.

10   Philosopher Alfred North Whitehead uses the term "concern" in "the Quaker sense" as a call to action, not simply as something to worry about; see: Alfred North Whitehead, *Adventures of Ideas* (New York: Free Press, 1967), 176 and 180. Bruno Latour—for whom Whitehead is an important thinker—regards design as a "matter of concern"; see: Latour, "A Cautious Prometheus? A Few Steps Toward a Philosophy of Design (with Special Attention to Peter Sloterdijk)," in Hackney, Glynne and Minton (eds.), *Networks of Design. Proceedings of the International Conference of the Design History Society* (Boca Raton, FL: Universal-Publishers, 2008), 2–10.

11   Arendt, *The Origins of Totalitarianism*, 458.

restless imaginations that ought to be considered, as previously anticipated, a necessary precondition for creative future production. These examples are deeply needed in these dark times, in which those of us not (yet) determined to become refugees often do not consider creative political action in our lives, as we are not (yet) urged toward it. Designers have the possibility today to learn from refugees how to train a restless imagination, which urges the broadening up of a public, creative, and political dignity. This is for designers, and all of us, a timely and, more than ever, necessary task.

Jamie Brassett

See also
ACTIVISM, COMPREHENSION, FREEDOM,
IMAGINATION, NATALITY, PARIAH

DEMOCRACY

DEMOCRACY

Let's imagine society as an interweaving mesh of networks of people intent on discussing and making decisions about what to do and doing (or trying to do) what they have decided. The environment in which this is happening may be more or less favorable, meaning that it may make it more or less probable that such conversations take place and that, focusing on the common interest, they become decisions and then collaborative actions. The environment in which all this can happen in the best way imaginable is democracy. More precisely, it is what I call a "project-centred democracy,"[1] meaning a participatory enabling ecosystem in which everybody can develop their projects and achieve their results, insofar as they do not reduce the possibility of other people doing the same. On the other hand, since we cannot design and produce alone, it is also a democracy that is born out of collaboration and produces collaboration. In doing so, it fosters the regeneration of social commons.

All this resonates with what Hannah Arendt wrote sixty years ago.[2] For her, democracy should be depicted as a complex mesh of conversations on themes of common "interest."[3] She also said that these conversations may emerge in public space and turn into concrete actions; that this passage from conversation to "action" is possible when people collaborate; and, finally, that this collaboration occurs when the common interest is made visible and representable. For Arendt, interest is never individual: it is always an inter-being, something that exists between different human beings, something that must be defined and recognized in its social nature. Because of this, pursuing this kind of interest always calls for collaboration between people, and it is this collaboration that gives people the power[4] to make things happen. This is a power that, writes Arendt, is not offered

1   Ezio Manzini, *Politics of the Everyday* (London: Bloomsbury, 2018), 174–84.
2   Hannah Arendt, *The Human Condition* (Chicago, IL: University of Chicago Press, [1958] 1998), 182–3.
3   Arendt, *The Human Condition*, 3.
4   Ibid., 200.

by others, but is born from their capacity to recognize common interests and collaborate to transform them into results.[5] With these thoughts Arendt offers us a useful background and language for our topic in a moment when, more than half a century later, what she imagined is, at least in principle, becoming technically possible: imagine a society of people who are capable of focusing on common interests and transforming them into actions on the world.

Adopting this approach and this terminology, project-centered democracy is therefore an environment that tends to give everybody the possibility of meeting and collaborating and, in so doing, to achieve objectives pursuing their interests (intending this term with Arendt's meaning of being both individual and collective interest). In this form of democracy, the coexistence of these two planes, one personal and the other collective, is the characterizing aspect. In fact, if the environment were only to provide favorable conditions for individual projects, it might appear to offer people greater freedom, but this would only occur within the limits of what the system in which they would be operating were able, and willing, to offer. On the other hand, an environment that provides favorable conditions for collaborative projects gives space to coalitions that have, or can assume, the power to carry out their decisions. In other words, they can themselves build the conditions by which to accomplish what they wish to achieve. This is why project-centered democracy is also an environment that facilitates the creation of the distributed systems in which people, collaborating, can make their own decisions on questions that concern them and have the power to implement them. Therefore, a project-centered democracy is a form of participatory democracy that, enriching the overall democratic ecosystem, can also support, integrate, and collaborate to regenerate other forms of democracy.

Given this conceptual framework, how can we create the conditions that make the existence of project-centered democracy more probable? How can we bring the group actions of active citizens and the practices of representative democracy together, so they can support each other? In very

5   Ibid., 7.

general terms the answer to these questions is the creation of a dedicated democratic infrastructure capable of enriching the overall democratic enabling ecosystem. In parallel to that, it requires also a diffuse design capability spread among a sufficient number of people. So, to increase potential, it is also necessary to increase the number of active citizens and for each of them to improve their design capability. This calls for appropriate intervention.

Nowadays, the already long experience in the field of participatory design and codesign can help by making numerous support tools available for designing projects (they could be scenarios, storytelling, prototypes, and whatever could be useful to make common interests more visible and tangible, and therefore capable to trigger and orient the needed conversations for action). These tools should be brought to a wider public, making them more accessible and easier to use, and hopefully become part of the normal basic culture of citizens. In addition, since every design activity is a question not only of tools but also of ideas, values, knowledge, critical sense, and creativity, it is necessary to develop some basic competence along these lines too. In other words, people also need cultural tools that enable them to recognize the current problems and opportunities and imagine possible futures (other than those normally proposed). Therefore, as well as the operational tools of codesign, it is crucial that an appropriate design culture be diffused among the people involved. To conceive, develop, and spread these tools and this design culture is, by all means, a main design expert's responsibility. That is, their main responsibility toward democracy.

Ezio Manzini

See also
IMAGINATION, IN-BETWEEN, TOGETHERNESS

EQUALITY
EVIL

EQUALITY

> The great challenge to the modern period, and its peculiar danger, has been that in it man for the first time confronted man without the protection of differing circumstances and conditions. And it has been precisely this new concept of equality that has made modern race relations so difficult, for there we deal with natural differences which by no possible and conceivable change of conditions can become less conspicuous. It is because equality demands that I recognize each and every individual as my equal, that the conflicts between different groups, which for reasons of their own are reluctant to grant each other this basic equality, take on such terribly cruel forms.
>
> Hannah Arendt, *The Origins of Totalitarianism*[1]

I bow, take off my shoes and socks, and gently walk through the words and worlds of Hannah Arendt—represented by a patchwork of copies of her writings that I have carefully placed on the floor. I invite my colleagues and students to walk with me, explaining the reverence I feel at these half-a-century-old works. A colleague of Indian origin explains walking on the work is not acceptable in her culture. We discuss such differences in showing reverence and practicing curiosity, my small ritual for getting closer to this body of work and her culture's long-standing tradition. I continue both literally and metaphorically gingerly walking around Arendt's notion of equality and how design might practice equality.

*

The quote from Hannah Arendt above pinpoints how, perversely, the diminishment of certain frameworks that upheld inequalities also fostered new inequalities, as human could meet human, so to speak, naked. Now, so many more feet are treading our world, and the weight of so many of us is so much heavier than

1   Hannah Arendt, *The Origins of Totalitarianism* (New York: Harvest Books, [1951] 1979), 54.

the weight of even the most privileged feet of Arendt's time. Now, through social media, there can be a semblance of being on the same plane, of the same weight, as people from all over the world. But, of course, we don't treat each other as equals: There is not one plane but multifold planes of complex intersections of power manifestations and oppressions. The responsibility of equality has become decentralized and blurry. Simultaneously, the opportunity for genuine meetings and brave negotiations is here—a hope.

*

Since *The Origins of Totalitarianism* was published in 1957, the "official" sites of totalitarianism have changed, with China's recent social credit system a current example of its expressions. In the last decades, seemingly mundanely, the adverb "totally" has become a frequent word of reinforcement. "I totally like this" or "I totally don't." It strikes me that this lack of nuance, if not overtly as sinister as the totalitarianism of Arendt's world and work, is still dangerous. "Totally" pushes away engagement with the wrongs that are part of the mostly rights and vice versa. Perhaps this everyday casual totalitarianism legitimizes, or is legitimized by, in Arendt's words, the "[lack of] the protection of differing circumstances and conditions." But it is also a product of a lack of situated ethical reflection, which is a prime condition for long-term equality.

*

At a demonstration against racism in 2017,[2] Sabby Dahlu, of Stand Up to Racism, offered a potent "come back line" for when we experience "racismglaze, sustaglaze, sexismglaze" (the glazing over of the eyes of the audience, as—name your cause— is mentioned).[3] When told that "you always keep banging on about racism," she responds with "well stop being racist then."

2   "The Battle of Wood Green 40th Anniversary," April 23, 2017, commemorating the day local shopkeepers and residents stopped a National Front march in North London.
3   The term "sustaglaze" was coined at Languaging Waste workshop organized by students of BA Design + Change, Linnaeus University, March 23, 2018.

This "come back" carries three vital messages. Firstly, that we are all complicit in inequality. Second, that "it ain't over 'til it's over"—in other words, until we have achieved equality, our work is not done. Third, that there is no middle ground when it comes to inequality; we are either against or for racism, against or for sexism, ablebodyism, ageism. Each of us must find agency for equality.

*

In metadesign we follow a trajectory "from me to we to world—and back again."[4] In practice it means that all our, mostly transdisciplinary, collaborations start with each individual exploring and sharing personal and professional values, interests, capabilities. These become the foundation for the common ground, which expands from the community *here*, to considering the world. The collapse of categories—differing circumstances and conditions—that the exploration entails, means stepping into a risky space with the potential of violent inequality but also with the potential of arriving at new configurations of equality. Each collaboration ends with revisiting individual personal and professional positions to explore how they have moved, and which agencies have opened—or closed. Equality is not a state; it is a practice. Practicing equality in the small and from the personal is a foundation for practicing equality in the world. Equality needs stretching, exercising, interrogating—playing with in the everyday as well as in the extraordinary. All life sites, personal and professional, are living laboratories of practicing equality.

Practicing equality entails risk-taking. These are not the heroics of the mountain climber, but accepting the social awkwardness and taking the risk of losing face, by biting our nails in public saying: "I am scared," "I feel unsure," or "I actually don't understand the term totalitarianism—can you explain?" Unless we are as generous with our experience of

4   On metadesign see: Hannah Jones and Anette Lundebye, "Metadesign: A Dynamic Framework for Seeding Socially Responsive Design." Paper presented at *Out of Control, the 8th International Conference on Design and Emotion*, Central Saint Martin's School of Art and Design, UK. September 11–14, 2012.

powerlessness as we are glorious when in our power, we are not
genuinely distributing the responsibility for equality. It is also my
responsibility to use the power I have been formally given, such
as in the academic institution, as a well as the freedom I have
from, for example, living in peaceful conditions and practicing
design. When we shrink from this power and freedom, pretend
we don't have it or don't practice it; we open up blurry territories
of "up for grabs." Formal power needs to be practiced with
responsibility and explicitness—so that the actions we make can
be contested. Equality is not about a lack of friction. Instead, it
is about transparency in how power is distributed and practiced,
and in how it can be redistributed.

I see one of the subtlest threats to equality today as
what I call epistemological inequality. This is seen in design's
meeting with other disciplines, and within design. It takes
many ways of knowing and the encouragement of many
knowledge holders' voices to practice equality. In recent years,
transdisciplinary collaborations have taught me valuable lessons
on epistemological inequality. I started collecting emails where
my team and I were called crazy or wishy-washy and to articulate
these adjectives as manifestations of knowledge oppression.
As I systematized them, I also discovered how the knowledge
oppression is intersected with sexism. I started crying when
I read yet another student essay using third person and passive
language. The very same student I had seen flourish through
transformative learning where context specificity had opened
up personal agency in a complex world, was too scared to leave
conventional epistemological hierarchies in the written work.

I started noticing how tired being in fields of power makes
me. And I have thought, if I, a person of significant privilege in
our world, can feel this tired from being in these fields of power,
how tired must you feel, you who are subjected to oppression
on many more, intersected grounds? And, how much of our
precious individual and collective energy is lost to inequality?
So here is a proposal for practicing equality in design: Care for
differing circumstances and conditions, and the situatedness of
each project, and protect it from the universal; Point to practices
of inequality and to practices of equality—we really need
informative and inspiring examples; Never think it's impossible

to recruit a competent person who is not like you; Be explicit when you use the power you have so that it becomes clear, to yourself and to the world, when you are overstepping; Use language as bridge instead of as barrier and ask questions about what constitutes respectful language. It is easy to feel you get the words wrong around race, gender and more—but not talking is not the answer. Walk barefoot, so you can sense the nuances between when equality or inequality is practiced.

Mathilda Tham

See also
BOURGEOIS, HUMAN RIGHTS, PLURALITY

EVIL

> In general, the degree of responsibility increases as we draw
> further away from the man who uses the fatal instrument
> with his own hands.
>
> Hannah Arendt, *Eichmann in Jerusalem*[1]

Evil, as a term, is used loosely these days by politicians and
commentators (such as in phrases like "the axis of evil"). This
vagueness is not a credible basis for social observation. In fact it
seems essential to define the term with precision, since otherwise
it becomes part of "a dangerous mentality—a mentality that
is drawn to absolutes, simplistic and clear dichotomies, and
alleged moral certainties."[2] One philosophical approach helpful
in defining evil is offered by Hannah Arendt, who considered
evil in terms of society, and in that sense, less as an individual
act of choice, and more in terms of the ways our actions are
linked to one another, generating consequences that are harmful,
consequences we do not acknowledge. Unseeing unthinking
actions generate evil. It is in fact the abuse of the word evil, by
creating simplistic oppositions, that prevents discussion, debate,
and reflection.

What Is Evil?

Arendt considers evil in two forms, as **radical evil** and **banal
evil**. Radical evil renders human beings superfluous through
three stages. First, you kill the juridical person, that is destroy
any notion of civil rights that legally protect all people. Then
you murder the moral person, that is break down solidarity,
such that we are essentially left with a choice between one form
of murder or another. Finally you destroy spontaneity, destroy

1   Hannah Arendt, *Eichmann in Jerusalem: A Report on the Banality of
Evil* (London: Penguin, [1963] 1994), 247 (original emphasis).
2   Richard Bernstein, "Are Arendt's Reflections on Evil Still Relevant?" *The
Review of Politics* vol. 70, no. 1 (Winter 2008): 66.

individuality, the capacity to create something new.[3] Radical evil was an evident quality of historical totalitarian systems, such as Nazi Germany, and Stalinist Soviet Union. What is key here is the matter of superfluousness, when our humanity is absolutely irrelevant in terms of the imperatives of a system within which we reside. Today the stateless, refugees, internally displaced persons, undocumented migrants, those stigmatized as a threat and deemed "unpeople," rendered as the other, are instances of those made superfluous, who end up without "legitimate legal or political status."[4]

Where radical evil points to the superfluousness of humanity and to acts of destruction that generate such superfluousness, banal evil considers the dreadful consequences of our routinized and habituated daily choices. Where the separation of children from their undocumented migrant families at the United States border represents radical evil, car usage and its effects on global warming would be an instance of what concerns Arendt as banal evil. "Normal people with banal motives and intentions can commit horrendous crimes and evil deeds."[5] Ultimately evil, in Arendt's view, does not originate in a core intention, from a root. Rather it spreads through inattention and conditions that encourage such inattention. And, as it spreads, it becomes pointless to locate the original location of contagion, and far more pressing to think of ways of halting further spread, with like a fungus.[6]

Arendt's discussion of evil challenges virtuous binaries of common parlance, which, by painting something else as evil, remind us that at least we are not so. In fact "we cannot rely on our traditional notion that evil deeds are committed by persons with evil intentions, that monstrous deeds are caused by monsters,"[7] and instead must "confront honestly the 'paradox' that even though normal persons may commit horrendous deeds without deliberate intention, they are, nevertheless, fully responsible for these deeds and must be held accountable."[8]

3   Bernstein, "Are Arendt's Reflections on Evil Still Relevant?"
4   Ibid.
5   Ibid., 73.
6   Ibid.
7   Ibid., 74.
8   Ibid., 75.

This is evil not in terms of appalling, visible, dramatic instances such as torture and bodily denigration alone; but also in terms of routine unthinking acts that aid and abet global warming, herding undocumented migrants into camps, separating refugee families, routinely treating Black people as potential criminals in white majority societies, arming teachers rather than restricting guns, polluting the planet, dispossessing people of their land ... the list is endless.

To Arendt evil has a particular relationship with the world around us. She distinguishes three realms of our world, labor (which relies on necessity), work (which relies on society), and action (which relies on politics). Labor emerges from a necessity imposed on us by nature, and it is through labor that we seek to defeat the constraints of nature that we face, repetitively, while ultimately failing to overcome them. In this way labor meets consumption in an endless circle. "The isolated and solitary character of labor marks it not only animal rather than human but also as pre-political."[9] Labor is an isolated, solitary repetitive activity, self-defeating in that it drives us toward satisfying our needs of consumption, endlessly.

In contrast "work elevates us beyond the repetitious and mute cycle of nature and gathers us into a common reality and shared objective space."[10] Unlike labor, work creates a world that we inhabit with one another. "Work makes a 'world' in which humans can live. What workers make are objects that are durable and have a measure of permanence."[11] But still "work is locked into a never-ending chain of means and ends and it is therefore chained to an instrumental view of life."[12] These means-end calculations, central to work, end up instrumentalizing social life.

To Arendt "unconstrained deliberation aimed at argument, persuasion and negotiation is the essence of political life."[13] In this way the realm of action allows for politics, and is uniquely capable of doing so, unlike those of labor and work.

9   Paul Voice, "Labor, Work and Action," in Patrick Hayden (ed.), *Hannah Arendt: Key Concepts* (Durham: Acumen, 2014), 38.
10 Voice, "Labor, Work and Action," 40.
11 Ibid., 39.
12 Ibid., 43.
13 Ibid., 47.

Such politics, in turn, relies on speech, common points of shared reference that allow for discussion. In this way action is privileged in Arendt's conception, as the realm of politics, creating a shared if fugitive notion of the commons. The relation between work and politics is that the former creates the conditions for the latter to occur through speech. Action is then the realm opposed to both necessity as well as to means-end instrumentalism, while dependent on both. In this sense applied disciplines like design offer opportunities for encouraging politics, since they contribute to shared points of reference through their attention to work.

But one of the poisoned blessings of applied disciplines such as design is that they also contribute to constructing worlds of tight interdependence, that ensure predictability and reliability, rendering their participants into tractable things, objects capable of being moved from a distance, in order to attain pre-established goals. This is why "the technocrat has no one to whom he can engage in a space of appearance (a polity) because he has objectified the individual for whom he claims to feel compassion."[14] Consider a policy design lab for instance and its own relation with a government body, and the particular categories of residents/citizens studied. Does it objectify its "clients" to achieve an established policy, or does it engage with them and their social and political needs, on their terms? Does it reproduce the structural inequality that is part of the larger society around it or challenge it?

"For compassion to lead to solidarity, it must go through the faculty of thinking"; which in turn requires recognizing "people in the plural" since otherwise "compassion collapses into pity."[15] Our contemporary society, with its formalized work structures and programmed interactions, its managers, settings designed for predictable reproduction, prefers abstract pity rather than

---

14   Gregory Feldman, "The Specific Intellectual's Pivotal Position: Action, Compassion and Thinking in Administrative Society, an Arendtian View," *Social Anthropology* vol. 21, no. 2 (2013): 145.

15   Feldman, "The Specific Intellectual's Pivotal Position," 149.

solidarity with those who suffer, and thus "sustains the certainty of the status quo rather than questions it."[16]

It could be argued that the sort of deliberation offered by the realm of politics, ensures reflection, thoughtfulness, mindfulness, the necessary care to make us capable of recognizing and avoiding banal evil. And the converse: to the extent we commit to realms of solely labor and work, we tend to generate the sort of thoughtlessness that will encourage banal evil. It is through the realm of action and politics that we can creditably address evil. A life we lead that relies solely on labor and work, and the more unthinking we choose to be in social life, the greater the banal evil we commit, as we exclude ourselves from the realm of politics.

What Is at Stake in Considering Evil?

The field of Design is overwhelmingly understood in terms of labor and work. For instance we can imagine product design in terms of devices that reduce labor, whether kitchen appliances, or information ordered for decision-making. We can think of design-methods that shape work, the ways decisions are made, and the ways work is allotted and its accomplishment acknowledged. We can think of design language, an aesthetic that shapes a line of products, from cutlery to coffee machines, into a recognizable brand.[17] It is in fact in terms of design and the political world that we face the greatest dilemma. Does design acknowledge what Arendt calls the realm of action? This would be a realm of contestation, where we consider the larger political and social questions that define our identity as inhabitants of a shared society, such as tolerance, migration, equality, taxation, the obligations of the state to its people, or the people to a shared planet. Is there enough discussion at present on how design can offer such a realm of contestation, where it could contribute to

16 Ibid., 145.
17 "Understanding design-intensive innovation," Report, Design council, last modified May 30, 2018, https://www.designcouncil.org.uk/resources/ report/understanding-design-intensive-innovation.

ways of reducing or mitigating banal evil in the world around us, whether in alliance with other modes of thought or by itself? An alternative and deeply troubling possibility emerges, that design (like other applied disciplines) may in fact encourage evil, contribute to it through a singular focus on labor and work.

For example, a recent polemic sharply criticizes the popular rhetoric of "design thinking" (DT),[18] arguing that it over-emphasizes individual creativity, values inner confidence at the expense of local knowledge. An inflation of design as a credible currency for applied success in all work settings, means that there is less attention to what designers actually do—their close understanding of user needs, grappling with the user's social world, and considering the tactility of materials in use. Instead the emphasis is on individual will and sincerity rather than on expertise and immersive experience. DT's adherents celebrate individuals as innovators but ignore politics and contestation. Since politics requires engaging with the world around us, and recognizing our social ties, a sole focus on individual entrepreneurial abilities can be misleading, and is socially corrosive.

What Do We Do about It?

Arendt's view of evil was shaped profoundly by her study of the modern world, of totalitarian political systems that eliminated all forms of freedom, of capitalist systems that channeled freedom toward solely consumption and routinized work and colonial systems that used totalitarian power for capitalist profits. We continue to inhabit such a world.

Our current model of capitalism, which relies on labor and work, on colonial legacies, contributes to banal evil. It is also a model now in crisis, with the frontiers for extracting further value greatly stretched, and to breaking point.[19] Like in Theodore

18   Lee Vinsel, "Design Thinking is Kind of Like Syphilis—It's Contagious and Rots Your Brains," *Medium*, December 6, 2017, https://medium.com/@sts_news/design-thinking-is-kind-of-like-syphilis-its-contagious-and-rots-your-brains-842ed078af29.

19   Immanuel Wallerstein et al., *Does Capitalism Have a Future?* (New York: Oxford University Press, 2013).

Géricault's famous painting, the capitalist raft on which our planet's inhabitants are perched, cannot hold all of us much longer, it is sinking.

Should designers champion efforts to generate further value, finding ways of extracting more profit from the tired avenues of the past, so that we can keep the raft afloat? Alternately should there be an effort to find alternative forms of value, through energy-efficient technologies, a kinder capitalism so to speak,[20] that will make the raft sturdier, wider? Or should we consider how designers can discuss an alternative to capitalism itself, promote resistance to our current world and its evils, encourage thinking on ways to address banal and radical evils more directly? Abandon the raft.

The designer has the potential to create spaces for encounters and dialog to explore such questions, to ask participants to reconsider their goals and professional roles. What would be the ways then of using design to encourage conversations among those deep in the realm of necessity, with their backs to the wall, their heads down in desperation? How could we use design to refract the realm of labor, so that unthinking actions and habituated choices are opened up for greater consideration? Ultimately these are political questions and this is the realm Arendt would advocate that we consider in terms of design—how designers and those claiming that word, can assiduously steer away from radical and banal evil, in these dark times.

Nidhi Srinivas

See also
COMPREHENSION, TOTALITARIANISM,
VIOLENCE

---

20 Navi Radjou, "Before We Reinvent the Economy, We Must Reinvent Ourselves," *Fastcompany*, June 20, 2018, https://www.fastcompany. com/40587024/before-we-reinvent-the-economy-we-must-reinvent-ourselves.

FABRICATION
FREEDOM

FABRICATION

The dark times we live in are a transition from the industrial to the postindustrial era. We are in *interregnum*, a transition period between two reigns, as Antonio Gramsci called it. Around the 1930s he wrote,

> The crisis consists precisely in the fact that the old is dying and the new cannot be born: in this *interregnum*, morbid phenomena of the most varied kind come to pass.[1]

One symptom of the transition is the gripping fear of losing jobs, a discussion that populates the public debate in almost any country and has given rise to populistic politics or hasty, short-sighted policies and public investment. Much less discussed is that we are potentially *being freed* from work or, more precisely in Arendt's terms, from labor. This is indicated in Arendt's critique of industrial society: "We live in a laborers' society because only laboring, with its inherent fertility, is likely to bring about abundance; and we have changed work into laboring, broken it up into its minute particles."[2] She juxtaposes labor with *homo faber*, the craftsman and his work. Craftsman's work has a definable beginning and end. Furthermore, the craftsman knows the relation of the process of fabrication to the durable end product. Instead of fabrication, in the industrial society, we have been subjected to repetitive and repeatable processes of labor, producing and consuming mere disposable "necessities." Now visions of full automation and digitalization bring great promise of liberating humans from labor.

The question is, liberating us to what? The fear of losing jobs is not just of losing income but of personal meaning, connection to a community, and the whole order of our societies, where so much is structured around work, from education to social security, from timetables to the way our cities have been

1   Antonio Gramsci, *Prison Notebooks Volume II* (New York: Columbia University Press, 2011), 32–3.
2   Hannah Arendt, *The Human Condition* (Chicago, IL: University of Chicago Press, [1958] 1998), 126.

designed. The Arendtian hope would be that we are being freed *to act*.

For Arendt, action happens between citizens, in the public realm beyond necessities where people are equal. Through action political community is made and maintained. In the core of action is speech. In the current society, in principle, the closest practice to the Arendtian ideal of action is democratic participation. When Arendt was writing *The Human Condition* in the 1950s, the number of democratically governed countries was only gradually growing and democracy overall just proving its capacity to organize fast-growing, industrial societies in a peaceful, egalitarian manner. Over the decades, the representative democracy established itself as an essential institution of an industrial society. In this transition, where the structures of industrial society are losing their functionality, so is the capacity of representative democracy to connect the political community of postindustrial society and provide solutions to contemporary challenges diminishing. This we have seen happening already for some time. In the society organized around work and consumption, work (in its conventional sense referring to employment, also income, and further to economy) and democracy are tightly intertwined. Representative democracy was one of the means resolving the societal tensions created by the industrial revolution. Another solution was the welfare state comprised of public services and social security benefits of which we decide upon through voting and of which many, like health care, daycare, or education system, are meant to create or maintain people's ability to work. If we look at how for the past decades we in democratic welfare states have organized our actions in politics, work has often been the common denominator: in labor and trade unions, in political parties, in structures of public sector.

From Arendt's perspective, the rupture of the linkage between work and politics is a positive development, because it should enable for more truly free action. But the problem is, we don't know, in a society that cannot structure around standardized paid employment, what should the democracy of this "workless," or postwork, system be like. The development of new forms of democracy is not keeping up the pace with the decline of the old, industrial-era structures of mass participation. Public realm, speech, immediacy, the presence of plurality are all key features of democratic participation that seem to be eroding in many ways in our societies. Even though some new practices have been introduced, democratic participation has become more and more unsatisfactory, departing ever farther away from these abstract ideals of Arendt. Most of all, it seems democracy's ability to begin something new has slowed down. For example, we urgently need profound reforms of our core institutions, such as our social security systems, as well as creation of completely new ones. But everywhere real reforms are stuck and eventually trust in democracy and its capacity to bring about progress is in decline.[3]

*

In Arendt's thinking, the essence and unique character of free action is its ability to create *the new*. In other words, the only true realm of novel is in the political realm, not in the markets, nor in organizations.[4] From there *new* spreads to other fields of human life—work and labor included. Reframing politics as free action poses a question: How is new born? Or better yet, how and where does people's ability to create new in the political sense develop? And, does that ability remain the same through time, or does it have various distinct iterations and manifestations in different periods of history?

Being political, that is, introducing something new into a given system, is and has always been difficult. It requires three things: tolerance for uncertainty of change, freedom to be able to

---

3   For example, postwar decades broadened education systems to include masses, introduced comprehensive social welfare and pension models, and created health care accessible to all, both geographically and socially. The last decades have mostly been incrementally adjusting or even eroding these systems. It is a widely debated question whether this is an intentional ideological project or mainly structural incapacity of political processes.

4   "However, of the three, action has the closest connection with the human condition of natality; the new beginning inherent in birth can make itself felt in the world only because the newcomer possesses the capacity of beginning something anew, that is, of acting. In this sense of initiative, an element of action, and therefore of natality, is inherent in all human activities." Arendt, *The Human Condition*, 9.

change, fearlessness toward the new future. Acting in the public realm is about constantly testing new ideas and being prepared to question old norms and conceptions. This is the very idea of free action: it is unsafe and beyond routines. Therefore the notion of free action easily carries with it an elitist, exclusive flavor: Who are the people that can afford to give up safety or think freely?

At least in an abstract sense, our societies are much more hospitable for free action than they were in Arendt's time. Just think of the "democratization of voice" enabled through the emergence of social media and the Internet, the emergence of global culture and its promise of breaking free from the boundaries of local and national culture. Yet we can seriously question whether people are free in Arendt's sense. Are they capable of initiating something truly new, willing to give up their safety? Further, has this group of free people grown, and who are the people capable of sacrificing the safety for the sake of something new and unforeseen? Even more importantly, who are not included in that group?

What we have recently seen in the political arenas around the world suggests that (the unsafe) world of free action is not seen as an optimal, dominant future by all. New forms of nationalism, the abandonment of liberal values (including human rights and rule of law), and the desire for a strong leader, these are all symptoms of this. Many people do not wish to encounter the constant flow of new things, nor do they wish to actively question their own views and habits for the sake of experimenting and transcending prior states of individual and collective being.

Can part of the explanation for the recent strengthening fear of new be in the fact that we have in general lost a sense of capacity *to make*? We have for long lived in ready-made societies, both materially (consumer society) and politically (mature welfare societies). Is *making* a key?

Hannah Arendt sets a stark distinction between fabrication and action, considering the former to be a domain of "means and ends" where goals are static and majority of activities hold merely an instrumental value. Both the distinction and its critique are emblematic to the late industrial era, an era that Arendt herself lived and where the most tangible reference points to the concepts she used are found. We need to consider that fabrication has changed since Arendt's times. Her notion of fabrication is tied to a certain era's idea of labor and work. For her, outside the realms of fabrication and work is free action, democratic participation. Today, fabrication is a way to create social action, make a statement of who I am, who we are. How then would Arendt have understood fabrication, had she seen the contemporary practices and movements around DIY fabrication, especially around digital fabrication, such as maker spaces, fab labs, GitHubs? Would it have shaken her distinctions? That remains to be an eternally unanswered scholarly question. However, we should ask, Can fabrication in its contemporary forms be seen as something where "new" is born, i.e., dismantling prevalent boundaries?

The communities of new fabrication we see formed all over the industrialized world could be interpreted as attempts to question and challenge industrialized work and consumption patterns of the late industrial era. Can they thus serve as incubators of free action, places where new emerges without being restricted and instrumentalized by clearly defined ends? When people together build crafty DIY solutions based on open source code and 3D printing, does it generate such experiences of action that permanently transform people to try new things in society and to step into unsafe territory outside routines and predictability? Can fabrication of tangible goods be seen as a way of reaching toward open, undefined future(s)?

Why should this matter? Arendt perhaps did not realize how closely linked work and democracy (labor and action) would become in the industrial society. One of the most tempting promises of democracy was mass employment and fulfillment of basic necessities, what the pay from work enabled. Also, the main promises of the welfare state such as health care and universal access to education, advocated by the labor movement too, were at least partially justified as a means that enhanced people's chances to earn decent income by making them more productive workforce. If in the postindustrial society work weakens as a fundamental institution around which the society revolves, action, politics by people, needs other initiators. Reinterpreting fabrication—providing access to it to all and reinforcing its ability to challenge both labor and consumption, and our thinking tied to them—could lead into cultures and communities of fabrication serving as environments of genuinely political holding power that make us free to begin something new.[5]

There are already some signs of this to happen. The biggest public building project lately in Finland has been Oodi, the new Helsinki City Central Library, completed at the end of 2018. Oodi aims to redefine how a library should be understood in the twenty-first century. Instead of being a building of books and online access to information, it is designed to be a new type of public space that will enable "focusing, learning and working," as well as "encountering, exploration and relaxation." Oodi is the new vanguard of Finland's comprehensive, high-quality network of public libraries, which citizens use extensively to recreate and develop themselves. Among many interesting things, Oodi provides modern tools for (digital) fabrication. The library offers this not only with an intention of providing public access for the fabrication of things, or teaching new technologies, but because fabrication has the power to convene people, create interaction and communities of citizens, like study circles did before. If today's Hannah Arendt would visit the new Helsinki City Library, she might label the fabrication she saw there, not economic or work, but political, the creator of the new.

Outi Kuittinen and Aleksi Neuvonen

See also
ACTION, FREEDOM, *HOMO FABER*, NATALITY, OBJECTIVITY

---

[5] This is something that we have depicted in a scenario called "Governing the Commons" that was part of *Scenarios for Sustainable Lifestyles 2050* report (Helsinki: Demos Helsinki, 2012) of Spread Sustainable Lifestyles 2050 project.

FREEDOM

> Because they are initium, newcomers and beginners by
> virtue of birth, men take initiative, are prompted into action
> … This beginning is not the same as the beginning of the
> world; it is not the beginning of something but of somebody,
> who is a beginner himself. With the creation of man, the
> principle of beginning came into the world itself, which, of
> course, is only another way of saying that the principle of
> freedom was created when man was created but not before.
> Hannah Arendt, *The Human Condition*[1]

All through the Western strive for modernity, the urge for new
beginnings has pervaded emancipatory thought. As Milan
Kundera has pointed out,[2] in the wake of modernism this
obsession with the new has become a sort of epistemology of
modern man to a degree where the commitment to novelty
obscures the capacity to judge what this novelty entails. Reading
Hannah Arendt's encomium to "beginning" may seem like yet
another iteration of the hope that humanity may lift itself out
of its own history to become free. Against the backdrop of the
multiple man-made crisis that humanity is facing today such a
hope appears at first sight like an attempt to escape or "make
over" the consequences of Western "modernization" in just the
same way that the modern world has again and again faced
challenges by pushing for "innovation." The idea of the "tabula
rasa" as a stepping out of the trajectories of tradition and the
cherishing of a freedom to fundamentally rethink what is at
hand are both traits of a modern thinking that for good reasons
are being questioned today. In this light one can ask if it is not a

---

1   Hannah Arendt, *The Human Condition* (Chicago, IL: University of
    Chicago Press, [1958] 1998), 177–8.
2   Kundera coined the derogative term "imagology" to characterize the
    restless production of new imagery of postmodernity reiterating a
    modernist epistemology yet cut loose from the grand ideologies of
    the twentieth century. Milan Kundera, *Immortality* (London: Faber &
    Faber, 1991).

commitment to what is already there and the acknowledgment of being deeply implicated in the complexities of the present that must be the precondition for responsible action.

Much of contemporary thinking points in similar directions.

Bruno Latour has claimed that the modern idea of the free individual acting at will with others in a social world clearly distinct from the natural substrate from which it feeds was always wrong.[3] He argues that modern thought fails both because it assumes that there is a place from which to act outside the networks in which the individual is embedded and because modern thought neglects the entanglement of the natural and the social. For Latour the consequence is that "we have never been modern." When modernity claimed to produce novelty in the social world through technological leaps in man-made things, it neglected the proliferation of consequences that made the social and the natural form ever more solid hybrids. When modern man is acclaimed for such achievements, it is, according to Latour, similarly ignoring how this agency is not the cause but the effect of the network of these hybrids.

Donna Haraway and other postfeminists have a slightly different take on some of the same issues. They object to the idea of stable epistemologies and argue for ontological worlds of becoming in which knowing and acting are inherently relational. For Haraway the web of relations that constitute agency extends beyond the human and is marked not by a strive toward effect but by a caring engagement with "significant others." In her *Companion Species Manifesto*[4] she takes the caring and loving between people and dogs as the constitutive example of such an engagement that is not constrained by but built upon the fundamental otherness of different lives that have been brought compassionately together. Where Latour would trace beginnings by "following the actors," Haraway urges us to "stay with the

3   I here draw loosely on Bruno Latour, *Reassembling the Social: An Introduction to Actor-Network-Theory* (Oxford: Oxford University Press, 2005) and Bruno Latour, *We Have Never Been Modern* (Cambridge, MA: Harvard University Press, 2012).

4   Donna Haraway, *The Companion Species Manifesto: Dogs, People, and Significant Otherness*, Vol. 1 (Chicago: Prickly Paradigm Press, 2003).

trouble"[5] in order to witness worlds unfolding. How much
both of these authors and with them also a vast array of other
contemporary writers direct us to (re-)think our being present in
entangled worlds of matter and bodies in ways that negate any
ideas of a tabula rasa, or of a license to enact a "total makeover"
of the ecology of which we are part, what we are left with as
unresolved, is the principle of freedom as it poses itself in the life
worlds of any "man."

Looking more closely at the concept of beginning that to
Hannah Arendt marks the principle of freedom, what comes
across as its dominant sense is more akin to the care and
friendship between companions hinted at by Haraway than to
the Machiavellian prince claiming to be modern in the writings of
Latour.

For Arendt freedom is first of all the freedom to move and to
take part. Contrary to the idea that we become free when we opt
out of the constraints imposed on us by the world, she insists that
it is only when we find ways to participate in the worlds *between*
us that we gain the power to move freely:

> Before it became an attribute of thought or a quality of the
> will, freedom was understood to be the free man's status,
> which enabled him to move, to get away from home, to go
> out into the world and meet other people in deed and word
> … Freedom as a demonstrable fact and politics coincide
> and are related to each other like two sides of the same
> matter.[6]

In this light it is "freedom" when a group of seniors and a group
of designers have worked together to connect and gather for
having fun in a public park, and one of the seniors declare that
"it is all already here." It is freedom that is invoked when a
call center worker, a municipal waste planner, and a garbage
collector act out a story about how they may engage tenants in a
high rise in recycling. And it is freedom as a new world becoming

5   Donna Haraway, *Staying with the Trouble: Making Kin in the
     Chthulucene* (Durham: Duke University Press, 2016).
6   Hannah Arendt, *Between Past and Future* (New York: Viking Press,
     1961), 148–9.

within reach when a group of design students transform a local library into a maker festival where young and old people from the neighborhood come together to repair cherished belongings and share stories about their life.

Arendt's thinking is strongly marked by her experience of being exiled as a Jew from Nazi Germany. To be forced to take on an identity imposed by an oppressive political regime, and in so doing to accept that this means having to radically opt out of the world she previously inhabited, becomes for her emblematic of an exclusion that cancels out any opportunities to act in the public sphere without addressing and redressing the label that marks this exclusion. In paralleling this experience of extreme exclusion with the exclusion of other groups she points to that, even if such exclusion may form the base for a strong sense of brotherhood and empathy, it is first when this exclusion is omitted and the excluding label is reinstated in a public dialogue that freedom can be regained. When designing in dark times where the exclusion of voices and the absence of open dialogues about pressing issues penetrate public life, the prerogative of design to speculate with others about the worlds that lie between us becomes a mandate to pursue a hopeful "What if?"

In designing, propositions are made that brings new realities within reach. Asking "what if" does not ensure that proposals are followed but imagining routes to take or practices to rehearse expands the horizon of the life worlds of those who engage with the proposals. More explicitly, to design for the "what if" can help to include voices, empower them to action and therefore to freedom (in its being political).

To design is to engage in free thinking when other realities are invoked as the possible toward which we can reach out. For Hannah Arendt the end point of such free thinking is never a truth or a definite solution to a problem. For her free thinking is the ongoing engagement with others to find new beginnings from where the present becomes open for our actions. Such free thinking does not stem from a bracketing off of the positions in which we are put by societal powers. We are still garbage collectors, elderly, or residents of a deprived neighborhood when we imagine how we can act differently in the here-and-now. As designers we are not generating proposals by drawing on a license to be creative in a space outside this here-and-now or envisioning new realities through empathizing with life worlds that are not our own. Instead free thinking unfolds as things are drawn together by people who acknowledge each other in friendship and sympathy across but not beyond differences in outlook to the realities that lie between them.

Addressing the loneliness and isolation among the elderly in the city is one among many pressing issues today. To design solutions to this problem is as futile as it is to gather people who will be comfortable with being labeled as elderly and lonely. Being invited to designing new beginnings in the everyday of senior citizens may transform alienation to agency if the coming together of different people transcends the categories that produce isolation. To concretely explore playgrounds for seniors and the lively exchanges of social media transposed to a loose network of people 70+ in gatherings where seniors, municipal caretakers, and designers all join in may provide for such a transformation. When Ketty, a woman of 83, after several of such gatherings, playfully performing what this may entail, announces that "it is all already here," we see for a moment such new beginnings.

Ecological imbalances and unsustainable economies surface on all levels of the societies we live in. There is no doubt that this calls for a radical rethinking of how we live our lives. Designers are promoting new frameworks for product service systems and engage in exposing and amplifying sustainable practices. When garbage collectors meet call center workers and tenants in a high rise struggling to get recycling right, it may seem a small step to make childish doll scenarios to envision a collaboration that makes garbage collectors the main protagonists of a more sustainable waste collection system. Yet again such visions are not solutions to a problem but a concrete rehearsal of other practices that open up toward dialogues in which all participants take on responsible agency.

Design students who partner with a local library to infuse creative making in a challenged neighborhood may seem like charity and short-lived empathizing with people living radically different lives. But designing is about connecting and the design schools and studios are barren facilities if they are not penetrated by voices and issues that let the students' aspirations and concerns blend with others. Designers need to reach out for the freedom to move with others and they must be aware that what they bring is not a privileged access to creativity but a commitment to and a culture of open experimentation in which new beginnings may be invoked, as Arendt does as she speaks of beginnings, by the power of a "hopeful if."

Thomas Binder

See also
COMMON WORLD, DEMOCRACY, *HOMO FABER*, IN-BETWEEN

HISTORY
HOMO FABER
HUMAN RIGHTS
HUMANITY

HISTORY

> Yet the meaningfulness of everyday relationships is
> disclosed not in everyday life but in rare deeds, just as the
> significance of a historical period shows itself only in the
> few events that illuminate it.
>
> Hannah Arendt, *The Human Condition*[1]

In the contemporary world of overwhelming events, we can
ask the question, Why study history? Without history we are
condemned to focus entirely on what's in front of us and not
to have the benefit of past experience. We can also ask the
question: What is experience? It is the awareness we accrue from
living through events. Experience is also the basis of wisdom. In
fact, we might say that wisdom is the distillation of experience
made available to enhance consciousness of the present and
make considered choices for the future.

The past has meaning for us in two senses. First, it is filled
with exemplary activity that can encourage present and future
actions. Second, it shows us events and actions that should not
be repeated. Specific actions or events in Arendt's terms become
dominant in certain periods. The need to bring the two senses to
present consciousness is crucial to making informed decisions
about how we currently live and how we might live in the future.
To those who say that history is not important one has to argue
that action without historical understanding is flying blind.

Knowledge of the past is necessary for the continuation
and development of social systems. Consider the power of the
U.S. Constitution. It is the bulwark of American democracy
without which there would be no anchor for sustaining
democratic values. How often have we needed to recount the
historical events that led to writing the Constitution in order to
understand the intent of its progenitors. Because we recognize

---

1   Hannah Arendt, *The Human Condition* (Chicago, IL: University of
     Chicago Press, [1958] 1998), 42.

the Constitution as the bedrock of American democracy, we have a clearer sense of when its values are abused or violated. Thus historical consciousness contributes to our understanding of the present as a sphere of action for the future.

In writing about the human condition, Hannah Arendt was aware of the past's importance for the present and future. Since the past as a totality is vast and impossible to recreate, we have to access past experience in the form of narratives about particular actions and events. These become the basis for a history of past experience that we believe has meaning for us. The questions we pose about which narratives to choose and validate emphasize events and actions that affect our emotions and feelings.

Ethnic genocides are examples of narratives that are remembered and described by those who believe they should never happen again. Those who are unsympathetic to their horrific consequences deny them. The most notorious example of ethnic genocide, at least in the West, is the Holocaust in Germany during the Second World War. Numerous Holocaust museums attest with photographs, films, and texts that the Holocaust did occur. Another narrative about which there have been conflicting views is slavery. We know that slavery extended back to the earliest civilizations and that it continued for many centuries. Contrary to the historical view that slavery was justified in economic terms, the abolition of slavery and the struggle for African American civil rights is a powerful story that is recounted in the recently established National Museum of African American History and Culture in Washington D.C. Where museums were once cabinets of curiosities or repositories of conventional artefacts, a new kind of museum embodies narratives of past events that in the cases of the Holocaust or slavery serve as repudiations of those who would deny or oppose their recognition.

*

As I am a design historian, I should say something about the importance of understanding the historical trajectory of design. Its history is essential to the formation of values. Design history

is replete with examples from the past that can and should
serve as inspiration for designers in the present and the future.
Consider William Morris. He exemplifies a designer whose
work was based on a powerful belief in justice and fairness.
While we may think of his designs, whether wallpaper, textiles,
or furniture, as no longer models for contemporary designers,
we still find his values to be highly relevant. Morris criticized
the inhumane conditions of factory labor and the exploitation
of workers by factory owners. He also condemned the poor
quality of many products made in factories as compared to those
that showed the hand of a craftsperson. Morris was involved
in the politics of his day and voiced strong opinions about the
policies of the British government. The way he defined his varied
activities can and should serve today as a model for the Citizen
Designer who can conceptualize her or his work in a larger
context of political and social values.[2] In Arendt's sense, Morris's
commitment to social justice invites our attention in more ways
than the accomplishments of many of his contemporaries.

Let us not forget that design has always been implicated in
the worst as well as the best of humanity's past actions. Waging
war has required weapons ranging from Roman catapults to
intercontinental ballistic missiles. The death camps established
by the Nazis depended on architects, engineers, and designers
to create the camp layouts, prisoner accommodations, and
even prisoner uniforms, and especially for the design of the
gas chambers in which so many prisoners were deprived of
life. The recognition of design's complicit involvement in such
activities was not part of the design history narrative told at its
inception. Yet it is important to incorporate this material. These
new additions expand the narrative and contribute to changing
its purpose from a chronology of aesthetic objects to a story
that seeks to explain the involvement of design in all aspects of
human life.

2   For biographical and critical accounts of Morris' life, see Jack Lindsay,
    William Morris: A Biography (New York: Taplinger, 1979) and Linda
    Parrey, ed., *William Morris* (New York: Harry N. Abrams, 1996).

Our expanding awareness of design history is now more than ever motivated by a desire to create an intersection between key objects, previously admired for their formal qualities, and actions that were once the exclusive purview of political and social historians. A consequence of this intersection is that we are beginning to understand more about how design is part of politics, and politics is part of design.

Victor Margolin[3]

See also
ACTIVISM, COMMON GOOD, STORIES

---

3   *Victor Margolin died just as this volume was going to press. We would like to take this opportunity to record our deep appreciation of his work and life in design history and design studies.—The Editors*

HOMO FABER

An *epistula* to Hannah

Dear Hannah,
    The Times They Are a-Changin.'[1]
    In our society, materializing any artefacts or systems has become technically possible, socially desirable, economically profitable. Through technology, it is possible to extract value from everything, even from human beings. Digitalization and automation change both work and labor. The *Animal Laborans* has been transformed into an exploited globalized human that fabricates artefacts and inequality at the same time.
    Empowered by the technology, speeding up the process as only a *Fabricator* could do, building and building things that have scarce collective meaning, *Homo Faber* has lost his way. The *acceleration* produces *dystopia*.[2] Seeking ways to find ways to escape to his destiny[3] but consuming everything in his path, destroying with an appetite for destruction that some still call *humanism*,[4] this inextricable relationship is crashing the ship that we are all in.

*

Dear Hannah, today we use terms like *Anthropocene*[5] and *Posthumanism*[6] to describe an era when the human condition

---

1   Bob Dylan, *The Times They Are a-Changin'* (New York: Columbia Records, 1964).
2   Benjamin Noys, *Malign Velocities: Accelerationism and Capitalism* (Winchester: Zero Books, 2013).
3   Mark Fisher, *Capitalist Realism: Is There No Alternative?* (Winchester: Zero Books, 2010) and Nick Srnicek and Alex Williams, *Inventing the Future: Postcapitalism and a World without Work* (London: Verso, 2015).
4   Timothy Morton, *Dark Ecology: For a Logic of Future Coexistence* (New York: Columbia University Press, 2016).
5   Will Steffen, Paul J. Crutzen, and John R. McNeill, "The Anthropocene: Are Humans Now Overwhelming the Great Forces of Nature?" *Ambio* vol. 36, no. 8 (December 2007): 614.
6   Rosi Braidotti, *The Posthuman* (Cambridge, MA: Polity Press, 2013).

impacts irreversibly on nature, space, and time and where desires go beyond the idea of species and the biological finiteness of the person.

But what could be the meaning of *vita activa* nowadays? What are the challenges for the future *Homo Faber*?

The role of the individual builder in a mass society could be indeed that of a spark, a spark of freedom in a world that values only money.

We must think forward with a broader perspective. Use the incredible transformative power of humanity to build more than the economic well-being that surrounds us. A new kind of *universalism* that connects the free empowered individual in a new way: the network. It is the independent power of these men together that could fight the *group-thinking* and *populist* society that is emerging from the ashes of the twentieth century.

The unique way to resist is not to believe that everything about our system is true.

It is the time for *skeptical citizens* who might discuss and rewire the work-laboring transformation process into a dynamic perspective: capitalism (in all of its configuration) could not be considered the unique and final possible political and socioeconomic regime.

They could open the *black boxes* sealed with *power*[7] and technology and discuss again the meaning of things, beyond the cruel illusions of the *comfort*.

We could work for being not alienated men. Rediscovering the idea that transformation could work for the *commons' sake*.[8]

Building a *new anthropology*[9] in which the transformation of the private sphere and public spaces requires this new critical action.

Crucial areas for the evolution of the transformative action of *Homo Faber* are the *body* and the *polis* in which the melting

---

7   *Public Enemy, Fight the Power in Fear of a Black Planet* (New York: Def Jam, 1990).

8   Yochai Benkler, *The Wealth of Networks: How Social Production Transforms Markets and Freedom* (New Haven, CT: Yale University Press, 2006).

9   Björk, *Hyper-Ballad* in *Post* (London: One Little Indian, 1995) and Timothy Morton, *Hyperobjects: Philosophy and Ecology after the End of the World* (Minneapolis: University of Minnesota Press, 2013).

and hybridization of life and work, of the private sphere and the public sphere, of nature and technology, is more visible.

A new evolutionary step of individuals and society requires to rethink the community understood as an ecosystem where the most advanced forms of the human condition coexist and where the human action takes shape through the most advanced forms of culture and material production.

It is a discussion that we must open about the value that we extract from these *commons*[10] and how the *Automaton* could help the man in changing the impact of the human in the world and the society.

We surely don't know if it is the *end of work as we know it.*
But surely of the *vita activa* as you know it.
Sincerely yours,
Stefano and Massimo

Stefano Maffei and Massimo Bianchini

See also
ANIMAL RATIONALE, ANTHROPOCENTRISM,
VIOLENCE

---

10   Michel Bauwens and Vasilis Niaros, *Value in the Commons Economy: Developments in Open and Contributory Value Accounting* (Chiang Mai: Heinrich-Böll-Foundation & P2P Foundation, 2017).

HUMAN RIGHTS

The fundamental deprivation of human rights is manifested first and above all in the deprivation of a place in the world which makes opinions significant and actions effective. Something much more fundamental than freedom and justice, which are rights of citizens, is at stake when belonging to the community into which one is born is no longer a matter of course and not belonging no longer a matter of choice, or when one is placed in a situation where, unless he commits a crime, his treatment by others does not depend on what he does or does not do. This extremity, and nothing else, is the situation of people deprived of human rights. They are deprived, not of the right to freedom, but of the right to action; not of the right to think whatever they please, but of the right to opinion. Privileges in some cases, injustices in most, blessings and doom are meted out to them according to accident and without any relation whatsoever to what they do, did, or may do.

Hannah Arendt, *The Origins of Totalitarianism*[1]

Arendt's sobering statement about the sense of agency that is stripped away when someone is robbed of their human rights represents an eerie and timely provocation. Her admonition evokes numerous circumstances during which designers engage with individuals who are at the center of situations where forces of inequity and/or social injustice are at play. We can think of the global refugee crisis; the plight of indigenous populations whose livelihood are affected by the cascading effects of climate change; enduring acts of race and gender violence— the examples abound in a world that is volatile, uncertain, and changing.

It is powerful to consider design as a field of research and practice fundamentally grounded in human dignity and

[1]   Hannah Arendt, *The Origins of Totalitarianism* (New York: Harvest Books, [1951] 1979), 296.

human rights.[2] Design for social innovation, by enabling right to actions, can also work for enhancing and protecting human rights. The resonance of Arendt's words is significant and is complemented by that of her friend and contemporary, the American philosopher Richard McKeon who, in another important body of work that contributed to the formulation of the 1948 Universal Declaration of Human Rights, highlights our ongoing difficulty of upholding the universal dimension of human rights for all. McKeon's key insight is to tell us how pluralistic the manifestation and interpretation of human rights can be across different cultural contexts and times:

> Human rights have a universal common basis in human thought and community; yet they are differently interpreted, and their recognition and practice depend on the development of a common understanding of rights and freedoms.[3]

Design for social innovation, a rapidly maturing field of design in which we situate our research and one that shares the ethos of Arendt and McKeon, can be leveraged to strengthen the moral principles and norms that have been identified by the United Nations Universal Declaration of Human Rights.[4] This is a field of design research and practice that is particularly prone to challenging our assumptions about designers' responsibilities and the many ethical issues they face as they navigate the ambiguity, tensions, and fluid conditions that often characterize many of the wicked problems of these design briefs.[5] How can design for social innovation enable rights to actions? The following three

2   Richard Buchanan, "Human Dignity and Human Rights: Thoughts on Principles of Human-Centered Design," *Design Issues* vol. 17, no. 3 (2001): 35-9.

3   Richard P. McKeon, "Philosophy and History in the Development of Human Rights," in McKeon (ed.), *Freedom and History and Other Essays* (Chicago, IL: University of Chicago Press, 1990).

4   "Universal Declaration of Human Rights," *United Nations*, accessed August 24, 2018, http://www.un.org/en/universal-declaration-human-rights.

5   For further reading on career pathways and roles of designers in an emergent field of design for social innovation, see: Mariana Amatullo, Bryan Boyer, Liz Danzico, and Andrew Shea, *LEAP Dialogues: Career Pathways in Design for Social Innovation* (Pasadena: Designmatters at ArtCenter College of Design, 2016).

examples show how design can function on different scales—
localized, systemic, and global—to support human rights.

Favela Painting Project

One example of a localized design intervention is the Favela
Painting Project.[6] In an effort to beautify Praça Cantão, located
within the Santa Marta favela near Rio de Janeiro, where
police and gangs often fought, the Dutch studio Haas&Hahn
partnered with community members to cocreate a mural that
features colorful rays and can be extended through the favelas
in the future. This kind of cocreating process ensures that the
insights and expertise of community members inform the design
solution. It also often promotes participants from residents to
neighborhood ambassadors. Next, Haas&Hahn employed local
youth to paint murals over 75,000 square feet of the public
square, thirty-four surrounding houses, streets, and the interior
of a popular samba studio. The murals transformed Praça Cantão
and have, in part, led to safer streets and a sense of belonging for
residents in the Santa Marta favela, who have taken more pride in
their neighborhood. They directly and indirectly support articles
of the UN Human Rights Declaration, including their standard of
living (Article 25) and their ability to participate in cultural life
(Article 27).

Lotus

A project that demonstrates design's ability to innovate an
existing system is Lotus,[7] a unique solar-powered irrigation
pump. The pump was designed by Proximity Designs, who
noticed that Myanmar farmers were switching to fuel engine
irrigation pumps that pollute, are heavy, difficult to operate, and
have high fuel costs and maintenance fees. This submersible
pump has a working depth of twenty-four feet, pumps over 15,000

---

6   "Praça Cantão," Haas&Hahn, accessed August 22, 2018, https://
     haasandhahn.com/Praca-Cantao.
7   "Farm Tech," Proximity Designs, accessed August 22, 2018, https://
     proximitydesigns.org/service/farm-tech.

liters of water each day, and fits into the tube wells commonly found in rural Myanmar. While most solar irrigation pumps cost several thousand dollars, the Lotus costs only US\$345, lasts for up to three years without needing a repair, enables small farmers to boost productivity and earn extra income, and promotes the right to own property (Article 17) and to just and favorable conditions of work (Article 23).[8]

Mine Kafon Drone

A third project that shows design's ability to advance human rights on a global impact is the Mine Kafon Drone,[9] which has been developed by two Afghan brothers who experienced the horrors of landmines. Landmines affect millions of people in over 60 countries who live with the risk of being killed, injured, or associated psychological trauma. The process of clearing the world's landmines using current techniques is extremely difficult, dangerous, and time consuming; it would take over 1,100 years. The Mine Kafon Drone maps an area for landmines, detects them, and then detonates them remotely, a process up to 20 times faster and up to 200 times cheaper. The drone can save thousands of lives around the world while providing communities with lasting benefits like security of person (Article 3) and more mobility (Article 13) and avoid deprivation of property (Article 17).

If we search for patterns among these three cases and many others from the design for social innovation field, we find that in addition to connecting directly with the universal principles of human rights, they share in common an ability to harness an element of agency—again, Arendt's idea of "action"—that may have been latent or even absent before the intervention. Oftentimes it is no mistake that some of the most promising solutions they propose are less about a top-down product or service innovation, but about a design intervention that creates

8   For further reading about this project, see: Mariana Amatullo, Bryan Boyer, Liz Danzico, and Andrew Shea, *LEAP Dialogues: Career Pathways in Design for Social Innovation* (Pasadena: Designmatters at ArtCenter College of Design, 2016).

9   "Mine Kafon Drone," Mine Kafon, accessed August 22, 2018, http://minekafon.org.

a positive impact by catalyzing qualities of self-reliance in the individuals that are touched, and by helping to reorient power structures, incentives, and privileges that are often intangible. In the aforementioned quote, Arendt speaks not only of the right to action, but of the right to opinion. What can design do for the right to opinion? Notoriously, design can help to make "things" visible and tangible. Critical works that focus on representation may empower individuals to become aware of their rights to act and opine as citizens with agency. Also, designers can contribute to creating environments where these rights are acknowledged. Design as "infrastructuring" can create the preconditions for "enabling ecosystems"[10] where these rights of opinion and action are fully articulated. In turn, this can lead to situations for dialogue and community building as well as actions that promote common interests, further empowering citizens who are now aware of their own rights. To design for human rights means then first to design the preconditions for opinions to be formed and actions to be undertaken. To borrow once again from Arendt, in these projects, design succeeds because of its agency and ability to counter the fundamental deprivation of human rights *by making opinions significant and actions effective.*

Mariana Amatullo and Andrew Shea

See also
CITIZENSHIP, CREATIVITY, DEMOCRACY, EVIL, PLURALITY

---

10 Ezio Manzini, *Design, When Everybody Designs* (Cambridge, MA: MIT Press, 2015).

HUMANITY

> Humanity is never acquired in solitude, and never by giving
> one's work to the public. It can be achieved only by one who
> has thrown his life and person into the "venture into the
> public realm."
>
> Hannah Arendt, *Hannah Arendt: The Last Interview and
> Other Conversations*[1]

For us, Arendt's words can serve as an invitation to designers
both to strive for humanity by throwing themselves into
encountering others and to design how to throw themselves
together with others. Others that are also other than human[2] and
into ventures with the potential for entanglements. In updating
this thought, we thus propose that the path toward humanity
lies more on entanglements (among bodies, things, feelings, and
actions) than on public-ness.

Drawing on Arendt, we look at humanity as an idea we
should strive for, an unfinished concept/state, always dynamic,
ongoing, and evolving. Thus, the path to humanity presents
itself as a process of constant change and movement. In
the same way, the quote we were assigned led to a venture
into designing toward humanity through the association of
concepts, juxtaposition, and at times pure gut feeling, based
on other excerpts and other thoughts in her work. Thus, we
delved into how these ideas and words resonate in us, in
the work we do as researchers and designers, and in how
they are diffracted by our hopes for new paths for designing
and researching with constantly renewed understandings of
humanity.

Inspired by the idea that words become part of lexicons
through various processes of borrowing, abbreviating, deriving,

---

1   Hannah Arendt, "What Remains? The Language Remains: A Conversation
    with Günter Gaus," in *Hannah Arendt: The Last Interview and Other
    Conversations* (Brooklyn, NY: Melville House, 2013), 18.
2   Marisol de la Cadena, "Runa: Human but Not Only," *HAU: Journal of
    Ethnographic Theory* vol. 4, no. 2 (September 1, 2014): 253–9.

agglutinating, and creating based on existing meanings and uses of other words, we put together our "Humanity" entry, by tracing the work that other words do for "Humanity." In this way, we also trace our paths toward humanity and draw meta-paths that we think help us make other journeys, in these difficult times.

The following aggregate of words and the words themselves constitute and emerge from entanglements that occurred in our design venture toward humanity. The reader should not see them as possibilities among which to choose.

*"Humanity is exemplified not in fraternity but in **friendship**."*[3]
Mano: São Paulo's slang for a friend worthy of trust and partner in everyday adventures.
Parcero: Colombian slang for good friend and close companion. It originally referred to a prisoner's cellmate.
Friendship: a relationship based on intimacy, disposition, and trust toward someone considered a friend and worthy of knowing one's own beliefs and sharing dreams and hopes.
*"**A trust**—which is difficult to formulate but fundamental—in what is human in all people."*[4]
Faith: the feeling and confidence about believing in something, i.e., in the collective action toward humanity.
Confianza/Confiança: the feeling of being able to trust fully, believe in another person, or thing.
Throw: to move (oneself) suddenly in reaction to some emotions or toward some emotions.
Jump: to proceed suddenly, ignoring the steps that should come between (something) or the thinking that should come before it. To leap or spring off the ground or other support by a sudden effort toward something.

---

3   Hannah Arendt, *Men in Dark Times* (New York: Harcourt, Brace, [1955] 1993), 25.
4   Arendt, "What Remains? The Language Remains: A Conversation with Günter Gaus," 18.

*"We **humanize** what is going on in the world and in ourselves only by speaking of it, and in the course of speaking of it we learn to be human."*[5]

*"The question of selflessness, or rather the question of openness to others, which in fact is the precondition for '**humanity**' in every sense of that word."*[6]

Voice: the sound or sounds uttered through the mouth of living creatures when speaking or singing. The right to present and receive consideration of one's desires or opinions.

Touch: a sense related to skin. A way to reassure, to share, to comfort. The action that connects one's extended mind to another's extended mind.

Silence: absence (of sound or noise).

Humming: to produce a wordless tone, often with a melody, forcing the sound to emerge from the nose.

Hummus: a delicious Levantine dip or spread made from cooked, mashed chickpeas or other beans, blended with tahini, olive oil, lemon juice, salt, and garlic.

"Humanity in the form of fraternity invariably appears historically among persecuted peoples and enslaved groups." [7] *'[…]'This [group] kind of organization has to do with a **relation** to the world."*[8]

Grope: to search uncertainly.

Entanglements: something that entangles. An involvement, a complication. Or even the situation of the filaments of a ball of wool.

Passion/Fire: a strong, powerful, compelling emotion, feeling, or interest. The outburst of strong emotion or feeling.

Unstable: a condition of something that could change or fluctuate quickly in an unforeseeable way.

*"[…] in every **action** the person is expressed as in no other human activity. Speaking is also a form of action. That is one*

---

5   Arendt, *Men in Dark Times*, 25.

6   Ibid., 15.

7   Ibid., 13.

8   Arendt, "What Remains? The Language Remains: A Conversation with Günter Gaus," 14.

venture. The other is: We start something. We weave our strand into a network of relations. What comes of it we never know."[9]

Unveil: to reveal or disclose by or as if by removing a veil or covering.

Sailing: any method for determining and undertaking courses of action and distances by means of charts and symbolic references.

In activity: the state or quality of being active or lively.

Performance: something accomplished, a completion of a task with application of knowledge, skills, and abilities.

Acaso: without definite aim, purpose, method, or adherence to a prior arrangement.

*"May I ask something? As a politically active being, doesn't man need commitment to a **group**, a commitment that can then to a certain extent be called love?"*[10]

Intimacy: the state of being intimate, an act that shows close feeling or intimate association.

Person: the body of a living human being, sometimes including the clothes being worn.

Action: a thing done or a doing thing.

Alteridade: the quality of being different or distinct in appearance, character, etc.

Mass: a body of matter of indefinite shape.

Ship: a large vessel, esp. one that travels on the ocean; the crew and passengers of a vessel.

Andrea Botero and Chiara Del Gaudio

See also
EQUALITY, SPEECH, TOGETHERNESS

---

9   Arendt, "What Remains? The Language Remains," 18.
10   Ibid., 14.

IMAGINATION
IMPERIALISM
IN-BETWEEN
INSTRUMENTALITY

I

IMAGINATION

"Imagination" was a text produced by Hannah Arendt in 1970 for a seminar on Kant's Critique of Judgement *at The New School in New York. Full details of the context of the work can be found in Hannah Arendt,* Thinking without a Banister, *ed. Jerome Kohn (New York: Schocken Books, 2018) pages 387–394, from which this slightly edited version is taken.*

I

Imagination, Kant says, is the faculty of making present what is absent, the faculty of re-presentation: "Imagination is the faculty of representing in intuition an object that is not itself present."[1] Or: "Imagination (*facultas imaginandi*) is a faculty of perception in the absence of an object."[2] To give the name "imagination" to this faculty of having present what is absent is natural enough. If I represent what is absent, I have an image in my mind—an image of something I have seen and now somehow reproduce. In the *Critique of Judgment*, Kant sometimes calls this faculty "reproductive"—I represent what I have seen—to distinguish it from the "productive" faculty—the artistic faculty that produces something it has never seen. But productive imagination (genius) is never entirely productive. It produces, for instance, the centaur out of the given: the horse and the man. This sounds as though we are dealing with memory. But for Kant, imagination is the condition for memory, and a much more comprehensive faculty. In his *Anthropology* Kant puts memory "the faculty to make present the past," together with a "faculty of divination," which makes present the future. Both are faculties of "association," that is, of connecting the "no longer" and the "not yet" with the present; and "although they themselves are not perceptions, they

---

1 Immanuel Kant, *Critique of Pure Reason*, trans. N. K. Smith (New York: St. Martin's Press, 1963), B151.

2 Immanuel Kant, *Anthropology from a Pragmatic Point of View*, trans. Mary J. Gregor (The Hague: Martinus Nijhoff, 1974), 28 (italics added).

serve to connect the perceptions in time."[3] Imagination does not
need to be led by this temporal association; it can make present
at will whatever it chooses.

What Kant calls the faculty of imagination, to have present
in the mind what is absent from sense perception, has less to do
with memory than with another faculty, one that has been known
since the beginnings of philosophy. Parmenides called it *nous*,
by which he meant true *Being* is not what is present, does not
present itself to the senses. What is not present is the *it-is*; and
the *it-is*, though absent from the senses, is present to the mind.
Or Anaxagoras' *opsis tön adēlōn ta phainomena*, "a glimpse
of the nonvisible are the appearances."[4] To put this differently,
by looking at appearances, which are given to intuition in Kant,
you become aware, catch a glimpse of something that does
not appear. This something is *Being* as such. From it comes
metaphysics, the discipline that treats what lies beyond physical
reality; and then, still in a mysterious way, what is given to
the mind as the nonappearance in the appearances becomes
ontology, the science of Being.

II

The role of imagination for our cognitive faculties is perhaps the
greatest discovery Kant made in the *Critique of Pure Reason*.
For our purposes it is best to turn to the "Schematism of the Pure
Concepts of Understanding."[5] To anticipate: the same faculty,
imagination, which provides schemata for cognition, provides
examples for judgment. You will recall that in Kant there are two
stems of experience and knowledge: intuition (sensibility) and
concepts (understanding). Intuition always *gives* us something
particular; the concept makes this particular known to us. If
I say: "this table," it is as though intuition says "this" and the
understanding adds "table." "This" relates only to the specific
item; "table" identifies it and makes the object communicable.

3   Kant, *Anthropology from a Pragmatic Point of View*, 34.
4   Hermann Diels and Walther Kranz, *Die Fragmente der Vorsokraiker*, 5th
     ed. (Berlin: Weidmannsche buchhandlung, 1934–7), B212a.
5   Kant, *Critique of Pure Reason*, B176ff.

Two questions arise. First, how do the two faculties come together? To be sure, the concepts of understanding enable the mind to order the manifold of the sensations. But where does the synthesis, their working together, spring from? Second, is this concept, "table," a concept at all? Is it not perhaps also a kind of image? So that some sort of imagination is present in the intellect as well? The answer is: "Synthesis of a manifold is what first gives rise to knowledge. [It] gathers the elements for knowledge, and unites them into a certain content"; this synthesis "is the mere result of the faculty of imagination, a blind but indispensable function of the soul, without which we should have no knowledge whatsoever, but of which we are scarcely ever conscious."[6] And the way imagination produces the synthesis is by "providing an image for a concept."[7] Such an image is called a "schema."

> The two extremes, namely sensibility and understanding, must be brought into connection with each other by means of imagination, because otherwise the former, though indeed yielding appearances, would supply no objects of empirical knowledge, hence no experience.[8]

Here Kant calls upon imagination to provide the connection between the two faculties, and in the first edition of the *Critique of Pure Reason* he calls the faculty of imagination "the faculty of synthesis in general [*überhaupt*]." At other places where he speaks directly of the "schematism" involved in our understanding, he calls it "an art concealed in the depths of the human soul"[9] (i.e., we have a kind of "intuition" of something that is never present), and by this he suggests that imagination is actually the common root of the other cognitive faculties, that is, it is the "common, but to us unknown, root"[10] of sensibility and understanding, of which he speaks in the Introduction to the *Critique of Pure Reason* and which, in its last chapter, without naming the faculty, he mentions again.[11]

---

6   Ibid., B103 (italics added).
7   Ibid., B180 (italics added).
8   Ibid., A124.
9   Ibid., B180.
10   Ibid., B29.
11   Ibid., B863.

III

Schema: The point of the matter is that without a "schema"
one can never recognize anything. When one says: "this table,"
the general "image" of table is present in one's mind, and one
recognizes that the "this" is a table, something that shares its
qualities with many other such things though it is itself an
individual, particular thing. If I recognize a house, this perceived
house also includes how a house in general looks. This is what
Plato called the eidos—the general form—of a house, which
is never given to the natural senses but only to the eyes of the
mind. Since, speaking literally, it is not given even to "the eyes of
the mind," it is something like an "image" or, better, a "schema."
Whenever one draws or builds a house, one draws or builds a
particular house, not the house as such. Still, how could one not
do it without having this schema or Platonic eidos before the
eye of one's mind? Kant says: "No image could ever be adequate
to the concept of triangle in general. It would never attain that
universality of the concept which renders it valid of all triangles,
whether right-angled, obtuse-angled, or acute-angled; the
schema of the triangle can exist nowhere but in thought."[12] Yet,
though it exists in thought only, it is a kind of "image"; it is not a
product of thought, nor is it given to sensibility; and least of all
it is the product of an abstraction from sensibly given data. It is
something beyond or between thought and sensibility; it belongs
to thought insofar as it is outwardly invisible, and it belongs to
sensibility insofar as it is something like an image. Kant therefore
sometimes calls imagination "one of the original sources of all
experience" and says that it cannot itself "be derived from any
other faculty of the mind."[13]

One more example:

> The concept "dog" signifies a rule according to which
> my imagination can delineate the figure of a four-footed
> animal in a general manner without limitation to any
> single determinate figure such as experience, or any
> possible image that I can represent in concreto, actually

12   Ibid., B180.
13   Ibid., A94.

presents—although as soon as the figure is delineated on paper it is again a particular animal!

This is the "art concealed in the depths of the human soul, whose real modes of activity nature is hardly likely ever to allow us to discover and to have open to our gaze."[14] Kant says that the image—for instance, the George Washington Bridge—is the product "of the empirical faculty of reproductive imagination; the schema [bridge] is a product of pure a priori imagination through which images themselves first become possible."[15] In other words: if I did not have the faculty of "schematizing," I could not have images.

IV

For us, the following points are decisive.

1. In perception of this particular table there is contained "table" as such. Hence, no perception is possible without imagination. Kant remarks that "psychologists have hitherto failed to realize that imagination is a necessary ingredient of perception itself."[16]
2. The schema "table" is valid for all particular tables. Without it, we would be surrounded by a manifold of objects of which we could say only "this" and "this" and "this." Not only would no knowledge be possible, but communication—"Bring me a table" (no matter which)—would be impossible.
3. Hence: Without the ability to say "table," we could never communicate. We can describe the George Washington Bridge because we all know "bridge." Suppose someone comes along who does not know "bridge," and there is no bridge to which I could point and utter the word. I would then draw an image of the schema of a bridge, which of course is already a particular bridge, just to remind him of

14   Ibid., B180–1.
15   Ibid., B181.
16   Ibid., A120 (note).

some schema known to him, such as "transition from one
side of the river to the other."

In other words: What makes particulars *communicable*
is (a) that in perceiving a particular we have in the back of
our minds (or in the "depths of our souls") a "schema" whose
"shape" is characteristic of many such particulars *and* (b) that
this schematic shape is in the back of the minds of many
different people. These schematic shapes are products of the
imagination, although "no schema can ever be brought into any
image whatsoever."[17] All single agreements or disagreements
presuppose that we are talking about the same thing—that we,
who are many, agree, come together, on something that is one
and the same for us all.

4. The *Critique of Judgment* deals with reflective judgments
   as distinguished from determinant ones. Determinant
   judgments subsume the particular under a general
   rule; reflective judgments, on the contrary, "derive" the
   rule from the particular. In the schema, one actually
   "perceives" some "universal" in the particular. One sees,
   so to speak, the schema "table" by recognizing the table as
   table. Kant hints at this distinction between determinant
   and reflective judgments in the *Critique of Pure Reason*
   by drawing a distinction between "subsuming under a
   concept" and "bringing to a concept."[18]
5. Finally, our sensibility seems to need imagination not
   only as an aid to knowledge but in order to recognize
   sameness in the manifold. As such, it is the condition
   of all knowledge: the "synthesis of imagination, prior
   to apperception, is the ground of the possibility of
   all knowledge, especially of experience."[19] As such,
   imagination "determines the sensibility *a priori*," i.e., it
   inheres in all sense perceptions. Without it, there would
   be neither the objectivity of the world—that it can be

17   Ibid., B181.
18   Ibid., B104.
19   Ibid., A118.

known—nor any possibility of communication that we can talk about it.

V

The importance of the schema for our purposes is that sensibility and understanding meet in producing it through imagination. In the *Critique of Pure Reason* imagination is at the service of the intellect; in the *Critique of Judgment* the intellect is "at the service of imagination."[20]

In the *Critique of Judgment* we find an analogy to the "schema": it is the *example*.[21] Kant accords to examples the same role in judgments that the intuitions called schemata have for experience and cognition. Examples play a role in both reflective and determinant judgments, that is, whenever we are concerned with particulars. In the *Critique of Pure Reason—where* we read that "judgment is a peculiar talent which can be practiced only, and cannot be taught" and that "its lack no school can make good"[22]—they are called "the go-cart *[Gängelband]* of judgment."[23] In the *Critique of Judgment*, i.e., in the treatment of reflective judgments, where one does not subsume a particular under a concept, the example helps one in the same way in which the schema helped one to recognize the table as table. The examples lead and guide us, and the judgment thus acquires "exemplary validity."[24]

The example is the particular that contains in itself, or is supposed to contain, a concept or a general rule. How, for instance, are you able to judge, to evaluate, an act as courageous? When judging, you say spontaneously, without any derivations from general rules, "This man has courage." If you were a Greek you would have in "the depths of your mind" the example of Achilles. Imagination is again necessary: you must have Achilles

---

20   Kant, *Critique of Judgment*, General Remark to §22, trans. J. H. Bernard (New York: Hafner, 1951).
21   Ibid., §59.
22   Kant, *Critique of Pure Reason*, B172.
23   Ibid., B173–4.
24   Kant, *Critique of Judgment*, §22.

present despite his absence. If we say of somebody that he is good, we have in the back of our minds the example of Saint Francis or Jesus of Nazareth. The judgment has exemplary validity to the extent that the example is rightly chosen. Or, to take another instance: in the circumstances of French history I can speak of Napoleon Bonaparte as a particular man; but the moment I speak of Bonapartism I make an example of him. The validity of this example will be restricted to those who possess the *experience* of Napoleon, if not as his contemporaries then as heirs of a particular historical tradition. Most concepts in the historical and political sciences are of this restricted nature; they have their origin in a particular historical incident and then proceed to make it "exemplary"—to see in the particular what is valid for more than one case.

Hannah Arendt

See also
COMPREHENSION, HISTORY, LAW, PUBLIC

IMPERIALISM

> Contemporary Historians, confronted with the spectacle of
> a few capitalists conducting their predatory searches round
> the globe for new investment possibilities and appealing to
> the profit motives of the much-too-rich and the gambling
> instincts of the much-too-poor, want to clothe imperialism
> with the old grandeur of Rome and Alexander the Great,
> a grandeur which would make all following events more
> humanly tolerable.
>
> Hannah Arendt, The Origins of Totalitarianism[1]

As Arendt makes brutally clear in her analysis, European
domination overseas was strongly motivated by greed.
Imperialism, or the notion that "only the unlimited accumulation
of power could bring about the unlimited accumulation of
capital,"[2] was the political means of securing unfettered access
to these sites of wealth. First put forward in the nineteenth
century by the emerging British bourgeois who were faced with
a saturated market, as the national demand was insufficient
to meet industry's capacity to mass produce, the expansion of
markets into the noncapitalist world became the logical move,
"the salvation of the nation,"[3] and the only way to prevent the
collapse of the system.[4] But what began as "the expansion of
markets" for goods to sell turned, in the late nineteenth and
early twentieth centuries, into the securing of territories from
which raw materials (rubber, diamonds, oil) could be extracted,
at extreme, as in the Belgian Congo, by slave labor and terror.[5]
What in turn was created to "legitimate" such exploitation were

1   Hannah Arendt, *The Origins of Totalitarianism*, 1st ed.
    (New York: Harcourt, Brace, Jovanovich, 1973), 132.
2   Arendt, *The Origins of Totalitarianism*, 137.
3   Ibid., 132.
4   Ibid., 148.
5   The arch example (though not at all the only one—earlier British
    Caribbean and American plantations, German and French colonies in
    Africa) is the Belgian Congo. On this see Adam Hochschild's study, *King
    Leopold's Ghost* (New York: Mariner Books, 1998). It is estimated that

ever more extensive theories and models of racial superiority and racial difference.

Arendt identifies in her essay the increasing popularity of "race thinking" across the years just before the First World War.[6] Growing in parallel to the development of imperialism, she sees this as a relevant component for the emergence of totalitarianism. She warns us that such ideologies become dangerous when they are taken seriously, for Hitler did not invent racism, he adopted it and placed it at the core of his totalitarian regime, and, as with imperialism, used racial difference as a legitimation for domination.

The consequences and implications of imperialism, and especially the attempt to legitimate exploitation by racial difference, have never gone away.[7] Leopoldo Zea, who traced its origin to the ancient Greek, argues that Western domination has always had the goal of attempting to make others—barbarians, pagans, natives, or the "undeveloped"—less like themselves.[8] The more that *apparent* "difference" between persons can be created the easier domination becomes; the harder, conversely to establish solidarity across and with peoples. Today, as global pressures increase, and racism becomes increasingly legitimate again as a tool of political power, it is easily possible to imagine

between the 1880s and c.1920 possibly 10 million Congolese died in Leopold's pursuit of wealth from rubber and other raw materials. The "colonization" of Congo had nothing to do with markets since nothing was exported back to it. It was run as an effective slave state.

6 Among a group of naturalists who supported the idea that instead of having a single ancestor, several ancestors had produced different human races (and the white European was the superior one), Arthur de Gobineau proposed that the mixture of blood caused the degeneration of (white) race, which would eventually lead to the fall of civilizations.

7 Uma Kothari explains that as (British) colonies gained their independence and the empire dissolved, violence was no longer needed; however, domination remained invisible, as former colonial officers became development workers, and development was promoted as something good. Thus, development work is often criticized for being a colonialist practice. See Uma Kothari, "From Colonial Administration to Development Studies: A Postcolonial Critique of the History of Development Studies," in Uma Kothari (eds.), *A Radical History of Development Studies: Individuals, Institutions and Ideologies* (London: Zed Books, 2005).

8 Leopoldo Zea, *Discurso desde la marginación y la barbarie* (Mexico City: Fondo de Cultura Economica, 1990).

a recurrence of some of the worst aspects of Imperialism's ideologies of racial difference.

*

When Arendt thought about ways that Dark Times might be engaged and contested, she thought not only at the largest but also at the smallest scales:

> That even in the darkest of times we have the right to expect some illumination, and that such illumination might well come less from theories and concepts than from the uncertain, flickering, and often weak light that some men and women, in their lives and their works, will kindle under almost all circumstances and shed over the time span that was given to them.[9]

Arendt writes this in her preface to "Men in Dark Times," but the idea that, even within the most difficult situations, it is possible to find and create moments that go against and in their own ways resist and become sites of alternative ways of thinking and acting can become a principle of design work that tries to explore moments of connection and "illumination" between persons.

*

Since 2012, the Aalto LAB Mexico (ALM) project aims at connecting a diversity of people, including students of different disciplines from Finland and Mexico and the inhabitants of the Mayan community called "20 de Noviembre" (located in Calakmul, Campeche, Mexico), under the shared cause of codesigning for a more sustainable living in the village. What ALM intends is better understood through Arendt's reflection that people are not born equal, but they become equal within a group.[10] When locals and strangers engage and collaborate to tackle a complex challenge together, they acknowledge each other as a special kind of experts, whose contributions are invaluable. By working together, as equal fellows, they cultivate friendship and sympathy, and eventually, they learn to value each

---

9 Hannah Arendt, Preface to *Men in Dark Times* (New York: Harcourt, Brace, [1955] 1993), ix.

10 Arendt, *The Origins of Totalitarianism*, 301.

other intrinsically, and they comprehend the meaning of "Volo ut sis" (I want you to be) (Augustine's words quoted by Arendt).[11]

Among others, ALM focuses on the community's intricate water challenges: scarcity and deficient quality. The local people are perfectly aware that the groundwater in the region is too hard for drinking, but they also admit that when facing a drought, and shortage of rainwater in their reservoirs, quality comes second. The laboratory analysis of water samples performed by ALM's participants between 2013 and 2017 confirmed that hardness is the greatest water quality challenge.

Elsewhere, ALM has been described as a longitudinal codesign process that aims at the empowerment of all participants.[12] Thus, following the idea that the community should be able to tackle their own issues by themselves, the team of 2018 explored the possibility of engaging the local youngsters in the construction of a filter (water softener) based on ash collected from the local kitchens. However, when the prototype did not perform as expected, the team decided to invite members of the community to take part in a workshop to collaboratively determine the direction of the project. Unexpectedly, the women participants revealed that ash as a water softener was an old Mayan laundry technique and that they determined the amount of ash by feeling the texture of soapy water. Nonetheless, when their capacity to harvest rainwater grew through the installation of big reservoirs, they abandoned that practice and started to use rainwater instead. The greatest finding from the workshop was that, given that the largest amount of potable water is currently used for laundry, if an ash filter could soften high volumes of groundwater to a level suitable for that, the families in the community could have enough potable water for the whole year.

*

This codesign workshop was an instance that left no room for any feeling of superiority; it was a humbling experience where both parts could be grateful of each other's existence. Only

11   Ibid.
12   Claudia Garduño García, *Design as Freedom* (Helsinki: Aalto ARTS Books, 2017).

through this dialogue did everyone realize the equal importance of both local wisdom and global science in preserving and perfecting the water softening technique. This is a minimal glimpse of how, by inviting people to be part of a creative group and by celebrating human diversity instead of fearing it, design experiences might prevent us from falling into dark times, simply by enabling us to fully comprehend the meaning of "Volo ut sis."

Claudia Garduño García

See also
CREATIVITY, EQUALITY, HUMANITY, STORIES

READING HANNAH ARENDT (POLITICALLY, FOR AN AMERICAN IN THE 21ST CENTURY)

Martha Rosler

Reading Hannah Arendt
(Politically, for an American in the 21st Century)
Martha Rosler

"At the present moment, thinking is greatly to be desired"[1]

Hannah Arendt was already a New Yorker when I first became aware of her writings, but it took some time before I was disposed to read European philosophers — as an undergraduate art and literature major, I was more interested in reading the ancient philosophers, on the one hand, and modern literature, on the other. Soon, however, we were engaging with the great flood of European philosophy in translation to help us understand and change the world, most prominently, the works of the Frankfurt School, among them Herbert Marcuse, who was also our mentor in San Diego. By the time I read Arendt's work, she was already chastising us students for the nature of our concerns and our forms of opposition to the Vietnam War. Her long essay on Eichmann in Jerusalem I read in book form, and I found it to be compelling — unlike many of its prominent Jewish critics, who, it seems, agreed neither with her thesis on the banality of evil (important enough to form the subtitle of the book) nor with what they took to be her accusation of Jewish complicity, however unwitting, with Nazi plans regarding extermination the Jews. Their anger seemed to be based on the dearth of information available then on the subject and also on her insistently accurate reportage of the arguments made during the trial.

This was not the first time, nor would it be the last, that her careful reasoning and philosophical distinctions would result in consternation on the part of readers, including me. Yet her discussions of politics, power, and public and private life were always worth reading with respect if not full assent. But it was her work on totalitarianism that I found most immediately compelling, for its weight of historical analysis as well as for its diagnoses of what I continue to regard as contemporary trends — especially in direct relation to the actions of my own government.

In the early 1980s I came across a short quotation from Arendt: one sentence or two on what amounts to international bullying, expressed through an analogy. Practically speaking, the totalitarian ruler proceeds like a man who persistently insults another man until everybody knows that the latter is his enemy, so that he can, with some plausibility, go and kill him in self defense. This certainly is a little crude, but it works. It derives from her work *The Origins of Totalitarianism* of 1951 and 1958. I used this quotation in 1985, in an exhibition, at the Alternative Museum in New York, entitled "Disinformation." Next to descriptions of the violence in the world, the quotations from Hannah Arendt seem more measured, even ironic. But her words put in starkly metaphorical terms the tactical behavior of many warlike regimes, such as my own — which seems to be unwilling to foreswear its warlike drive toward global dominance.

At the present moment, thinking is greatly to be desired. In current times nothing seemed more appropriate than to present a series of passages from her work, to help us think through this moment and to act, as citizens and interested persons, to play our part, however small, in determining the fate of the world's peoples.

1   A version of this text, and the 13 pages of quotations that follow, were part of Martha Rosler's contributions to the exhibition "Hannah Arendt Denkraum"/ "Hannah Arendt Thinking Space" in Berlin in 2006 which marked the centenarty of Arendt's birth. For this exhibition, Rosler chose a number of texts that Arendt had published, in both English and German, which she printed on transparent vinyl sheets. The work, in expanded form, was also displayed at her two-person exhibition, "War Games," at the Kunstmuseum Basel in 2017 and at her solo "Irrespective" exhibition at the Jewish Museum in New York (Nov 2, 2018 -Mar 3, 2019). The full text of Martha Rosler's statement on Arendt is available on the web-site for the Berlin exhibition http://www.wolfgang-heuer.com/denkraum/eng/rosler. htm. We are extremely grateful to Ms. Rosler for allowing us to reproduce a typographic version of some of the panels that she exhibited there.

Die anarchische Verzweiflung, die sich in diesem Zusammenbruch

This breakdown, when the smugness of

der Massen des Volkes bemächtigte, schien der revolutionären

spurious respectability gave way to anarchic

Stimmung der Elite ebenso entgegenzukommen wie den

despair, seemed the first great opportunity for

verbrecherischen Instinkten des Mob. Daß der Mob hier seine

the elite as well as the mob. This is obvious

erste große Gelegenheit erblicken mußte, liegt auf der Hand.

for the new mass leaders whose careers

Die Führer des Mob hatten zum ersten Male die Chance, nicht nur

reproduce the features of earlier mob leaders:

das Gesindel, sondern große Massen des Volkes zu organisieren.

failure in professional and social life,

Die Tatsache, daß sie meist in die politische Laufbahn nur

perversion and disaster in private life.

gekommen waren, weil sie in einer normalen beruflichen Karriere

The fact that their lives prior to their political

Schiffbruch erlitten und als Sexualverbrecher, Rauschgiftsüchtige

careers had been failures, naively held

oder Pervertierte sich in einem normalen Privatleben nicht hatten

against them by the more respectable leaders

zurechtfinden können – Tatsachen, mit denen naiverweise

of the old parties, was the strongest factor in

die Leiter der traditionellen politischen Parteien sie bei der Masse

their mass appeal. It seemed to prove that

zu diskreditieren hofften -, bildete ihre größte Anziehungskraft

individually they embodied the mass destiny

auf die Massen. Schien dieser Tatbestand doch zu beweisen,

of the time. ...

daß sich in ihnen das Massenschicksal der Zeit verkörperte....

Der Philister, der sich ins Privatleben zurückgezogen hatte,

The philistine's retirement into private life,

einzig besorgt um Sekurität und Karriere, war das letzte und

his single-minded devotion to matters of

bereits entartete Produkt der Bourgeoisie und ihres Glaubens

family and career, was the last, and already

an das absolute Primat der sozialen und ökonomischen Interessen

degenerated, product of the bourgeoisie's

vor den Ansprüchen des öffentlichen und staatlichen Lebens.

belief in the primacy of private interest.

Der Spießer ist der Bourgevwois in seiner Isolierung, in seiner

The philistine is the bourgeois isolated from

Verlassenheit von der eigenen Klasse. Als solcher,

his own class, the atomized individual who is

als ein atomisiertes Individuum, entstand er in Massen erst durch

produced by the breakdown of the bourgeois

den Zusammenbruch der Bourgeoisie als Klasse.

class itself. The mass man whom Himmler

Der Massenmensch, den Himmlers Organisationskünste unschwer

organized for the greatest mass crimes ever

zum Funktionär und willigen Komplicen der größten Verbrechen,

committed in history bore the features of the

welche die Geschichte kennt, machten, trug deutlich die Züge

philistine rather than of the mob man,

des Spießers, nicht die Züge des Mob; hier waren keine

and was the bourgeois who in the midst of the

Leidenschaften, verbrecherische oder normale, im Spiel,

ruins of his world worried about nothing so

sondern lediglich eine Gesinnung, die es selbstverständlich fand,

much as his private security, was ready to

bei der geringsten Gefährdung der Sekurität alles – Ehre, Würde,

sacrifice everything — belief, honor, dignity—

Glauben – preiszugeben. Nichts erwies sich leichter zerstörbar

on the slightest provocation. Nothing proved

als die Privatmoral von Leuten, die einzig an die ununterbrochene

easier to destroy than the privacy and private

Normalität ihres privaten Lebens dachten, nichts konnte leichter

morality of people who thought of nothing

gleichgeschaltet, öffentlich uniformiert werden als dieses

but safeguarding their private lives.

Privatleben.

Geistige und künstlerische Initiative ist der totalen Herrschaft

Intellectual, spiritual, and artistic initiative is as

nicht weniger gefährlich als die Gangsterinitiative des Mob,

dangerous to totalitarianism as the gangster initiative

und beide sind ihr bedrohlicher als bloß politische Gegnerschaft.

of the mob, and both are more dangerous than mere

Die konsequente Unterdrückung aller höheren Formen geistiger

political opposition. The consistent persecution of

Aktivität durch die modernen Massenführer hat tiefere Gründe

every higher form of intellectual activity by the new

als die natürliche Abneigung gegen das, was man nicht versteht.

mass leaders springs from more than their natural

Totale Beherrschung kann freie Initiative in keinem

resentment against everything they cannot

Lebensbereich erlauben, weil sie kein Handeln zulassen darf,

understand. Total domination does not allow for free

das nicht absolut voraussehbar ist. Die totalitäre Bewegung

initiative in any field of life, for any activity that is not

muß daher, wenn sie erst einmal die Macht in der Hand hat,

entirely predictable. Totalitarianism in power invariably

unerbittlich alle Talente und Begabungen ohne Rücksicht auf

replaces all first-rate talents, regardless of their

etwaige Sympathien durch Scharlatane und Narren ersetzen;

sympathies, with those crackpots and fools whose lack

ihre Dummheit und ihr Mangel an Einfällen sind die beste

of intelligence and creativity is still the best guarantee

Bürgschaft für die Sicherheit des Regimes.

of their loyalty.

Imperialismus ist nicht Reichsgründung, und Expansion ist nicht

Imperialism is not empire building and expansion is not

Eroberung. ...

conquest. ...

Daß gerade der Nationalstaat, der mehr als irgendeine andere

That a movement of expansion for expansion's sake

Staatsform auf Begrenztheit des Territoriums und einer mit

grew up in nation-states which, more than any other

dem Territorium gegebenen homogenen Bevölkerung beruht,

political bodies were defined by boundaries and the

den Boden abgeben sollte, auf dem die imperialistische

limitations of possible conquest, is one example of the

Expansionsbewegung erwuchs, gehört zu jenen anscheinend

seemingly absurd disparities between cause and effect

absurden Diskrepanzen von Ursache und Wirkung,

which have become the hallmark of modern history. ...

an denen die neueste Geschichte so reich ist.

Die Historiker unserer Zeit haben, verständlich genug,

Contemporary historians, confronted with the

immer wieder versucht, dieses Element des blutigen Narrenspiels

spectacle of a few capitalists conducting their

zu verdecken, auszulöschen und den Geschehnissen eine Größe

predatory searches round the globe for new investment

zu verleihen, die sie nicht haben, die sie aber menschlich

possibilities and appealing to the profit motives of the

erträglicher machen würde. So haben sie das kuriose Gemisch

much-too-rich and the gambling instincts of the

von Kapital-Export, Rassen-Wahnsinn und bürokratischer

much-too-poor, want to clothe imperialism with the old

Verwaltungsmaschine, das sich selbst den großartigen Namen

grandeur of Rome and Alexander the Great, a grandeur

Imperialismus gab, verdeckt mit Vergleichen, in denen die

which would make all following events more humanly

Eroberungen von Alexander oder Cäsar oder die Reichs-

tolerable.

gründungen des Altertums heraufbeschworen werden.

In einer fiktiven Welt gibt es gar keine Instanz, die Misserfolge

In a totally fictitious world, failures need not be

als solche verbuchen könnte; ja selbst der einfache Unterschied

recorded, admitted, and remembered. Factuality itself

zwischen Erfolg und Misserfolg hängt von dem Fortbestand einer

depends for its continued existence upon the existence

tatsächlichen und damit von der Existenz einer nichttotalitären

of the nontotalitarian world.

Welt ab.

...

Das Resultat dieses verblüffend einfachen Systems ist,

The gullibility of sympathizers makes lies credible to the

daß die Sympathisierenden wirklich bis zu einem gewissen

outside world, while at the same time the graduated

Grade der außenstehenden Welt Lügen glaubhaft machen,

cynicism of membership and elite formations eliminates

die ohne sie nicht geglaubt werden würden, während auf der

the danger that the Leader will ever be forced by the

anderen Seite der gradulerte Zynismus innerhalb der Bewegung

weight of his own propaganda to make good his own

die Gefahr bannt, daß der Führer durch das Gewicht seiner

statements and feigned respectability....

eigenen Propagandalügen gezwungen werden könnte,

The totalitarian system, unfortunately, is foolproof

seine Erklärungen wahrzumachen und aus der gespielten

against ... normal consequences; its ingeniousness rests

Ehrenhaftigkeit in eine echte hineinzugleiten. ...

precisely on the elimination of that reality which either

Leider sind totalitäre Systeme gegen derartige normale

unmasks the liar or forces him to live up to his pretense.

Konsequenzen geschützt; insofern sie jede Realität eliminiert

While the membership does not believe statements

und durch eine Fiktion ersetzt haben, haben sie es auch erreicht,

made for public consumption, it believes all the more

jene Macht der Wirklichkeit auszuschalten, die dem Lügner

fervently the standard clichés of ideological explanation,

entweder die Maske vom Gesicht reißt oder ihn zwingt,

the keys to past and future history which totalitarian

seine Lügen wahr zu machen. Die Mitgliedschaft, die allen

movements took from 19th-century ideologies and

aktuellen öffentlichen Kundgebungen prinzipiell misstraut,

transformed, through organization, into a working reality.

glaubt um so fester an jene ideologischen Klischees und

Pauschalerklärungen aller vergangenen und zukünftigen

Geschichte, welche die totalitären Bewegungen aus dem

neunzehnten Jahrhundert erbten und sie mittels ihrer

Organisation in die Wirklichkeit umgesetzt haben.

From *The Origins of Totalitarianism*, pp. 388, 384

Bevor die totalitären Bewegungen die Macht haben,
Before they seize power and establish a world
die Welt wirklich auf das Prokrustesbett Ihrer Doktrinen zu
according to their doctrines, totalitarian movements
schnallen, beschwören sie eine Lügenwelt der Konsequenz herauf,
conjure up a lying world of consistency which is more
die den Bedürfnissen des menschlichen Gemüts besser entspricht
adequate to the needs of the human mind than
als die Wirklichkeit selbst. ...
reality itself. ...
...besitzt totalitäre Propaganda bereits die Kraft,
The force possessed by totalitarian propaganda ...
die Massen imaginär von der wirklichen Welt abzuschließen.
lies in its ability to shut the masses off from the real
Das einzige, was sich dem Verständnis der Massen, die mit jedem
world. The only signs which the real world still offers
neuen Unglücksschlag leichtgläubiger werden, von der wirklichen
to the understanding of the unintegrated and
Welt noch darbietet, sind gleichsam ihre Lücken, das heißt die
disintegrating masses — whom every new stroke of ill
Fragen, die die Welt nicht öffentlich diskutieren will, oder die
luck makes more gullible — are, so to speak,
Gerüchte, denen sie nicht öffentlich zu widersprechen wagt,
its lacunae, the questions it does not care to discuss
weil sie, wenn auch in entstellter Weise, irgendeinen wunden
publicly, or the rumors it does not dare to contradict
Punkt berühren.
because they hit, although in an exaggerated and
Aus diesen wunden Punkten ziehen die Lügen der totalitären
deformed way, some sore spot. From these sore
Propaganda jenes Minimum an Wahrheit und realer Erfahrung,
spots the lies of totalitarian propaganda derive the
dessen sie bedürfen, um die Brücke schlagen zu können von der
elements of truthfulness and real experience they
Realität in die totale Fiktion.
need to bridge the gulf between reality and fiction.
Selbst die durch Terror unterbauten lügenhaften Fiktionen
Only terror could rely on mere fiction, and even the
totalitärer Regierungen sind bis heute noch nicht ganz und gar
terror-sustained lying fictions of totalitarian
von Willkür diktiert.
regimes have not yet become entirely arbitrary. ...

From *The Origins of Totalitarianism*, p. 353

Es ist immerhin merkwürdig, daß es nie eine wirklich populäre Opposition gegen

The curious weakness of popular opposition to imperialism, the numerous

imperialistische Politik gegeben hat. Die zahlreichen Inkonsequenzen, nicht eingehaltenen

inconsistencies and outright broken promises of liberal statesmen,

Versprechungen und Vertrauensbrüche liberaler Staatsmänner, die, wenn sie an die Macht

frequently ascribed to opportunism or bribery, have other and deeper

kamen, eben auch nur imperialistische Politik machen konnten, kann man schwerlich einfach

causes. ... [These men] shared with the people the conviction that the

als Opportunismus oder gar Bestechung erklären. ...

national body itself was so deeply split into classes ... that the very cohesion

Das Volk wie die Staatsmänner wussten, dass der Klassenkampf den Körper der Nation selbst

of the nation was jeopardized. Expansion ... appeared as a lifesaver,

zersplittert hatte und das gesamte politische wie gesellschaftliche Gefüge in äußerster Gefahr

if and insofar as it could provide a common interest for the nation as

war. Expansion schien der zersplitterten Nation ein einheitliches Interesse wiederzugeben

a whole, and it is mainly for this reason that imperialists were allowed

und sie aufs neue zu einen. Die Imperialisten wurden zu einem so gefährlichen Feind

to become "parasites upon patriotism."

im Innern der Nation, weil sie in der Tat, wie Hobson meinte, »Parasiten des Patriotismus«

Partly, of course, such hopes still belonged with the old vicious practice

waren und sich der aufrichtigen Sorge der Patrioten um den Fortbestand der Nation nährten.

of "healing" domestic conflicts with foreign adventures. The difference,

Es ist keine Frage, dass die patriotischen Hoffnungen auf den Imperialismus etwas mit der

however, is marked. Adventures are by their very nature limited in time

alten vergeblichen Praxis zu tun haben, innerpolitische Konflikte durch außenpolitische

and space; they may succeed temporarily in overcoming conflicts, although

Abenteuer beizulegen. Aber der Unterschied zu früheren Zeiten ist bezeichnend.

as a rule they fail and tend rather to sharpen them. From the very

Abenteuer sind ihrer Natur nach zeitlich und räumlich beschränkt, und die Lösungen,

beginning the imperialist adventure of expansion appeared to be an eternal

die sie mitunter bringen können, sind immer darauf berechnet, Zeit zu gewinnen.

solution, because expansion was conceived as unlimited. Furthermore,

Das imperialistische Abenteuer einer permanenten Expansion wurde hingegen von Anfang an

imperialism was not an adventure in the usual sense, because it depended

für unbegrenzt gehalten, es sollte in den Bewegungsprozess der kapitalistischen Produktion

less on nationalist slogans than on the seemingly solid basis of economic

selbst eingeschaltet werden und nicht lediglich eine zeitweilige Krise beseitigen. Auch war

interests. In a society of clashing interests, where the common good was

der Imperialismus kein Abenteuer, wie man es gewöhnt war, weil er weniger nationalistische

identified with the sum total of individual interests, expansion as such

Schlagworte der Außenpolitik benutzte, als sich auf eine angeblich solide Basis wirtschaftlich

appeared to be a possible common interest of the nation as a whole.

materieller Interessen berief. In einer Gesellschaft von Klassengegensätzen, deren

Since the owning and dominant classes had convinced everybody that

Gemeinwohl sich angeblich aus einer Addition aller Einzelinteressen ergab, konnte Expansion

economic interest and the passion for ownership are a sound basis for

wiederum nur als Interesse erscheinen, aber nun als Interesse der Nation als Ganzes.

the body politic, even non-imperialist statesmen were easily persuaded

Da die besitzenden und herrschenden Klassen alle anderen davon überzeugt hatten,

to yield when a common economic interest appeared on the horizon.

dass ein Staat ohnehin nur der Ausdruck ökonomischer Interessen sei und jedenfalls auf

... The more ill-fitted nations were for the incorporation of foreign

einer materiellen Grundlage beruhe, lag es auch nichtimperialistischen Staatsmännern nahe,

peoples..., the more they were tempted to oppress them. In theory, there is

die Rettung der Nation in einem angeblich allen gemeinsamen, nationalen Interesse zu

an abyss between nationalism and imperialism; in practice, it can and has

erblicken.

been bridged by tribal nationalism and outright racism.

... Je weniger der Nationalstaat sich für die Eingliederung fremder Völker eignete, desto

größer war die Versuchung, sie einfach zu unterdrücken. Nationalismus und Imperialismus

sind theoretisch durch einen Abgrund immer wieder durch rassisch oder völkisch orientierte

Nationalismen überbrückt worden.

Das beunruhigende an der Person Eichmanns war doch gerade,

The trouble with Eichmann was precisely that so many

dass er war wie viele und dass diese vielen weder pervers noch

were like him, and that the many were neither

sadistisch, sondern schrecklich und erschreckend normal waren

perverted nor sadistic, that they were, and still are,

und sind. Vom Standpunkt unserer Rechtsinstitutionen und an

terribly and terrifyingly normal. From the viewpoint of

unseren moralischen Urteilsmaßstäben gemessen,

our legal institutions and of our moral standards of

war diese Normalität viel erschreckender als all die Greuel

judgment, this normality was much more terrifying

zusammengenommen.

than all the atrocities put together.

From *Eichmann in Jerusalem*

Die traurige Wahrheit ist, dass fast alles Schlechte von Menschen

The sad truth is that most evil is done by people who

getan wird, die sich nie dazu entschlossen haben,

never make up their minds to be either good or evil.

gut oder böse zu sein oder zu handeln.

Insofern die Bourgeoisie sich als Hüterin der abendländischen
Since the bourgeoisie claimed to be the guardian of
Tradition aufspielte und öffentlich mit Tugenden prunkte,
Western traditions and confounded all moral issues by
die sie nicht nur im privaten und geschäftlichen Leben nicht
parading publicly virtues which it not only did not
ausübte, sondern in Wirklichkeit sogar verachtete, erschien
possess in private and business life, but actually held in
ein gewisses Prahlen mit Grausamkeit, Unmenschlichkeit und
contempt, it seemed revolutionary to admit cruelty,
Amoralität als revolutionär; zumindest beseitigte es die
disregard of human values, and general amorality,
Doppelzüngigkeit, auf der die bestehende Gesellschaftsordnung
because this at least destroyed the duplicity upon which
zu beruhen schien. Gerade weil die Elite die Brüchigkeit dieser
the existing society seemed to rest. What a temptation
Gesellschaft nicht erkannte, weil sie sich einbildete, immer noch
to flaunt extreme attitudes in the hypocritical twilight of
in dem heuchlerischen Zwielicht einer doppelten Moral zu leben,
double moral standards, to wear publicly the mask of
erschien ihr die Maske der Grausamkeit so verführerisch:
cruelty if everybody was patently inconsiderate and
Wie herrlich erschien das Böse in einer Welt, in der es nur noch
pretended to be gentle, to parade wickedness in a world,
zur Gemeinheit langte.
not of wickedness, but of meanness!

„Objektivität und Gleichmut" angesichts unerträglichen Leidens
"Detachment and equanimity" in view of "unbearable
können in der Tat mit Recht „Furcht erregen". (Siehe Noam
tragedy" can indeed be "terrifying." (I am paraphrasing
Chomsky (...), der die „Fassade der Härte und pseudowissen-
a sentence of Noam Chomsky, who is very good in
schaftlichen Objektivität", hinter der sich nichts als geistige
exposing the "façade of toughmindedness and pseudo-
Leere verbirgt, entlarvt.)
science" and the intellectual "vacuity" behind it, especially

in the debates about the war in Vietnam.)

From *The Origins of Totalitarianism*, p. 334; *On Violence*, p. 64

The survivors of the extermination camps, the inmates of concentrations and

Die Überlebenden der Vernichtungslager, die Insassen der Konzentrations- und

internment camps, and even the comparatively happy stateless people could see

Internierungslager, ja selbst die noch verhältnismäßig glücklichen Staatenlosen mussten

... that the abstract nakedness of being nothing but human was their greatest

erkennen, dass die abstrakte Nacktheit ihres Nichts-als-Mensch-Seins ihre größte Gefahr

danger. Because of it they were regarded as savages and, afraid that they might

war. Die zivilisierte Welt behandelte sie als unerwünschte Barbaren und so bestanden sie

end by being considered beasts, they insisted on their nationality, the last sign

umso heftiger auf ihrer Nationalität, dem letzten Zeichen ihrer früheren

of their former citizenship, as their only remaining and recognized tie with

Staatszugehörigkeit, auf dem letzten verbliebenen und anerkannten Bande, das sie an

humanity. Their distrust of natural, their preference for national, rights comes

die Menschheit knüpfte. Ihr Misstrauen gegen Natur- und ihre Bevorzugung nationaler

precisely from their realization that natural rights are granted even to savages....

Rechte entspringt gerade ihrer Einsicht, dass natürliche Rechte auch dem Wilden

zugesprochen werden. [...]

From *The Origins of Totalitarianism*, p. 300

Verliert ein Mensch seinen politischen Status, so sollte er sich – folgt man dem Konzept
If a human being loses his political status, he should, according to the
der angeborenen und unabdingbaren Menschenrechte – in eben jener Situation
implications of the inborn and inalienable rights of man, come under exactly the
befinden, in welcher diese allgemeinen Menschenreche greifen. Das Gegenteil ist jedoch
situation for which the declarations of such general rights provided. Actually the
der Fall. Es scheint, als mangele es einem Menschen, der nichts als ein Mensch ist, an
opposite is the case. It seems that a man who is nothing but a man has lost the
genau jenen Qualitäten, die es anderen ermöglichen, ihn wie einen Mitmenschen zu
very qualities which make it possible for other people to treat him as a
behandeln. Dies ist einer der Gründe dafür, dass es weitaus schwerer ist, die
fellow-man. This is one of the reasons why it is far more difficult to destroy the
Rechtspersönlichkeit eines Verbrechers – eines Menschen, der Verantwortung für eine
legal personality of a criminal, that is, of a man who has taken upon himself the
Tat übernimmt, deren Konsequenzen nun sein Schicksal bestimmen – zu zerstören, als
responsibility for an act whose consequences now determine his fate, than of a
die eines Menschen, dem jegliche menschliche Verantwortung abgesprochen wurde.
man who has been disallowed all common human responsibilities.

IN-BETWEEN

The world and the people who inhabit it are not the same.
The world lies between people, and this in-between—much
more than (as is often thought) men or even man—is today
the object of the greatest concern and the most obvious
upheaval in almost all the countries of the globe. Even
where the world is still halfway in order, or is kept halfway
in order, the public realm has lost the power of illumination
which was originally part of its very nature. More and
more people in the countries of the Western world, which
since the decline of the ancient world has regarded
freedom from politics as one of the basic freedoms, make
use of this freedom and have retreated from the world
and their obligations within it. This withdrawal from the
world need not harm an individual; he may even cultivate
great talents to the point of genius and so by a detour be
useful to the world again. But with each such retreat an
almost demonstrable loss to the world takes place; what
is lost is the specific and usually irreplaceable in-between
which should have formed between this individual and his
fellow men.

Hannah Arendt, *Men in Dark Times*[1]

No concept in Arendt's conceptual vocabulary is more germane
to design—or to our times. In her later work Arendt sensed
this, which is why in these sentences she gives it such priority.
The concern is no longer, she recognizes, as it always was, for
"man" or even "men" (in their subjectivity—in their knowing,
their aspirations, their limits, and their failures, individual or
collective) but rather it is for all that lies "between" persons.
What lies between persons is the "world." But the world,
for persons, has never been only nature. "World" means
everything, from language outward, that mediates relations.

1   Hannah Arendt, *Men in Dark Times* (New York: Harcourt Brace, [1955]
     1993), 4.

Until comparatively recently, at least in thought, "world" is split (or rather, "subjects" are split from world). On the one side language, subjectivity, communication, the "infinite character of practical reason" (morality, ethics) all that pertains to mind, consciousness, and its externalization in action (Arendt herself focuses here). On the other (to caricature the divide) the "dull" objectivity of nature: the a-subjective, or at the least the necessarily limited, realms of labor and work (again Arendt).

The problem has always been that, in their lived actuality, persons have never been able to separate "labor, work and action."[2] Consciousness does not form sui-generis; it is not *only* an internal process. As Hegel argued so strongly in the memorable section on "Lordship and Bondage" in the *Philosophy of Spirit*, self-consciousness is formed in reflection on externalization, formed indeed *through* work.[3] In dealing with the necessities of life, "labor" is never distinct from mind. The separation of servitude may have made this a desirable ideology for those who were served but it remains a fantasy that reflects poorly on those who advanced it. Today, the internalization of technology, which has proceeded apace since the latter to move from the factory into the home at the beginning of the last century—and then with rapidity into consciousness (the "culture industry") and the body, is "completed" at the point where subjects (as data and made over as data) are no longer distinguishable in absolute terms from artifice. At this point, all prior assumptions that the "in-between" is a purely subjective relation—"to the other"—fall by the wayside. The subject made over through artifice never stands outside of artifice. The "in-between" is therefore not merely the purely subjective relation to the other; it stands for everything that today (but in truth across all of history) objectively as well as subjectively mediates these relations.

Heidegger, by the 1940s, had already understood this in regard to technology:

---

2   Or, to give Habermas's later, if simpler version, "work" and "interaction." See Jürgen Habermas, trans. Thomas McCarthy, *Theory of Communicative Action* (2 vol.) (Boston: Beacon Press, 1984).

3   G. W. F. Hegel, *Phenomenology of Spirit*, trans A. V. Miller (Oxford: Oxford University Press, 1977), 117–19.

This name … does not signify here the separate areas of
the production and equipment of machines … [rather it]
includes all the areas of beings which equip the whole
of beings: objectified nature, the business of culture,
manufactured politics, and the gloss of ideals overlying
everything. Thus "technology" … is understood here in such
an essential way that its meaning coincides with the term
"completed metaphysics."[4]

Jamer Hunt renders the same perception in more
contemporary terms:

The designed, artificial world that envelops us is coming
alive with communicative possibilities. There was a time
when our tools of communication were distinct from our
bodies: we spoke into a telephone wired into the walls
of our home, or we hunted and pecked and clicked at
a keyboard to type data into a personal computer. That
era is vanishing as quickly as it arrived. Instead we are
drifting into a new alignment, in both mind and body, with
technology that is far more immersive, encompassing, and
confounding.[5]

Designers have always known this. Design is nothing
other than mediation, what Simon called a "meeting point" or
"interface" between the inner (the substance and organization
of the artefact itself) and outer environments.[6] Design, in this
sense, does not exist. Design disappears into the configuration
of that which mediates. Today, there is nothing in the world
that is not mediated. The transition to the world in which
the artificial provides the horizon, medium, and condition
of existence ontologically confirms this point. In the past it
seemed possible to disdain artifice and the artificial. Not only
did the contingency of the artificial create doubts whether it

4   Martin Heidegger, "Overcoming Metaphysics," in Stambaugh (trans. and
    ed.), *The End of Philosophy* (New York: Harper & Row, 1973), 93.
5   Jamer Hunt,"Nervous Structures and Anxious Infrastructures," in
    Antonelli (ed.), *Talk to Me* (New York: MoMA, 2011), 48.
6   Herbert Simon, *The Sciences of the Artificial*, 3rd ed. (Cambridge,
    MA: MIT Press, 1996), 6.

could fall within the compass of science (or philosophy)[7] but
the artefact too—with a few notable exceptions—suffers equal
disdain—as in Simon's wonderfully dismissive comment on the
artefact seen from the perspective of science.[8] The exceptions
(those most extraordinary remains of human consciousness)
should have told a different story.[9] All human artefacts are
mediations. All mediate, ultimately, subject and object. If we
constructed the modern world on the created and maintained
illusion of that separation (which, in industrialization called
forth the necessary invention of Design to mediate its effects)[10]
today the self-dissolution of that world requires the opposite
momentum. Adorno (in *Negative Dialectics*) gives this necessity
philosophical expression:

> Mediation of the object means that it must not be statically
> dogmatically hypostatized but can be known only as
> it entwines with subjectivity; mediation of the subject
> means that without the moment of objectivity it would be
> literally nil.[11]

But, as every designer will instantly grasp, what Adorno
posits theoretically (as absolute demand for going forward
in thinking) is perpetually and in every moment realized in
designing. Designing is the negotiation of incommensurable
requirements. The ultimate incommensurability is subject
and object. But incommensurable too, and requiring acute

7   Simon, *The Sciences of the Artificial*, xi.
8   "The peculiar properties of the artefact lie on the thin interface between
     natural laws within and natural laws without. What can we say about it?
     What is there to study besides the boundary sciences—those that govern
     the means and the task environment." Ibid., 111. It will be noted that in this
     equation configuration is no account. This is not to say that things were
     any different in the Humanities (save incidentally in some moments in the
     history of art or architecture). Nor are they substantially different in the
     social sciences for whom, even in anthropology and the study of material
     culture, the artefact is little more than a fact (or, worse, a "symbol").
9   Thomas Crow, *The Intelligence of Art* (Chapel Hill: University of North
     Carolina Press, 1999).
10   Clive Dilnot, "The Matter of Design," *Design Philosophy Papers* vol. 13,
     no. 2 (2015): 115–23.
11   Theodor Wiesengrund Adorno, *Negative Dialectics*, trans. E. B. Ashton
     (New York: Continuum, 1973), 186.

negotiation (reconciliation, attunement) are subject–subject relations (think only of translation, in all senses). No less acute is the constant necessity to face the diremptions of the "in-between" that makes human intercourse possible both immediately and as politics.

What design instinctively understands (though often badly) is what politicians also often grasp (though again sometimes scarcely without full consciousness), that is, that the *forms* in which (to speak only at this level) "material human needs" are met *matters.* Completely privatized health care; Medicare and "Obama-care"; single-payer systems; configurations of state, private, and charitable religious institutions; the National Health Service (UK) are all ways of meeting the needs for health care; however, they are obviously not the *same* ways—a society in which one form is dominant and the other recessive would not be the same as one in which roles are reversed.[12] What matters then, politically, socially, *for* persons is the form—or better the configuration—through which needs are met. The crucial question *for persons* (and no less for economic interests) is the *ways* that the world *lies between* and *act towards* persons (and, we should add, crucially, how it will lie between and act toward nature).

Today, politics is the fight for ways the "in-between" will be constituted. This is why Arendt is correct when she says that "this in-between—much more than (as is often thought) men or even man—is today the object of the greatest concern." It is of concern because everything for us lies in the "in-between." Everything depends, for our futures, on the ways in which the almost infinite moments of the "in-between" are constituted and configured; depends on how the equally complex incommensurabilities of our existence are negotiated. *designing* (lower case) is not "the" answer to this question. But it is a capability or a capacity (even a skill) that is not irrelevant to constituting answers to these dilemmas. But this also means

12 Stephen Yeo, "State and Anti-State: Reflections on Social Forms and Struggles from 1850," in Phillip Corrigan (ed.), *Capitalism, State Formation and Marxist Theory* (London: Quartet, 1980), 115.

that designing is no longer outside of the "in-between." One of
the requirements placed on it today is to attempt to come to
consciousness of this; to explore and examine in what ways,
today, some "power of illumination" in Arendt's term can be
cast on the possibilities of how we can negotiate the necessary
diremptions of the "in-between" well.

See also
COMMON GOOD, IMAGINATION, PUBLIC

INSTRUMENTALITY

The discussion of the whole problem of technology, that is, of the transformation of life and world through the introduction of the machine, has been strangely led astray through an all-too-exclusive concentration upon the service or disservice the machines render to men. The assumption here is that every tool and implement is primarily designed to make human life easier and human labor less painful. Their instrumentality is understood exclusively in this anthropocentric sense. But the instrumentality of tools and implements is much more closely related to the object it is designed to produce, and their sheer "human value" is restricted to the use the animal laborans makes of them. In other words, *homo faber*, the toolmaker, invented tools and implements in order to erect a world, not—at least not primarily—to help the human life process. The question therefore is not so much whether we are the masters or the slaves of our machines, but whether machines still serve the world and its things, or if, to the contrary, they and the automatic motion of their processes have begun to rule and even destroy the world and things.

Hannah Arendt, *The Human Condition*[1]

One name by which Ulysses, the protagonist of Homer's epic poem, is known is *polymechanos* (πολυμήχανος, i.e., resourceful, inventive), a personage capable of a thousand artifices. The term *mechanos* derives from the same root as *machina* (machine). This gives the crux of Arendt's discourse concerning the global issue of technology. *Machina* is a technological device and Ulysses is *polymechanos* primarily because of the expedient of the Trojan horse, a ruse at the Trojans' expense that would turn the course of the war in the *Achaeans'* favor.

---

[1] Hannah Arendt, *The Human Condition* (Chicago, IL: University of Chicago Press, [1958] 1998), 151–3.

The machine, then, may be an item of use but it is also a device that deceives, tricks, plays. The philosopher Vilém Fussler reinforces this aspect of technology. In *The Shape of Things* he notes how it invents devices capable of cheating and surpassing human limits.[2] All of which, this cheating of limits, is achieved through the instrumentalism described by Arendt: the instrumentalism through which—with a Promethean attitude— humanity enslaves and destroys nature, God's creation, so as to transform it with the aim of improving its existential conditions and lighten the toil of labor. Nevertheless, the automation of production processes, according to Arendt, "unties" machines from such ends and from the human will. A mega-machine creates objects, other tools, and other implements, designed for their operational capacity as opposed to specific ends which today we would call human centered. In short, what is created to overcome and "cheat" limits create new, completely unprecedented limits.[3]

What this means is that instrumentality is an activity and discipline of the limit that progress and complexity—fueled by exponentially developing phenomena—tend to recast into new, variously structured forms.

Toward a New Model of Instrumentality

In her work, Arendt accurately forecasts a number of evolutionary aspects of society and technology—and their consequences for instrumentality—yet is only able in part to anticipate what we experience today in our day-to-day experience. The degree of violation of and violence against nature—of the dominance of instrumentality—is clear when dealing with issues of environmental sustainability. Utility and expediency in the use of natural resources have led us to the cusp of an irreversible process of exploitation, which was

2   Vilém Flusser, *The Shape of Things: A Philosophy of Design* (London: Reaktion Books, 1999).

3   An interesting essay on "limits" and their relationship with the idea of progress is in: Raj Patel and Jason Moore, *A History of the World in Seven Cheap Things: A Guide to Capitalism, Nature, and the Future of the Planet* (Berkeley: University of California Press, 2017).

only accorded significant scientific and political recognition internationally at the beginning of the 1970s. The forces of nature—considering the physics of matter—enter the processes of instrumentality ever more pervasively. Matter is no longer simply obtained from nature but created by intervening at the subatomic scale, according to the specific performance characteristics required in terms of function and use, in some cases even blurring the boundaries between organic and inorganic life.

What is being achieved here is what Arendt, citing Heisenberg, herself prophesied, a biological evolution of humanity in which "the innate structures of the human organism are transplanted in an ever-increasing measure into the environment of man."[4] New computational models promise, through artificial intelligence, to replicate and surpass the processing power of the human mind, simulating the same adaptive, evolutionary learning processes of the brain. Posthumanism posits the merging of biology and technology, to enhance human potential and performance.

The idea of limit engages with the theme of means–end, which is the ontological dimension of technology and design. Indeed, Arendt's *homo faber* instrumentalizes, using tools and implements—i.e., means—in order to achieve an end. Yet what he creates is sometimes a means for someone else. The craftsman, for example, using wood from a tree, makes a chair. For him the chair is an end, while for other users it is a means to be able to guarantee a certain service: for example, comfortably waiting one's turn in the doctor's waiting room. The work of *homo faber* creates an artefact—in this case a chair—yet often fails to grasp the meaning that this new object of daily use may have. The meaning that is associated with the object is that of utility; yet who decides what is useful and what is not?

This theme opens itself to a specific aspect of contemporary consumption: a plethora of often-undifferentiated goods of which it is not possible to grasp a sense/meaning that is capable of creating distinction. *Homo faber* instrumentalizes, but no

4   Werner Heisenberg, *Das Naturbild der heutigen Physik* (Hamburg: Rowohlt, 1957), 14–15.

longer knows why he is doing so, what reason-why exists, in many cases, behind the sense of what he is creating, with his action, resulting in the process of instrumentality becoming progressively meaningless. Sometimes it is the aspect of the challenge that lies behind an instrumental action that leads to certain choices being made without asking why. Robert Oppenheimer's testimony before a government commission in 1954 is significant in this regard: "When you see something that is technically sweet, you go ahead and do it and you argue about what to do about it only after you have had your technical success. That is the way it was with the atomic bomb."[5] Sometimes the technical satisfaction felt for something which puts us to the test and which emphasizes our mastery leads us to lose sight of the ethical dimension of a choice.

In a recent conference held by Emergency (an ONG ONLUS Life Support for Civilian War Victims)[6] to launch its "design against the war" initiative, a designer publicly extolled the qualities of weapons in terms of their technology, manufacture, and materials. The statement is correct; yet may a designer legitimately deal with such instruments?

Designers are often attracted to equally technically sweet challenges (as Oppenheimer's quotation) but these challenges ask for more critical attitude and understanding of context, situations, and implications related to their design choices. The pragmatism to which Arendt alludes links utility with the need to ask oneself equally forceful ethical and political questions and what a specific work is worth or meaning it possesses. That's truer for those primarily involved in the process of instrumentality as technicians and designers.

Instrumentality, moreover, through a set of tools and implements, results in the creation of an artefact. Each artefact is inspired by an image that guides and steers action: a specific reference model exists for each thing that guides and instructs *homo faber*. Instrumentality is fed by these reference models.

5   *In the Matter of J. Robert Oppenheimer*, USAEC Transcript of Hearing before Personnel Security Board (1954).

6   "Design against the War," SOS design for EMERGENCY—second edition, accessed November 26, 2018, https://eventi.emergency.it/event-pro/design-contro-la-guerra-call-for-ideas/.

Yet is this model still true today? The abundance of available technologies—ubiquitous, miniaturized, low-cost—tends to enable processes of meaning discovery that are unshackled from the traditional production mechanisms and to these reference models. Today, many are invited to the "banquet" of making artefacts (the goal of every instrumentality) no longer only the traditional agents of design and production. Designers, as a consequence, are transforming their way of designing, considering this wide request of making artefacts. The traditional "stopping rule"[7] in the design process seems to be transformed into an enabling rule and creates "platforms" that enable and engage other actors and private citizens.

This enabling aspect is amplified by the digital transformation and transforms the idea of instrumentality: tools and implements become ICT microdevices, MEMS, memories, sensors, actuators. Object-oriented or simplified programming languages enable ever greater numbers of people to use these objects, recombining them to respond to various requirements, discovering the meaning of these new compositions, without necessarily having models. A notable example is Arduino, an open source computer hardware and software set, created by Massimo Banzi and others in 2004, within the Interaction Institute in Ivrea.

Technology, this type of technology, seems, in some ways, to be becoming more inclusive and encouraging many more people into doing and making than in the past. Richard Sennett, Hannah Arendt's pupil, emphasizes this aspect and presents the artisan—looking at the world of open source and programming—as an example that can save modern man from a situation of perpetual dissatisfaction, which in his view is precisely the outcome of the separation between thinking and making.[8] Possibility through making, with the digital transformation, offers new goals to give hopefulness, initiative, optimism back to contemporary humanity.

7 Horst W. J. Rittel and Melvin M. Webber, "Dilemmas in a General Theory of Planning," *Policy Sciences* no. 4 (1973): 155–69.
8 Richard Sennett, *The Craftsman* (New Haven, CT: Yale University Press, 2009).

An interesting example is "Manifattura Milano,"[9] supported by the Municipality of Milan, where thinking and making together are seen as levers for urban regeneration. MM built a community composed of individuals, micro, small and medium enterprises, research centers, learning agencies, fab labs, and maker-spaces, to promote the exchange of experiences and new forms of socialization.

It seems that this new model of instrumentality, without models and in search of new meanings, is shaping up to be an unprecedented, active process of social inclusion.

Francesco Zurlo

See also
BEGINNINGS, METABOLISM, OBJECTIVITY,
THOUGHTLESSNESS

9   "Manifattura Milano," Facebook, accessed November 26, 2018, https://it-it.facebook.com/ManifatturaMilano/.

LABOR
LAW

LABOR

Labor has always been ambiguous: recognized as essential, yet avoided whenever possible. The getting of food and shelter is burdensome. It can be avoided by forcing others to do it—this is slavery,[1] or by reducing the burden by inventing and using tools. Is the history of technology a history of the avoidance of labor? Perhaps we could rewrite human history in terms of the productive power of laziness? This is going too far, but we do need antiproductivist narratives of labor, especially at this time of its imminent disappearance.

Labor carries a heavy burden of accumulated economic theory and romanticized imagery, to say nothing of its sociological character whereby the respect of others and sense of self are intimately tied up with "having a job" and the type of job one does. Within political economy the concept of labor had its full glory in Marx's theorization of the relation between modes of production and social classes, from slave societies through to capitalism. Hannah Arendt criticized Marx for conflating labor and work, but gave him credit for noticing the excess productivity of labor—the human capacity to produce much more than required for subsistence; for Marx, the issue was how and by whom this surplus is appropriated.

Yet, to what extent does Marx's famous distinction—between capitalists, as owners of the means of production, and workers, as those who have only their labor power to sell—still apply? Less and less, if you consider that the purpose of capitalist production is not the meeting of human needs but the creation of wealth, and that today cognitive labor is the main generator of wealth. The economic game is no longer about producing more and more of a standard product at a lower cost, e.g., by replacing live workers with automation, rather it's about constant

---

1   In premodern times the only freedom from the necessary toil and drudgery of labor came from the taming of animals or of dominating another human being to the level of a tame animal, as described by Hannah Arendt in *The Human Condition* (Chicago, IL: University of Chicago Press, [1958] 1998). She adds that the modern age forgot the link between labor and slavery.

innovation and the leveraging of intangibles: how to harness
affects, emotion, and aesthetics for the design of new services
and experiences. Many cognitive laborers who do this, designers
prominent among them, own portable "means of production,"
allowing them to move from place to place while working
for clients who could be somewhere else (Bali is a popular
location for creative digital nomads). Yet the same global digital
infrastructure that facilitates serendipitous mobile work also
delivers more of the same, slightly repackaged: low-paid micro-
tasking, outsourcing, and freelancing with transactions between
buyers and sellers managed by profit-making intermediaries for
the usual percentage fees.

Hannah Arendt differentiates labor and work: labor is what
has to be done in order to subsist, it is tied to biological necessity,
it is repetitive, and it has no product, whereas work is an activity
of producing something, transforming the given materials of the
earth into things of use to humans, to create a durable *world* of
shelter, artefacts, and meanings. Arendt recognized that labor
and work became blurred in the modern world: the durable
product of work gets demolished by the flow of consumable
things to meet "needs," thereby reducing work to labor. Arendt
is not speaking of political economy; her concern is with the
human condition, which is not reducible to essentialized human
nature. She talks of the conditioning "force" and "power" of given
conditions, and things made by human beings "possessing the
same conditioning power as natural things."[2]

While conditions condition, they do not overdetermine, and
this is crucial for Arendt because what is at stake is freedom and
the possibility of the unexpected that comes from the plurality of
human beings.[3] And this returns us to labor which, as the toil of
mundane subsistence relegated to slaves and servants (and in the
modern era to "labor-saving" devices), is unfree. Historically (and
we are not post this) there was also the Fordist moment of the
initiation of assembly-line production whereby workers traded

2   Arendt, *The Human Condition*, 9.
3   Plurality is not the same as pluralism or "the diversity of cultures" but the
    more fundamental fact that no two human beings are ever exactly alike,
    and from that difference, the possibility of the emergence of the new is
    kept open. This she named natality. See ibid., 246–7.

away relative freedom over working conditions for higher wages that allowed "freedom to consume."

*

The un-freedom of labor links to Arendt's other major concern, which was the nature of totalitarianism which "strives not toward despotic rule over men, but towards a system in which men are superfluous."[4] Is this not the logic of digital capitalism? Consider the digital automation of so much of the operational labor of infrastructure, transport, finance, communication, retailing, distribution, administration, education, and much more. Industrial robotics also renders people superfluous. Rather than humanoid robots envisaged by earlier generations, industrial robots mimic only those parts of the body required—"arms" that lift and place, and "hands" that assemble components in computer-controlled sequences of precision movements. What is eerie about automated factories is not that all the people have gone but that what remains are only those parts of the human being (rationalized and redesigned) that were ever required for profit-making production.[5]

Perhaps Arendt's characterization of totalitarianism is more pertinent here:

> Total power can be achieved and safeguarded only in a world of conditioned reflexes, of marionettes without the slightest trace of spontaneity.[6]

Despite infinite variety of applications and content, globally connected computation is a totalizing system that has become a meta-condition. This system has no interest in human beings, only disaggregated human functions or the actions of marionettes—a glance of idle curiosity registered as a touch at an interface relaying through invisible pathways of time and space. Spontaneous actions are harvested in order to turn them into

4   Hannah Arendt, *The Origins of Totalitarianism* (New York: Harvest Books, [1951] 1979), 588.

5   This having been prefigured more than a century ago by Frederick Winslow Taylor's "Scientific Management" that studied and then redesigned the movements of assembly-line workers so as to maximize outputs.

6   Arendt, *The Origins of Totalitarianism*, 588.

programmed actions. Who is producer or consumer? Sender or receiver? Slave or slave-owner? The attention economy exhausts these distinctions. It feeds on acquisition of fine-grained, real-time data to reveal habits and dispositions. Scrolling, swiping, liking, commenting could be regarded as actions in the Arendtian sense of free expressions in a public sphere. Yet these expressions of taste, opinion, mood become acts of inadvertent labor that can be harvested and converted into exchange value— just as specks of gold are extracted from the grime of the alleys of Mumbai's jewelry bazaar by artisanal scavengers.[7] And, in both cases, the extraction of value requires a fatal interdependence of economic actors that blurs the distinction not only between labor and slavery, as Arendt would say, but also between labor, slavery, and consumption.

Anne-Marie Willis

See also
ALIENATION, *ANIMAL LABORANS*,
SUPERFLUITY, THOUGHTLESSNESS

---

7   Linking this example to the wider discussion of labor: in the first draft of this essay I described such people as "informal" workers, which prompted one of the editors to ask whether I could substitute "a term closer to destitute." Both descriptions are inadequate, revealing how Eurocentric categorizations of the labor of the Global South cannot capture its complexity. Informal refers to the formally unorganized economic activities of day laborers, street vendors, scavengers, trash collectors, and the like who make up the majority of the working population of many nations of the global south; there is no collective noun that can adequately describe the gradations of difference of artisanal skill, entrepreneurial ability, income, and social status, among which the destitute are a subcategory.

LAW

Design and the law: two fields whose constituent communities have, in the common course of things, little to do with one another and whose perspective on the world, on the "things" it comprises, might differ quite markedly. If one is concerned with humans, environments, and artefacts, the other sees in terms of institutions, rules, and precedents. Ontologically and epistemologically there is not much shared ground. So, what might be gained from colliding these two terms? In what ways might we relate design and the law?

The first, most obvious point of contact is where design activity is regulated by law: by the rules around intellectual property and protection thereof, by agreed standards around safety and interoperability, by the demands placed on designers and manufacturers and with which they must comply.[1] This relation illustrates Hannah Arendt's characterization of the modern understanding of law as a "catalogue of prohibitions … the Thou Shalt Nots."[2] As a matter of professional practice, designers must be aware of the legal parameters of their chosen field (not always clear or easy in emergent design terrains). A recurring question for design is whether the bare minimum of compliance with the law goes far enough in terms of an acceptable code of practice or professional ethos.[3],[4]

Second, we can see the making of laws as a kind of designerly activity in itself. The crafting of a text via the back and forth of parliamentary dialogue, the modifying, essaying, and critiquing that goes on between the chambers of the house and the institutions of the civil service, can be seen as a design

1   Carma Gorman, "Law as a Lens for Understanding Design," *Design and Culture* vol. 6, no. 3 (2015): 269–90.
2   Hannah Arendt, *The Human Condition* (Chicago, IL: University of Chicago Press, [1958] 1998), 63.
3   Phil McCollam, "Redefining Design Ethics," *Design and Culture* vol. 6, no. 3 (2014): 315–25.
4   Cameron Tonkinwise, "Ethics by Design, or the Ethos of Things," *Design Philosophy Papers* vol. 2, no. 2 (2004): 129–44.

process, and in fact can be modeled as one without too much difficulty.[5] This relation illustrates Arendt's characterization of law as "the content of political action." In a modern democracy, active participation in legislative ritual is central to formal political "work."

But Arendt would have us—for a moment at least—set aside these two ideas and think of the law according to its etymological origins in the ancient *polis*, as a kind of boundary, or wall, demarcating public from private, and defining the lines of a political community; in other words, a "caesura," a demarcation line including but therefore also excluding:

> It was quite literally a wall, without which there might have been an agglomeration of houses ... but not a political community. This wall-like law was sacred ... without it a public realm could no more exist than a piece of property without a fence to hedge it in. The one harbored and enclosed political life as the other sheltered and protected the biological life process of the family.[6]

This idea of the relationship of the law to a political community and a public realm—as a physical, spatial thing *that needs maintaining*—is a useful provocation to the design community, following Arendt's exhortation to "think what we are doing," to reflect on how we conceive of and address some of these things through our work. Are we maintaining and repairing the wall? Or are we chipping away at the foundations? And how would we know, in the context of a single, bounded project, the difference?

To think about something, we first have to perceive it, to have an idea of it as a thing that exists, to stretch our "ontological imagination."[7] Arendt is here describing in material and spatial terms something that is now (vellum parchment scrolls notwithstanding) largely intangible. Making things visible and tangible is one of the great strengths of design, but does our

5   Darren Umney and PeterLloyd, "Designing Frames: The Use of Precedents in Parliamentary Debate," *Design Studies* vol. 54 (2018): 201–18.
6   Arendt, *The Human Condition*, 64.
7   Andrew Barry, Georgina Born, and Giza Weszkalnys, "Logics of Interdisciplinarity," *Economy and Society* vol. 37, no. 1 (2008): 20–49.

palette stretch to being able to perceive and articulate these sorts of things? We are trained to understand and manipulate certain human–thing relationships: buildings, imagery, products, etc., and we are expanding our repertoire to incorporate more complicated human—nonhuman configurations, such as services. We have even started talking about "systems" as design objects (which is somewhat simplistic). But the human is the consistent point of reference; we see through the lenses of interactions, psychologies, behaviors, journeys, experiences. Our methods lead us inexorably back to humans and their life-worlds—this is both design's strength and also its blind spot. Even when adopting a consciously social raison d'être, design seems to lack the ability to deal with the social—or the public realm—beyond small groups of individuals. As Christopher Alexander says, "A city is not a tree."[8] Anything more complex than a village eludes design's methods.[9]

What are we doing to the humans we are acting on? Arendt describes the law as a wall—a line that creates a space of possibility, but not one that determines what must take place within it. It is a guarantee of plurality, which in her account is our primary source for hope: the originality of human beings. There, other logics besides the binary are allowed. In design we are not habitually working with this space of possibility in mind. Instead, we have become expert at targeting individuals, predicting and prefiguring responses and behaviors, promising impact to clients, and mitigating the risk of the unknown future. In all this we are limiting action rather than making and protecting space for it.

But what if, instead, we focused our efforts on creating spaces of possibility? Expanding our gaze beyond the human, what other "things" are there, and what is our understanding of them? Society, the law, politics, the public realm, culture, norms, power, governance, labor, work, institutions, discourse, colonialism, class, ideas: one might imagine acting on the

8   Christopher Alexander, "A City Is Not a Tree." *Design*, London: Council of Industrial Design, no. 206 (1966).

9   Dung-Sheng Chen et al., "Social Design: An Introduction," *International Journal of Design* vol. 10, no. 1 (April 2016): 1–5.

relations between some of these things, but that would require critical engagement with them. At present, while we may mobilize some of these terms in the pursuit of a project, the instrumentalizing mode of design practice tends to take a working definition as satisfactory. Terms are rarely opened up for examination.

Unless we start to perceive these things, and the connections between them, and educate ourselves in this regard, we may easily be eroding, through our micro-focus on individuals, the intangible things[10] that support and protect the public realm and political community.[11] This is especially so in the context of the contemporary condition of neoliberalization, a process that serves, through the introduction of competition to every sphere of life, to chip away at the existence of a shared, collaborative, protected public realm.[12] We need to be alert to the mechanisms of neoliberalism, to become attuned to its language.

The task of sensitizing ourselves to an expanded set of things—of seeing connections between micro and macro, of hearing the ideologies that are coded into design briefs, and, finally, of considering design and law in this unconventional pattern—has implications for education, of course, but also professional practice. For instance, the "subaltern" position of design in economic terms severely limits the agency of the design professional. We need some structurally different ways of engaging and being acknowledged for our work.[13] It also has implications for the personal. It means having a view beyond some vague commitment to "social good" and taking seriously

10 To further describe the delicate balance between those "intangible things," one can recur to Giorgio Agamben's idea of "*tensio*" being a tension that keeps things together. Giorgio Agamben, *La Natura delle Cose* (Brossura: Maschietto Editore, 2008).

11 Liesbeth Huybrechts, Henric Benesch, and Jon Geib, "Institutioning: Participatory Design, Co-Design and the Public Realm," *CoDesign* vol. 13, no. 3 (2017): 148–59.

12 William Davies, *The Limits of Neoliberalism: Authority, Sovereignty and the Logic of Competition* (London: Sage, 2014); Guy Julier, *Economies of Design* (London: Sage, 2017).

13 Clive Dilnot, "The Matter of Design," *Design Philosophy Papers* vol. 13, no. 2 (2016): 115–23.

the cognitive dissonance that arises through the course of work. And it might sometimes mean, as recommended by Mahmoud Keshavarz, dropping design for a moment and using our privileged bodies in different ways.[14] Considering our being designers in this *caesura* might lead us to unconventional, still unexplored patterns.

Jocelyn Bailey

See also
BUREAUCRACY, IN-BETWEEN, OBJECTIVITY,
TOTALITARIANISM

14   Mahmoud Keshavarz, "Care/Control: Notes on Compassion, Design and Violence," Keynote presentation at *Nordes 2017: Design + Power*, accessed February 5, 2018, http://www.nordes.org/nordes2017/assets/ keynotes/Keynote_Mahmoud_Keshavarz.pdf.

METABOLISM
MORTALITY

METABOLISM

> Labor is the activity which corresponds to the biological
> process of the human body, whose spontaneous growth,
> metabolism, and eventual decay are bound to the vital
> necessities produced and fed into the life process by labor.
> The human condition of labor is life itself.
>
> Hannah Arendt, *The Human Condition*[1]

Labor is metabolism is labor. In times where there are seemingly
no limits to design, and designers take on any issue with the
same happy naïveté, this has implications for life itself. When
designers can no longer imagine meaningful existence beyond
consumerism, the very metabolism of life is designed to sustain
the barest form of life. When the growth and sustainment of
the organism is coupled to economic success that equates
to accumulation of more life (acquire more points, avoiding
depression, damnation, death), there can be no "meaning" in
Being beyond hoarding. Design has become the manipulation
of the Spinozan conatus, designating the labor of life as a
gamble, setting life up for speculation. When IDEO designs life,
perhaps design itself is dead. *Design makes living and labor
the same: user-friendly, invisible, and impossible to turn into
praxis.*

Design theorists Harold Nelson and Erik Stolterman posit in
The Design Way, "Design ... is different from other traditions of
inquiry and action in that *service* is a defining element. Design
is, by definition, a service relationship."[2] To Arendt, the labor
of slavery is a service: an unconscious societal metabolism
serving the higher purpose of the *polis*. Yet not only is labor
serving design, it is Being itself shaped to serve; the striving
for life is designated to subsume into servitude, to serve the
accumulation of more and more life for another. Sustainable

1   Hannah Arendt, *The Human Condition* (Chicago, IL: University of
    Chicago Press, [1958] 1998), 7.
2   Harold G. Nelson and Erik Stolterman, *The Design Way* (Cambridge,
    MA: MIT Press, 2012), 41.

design means everlasting servitude where metabolism and vital necessities are recruited to keep on serving their prescribed function. The organism's metabolism itself is now the realm of artifice, merging life, labor, and Being. Salvation is replaced by design. "In a society in which design has taken over the function of religion," cultural theorist Boris Groys posits, "self-design becomes a creed."[3] Design is homeostasis, at the core of cellular autopoieis: life as a content provider for itself. *There can be no enjoyment of life by designing for a future. To live is to have no future.*

Affective labor, viral labor, petro labor, chthulu labor: if labor is a striving for life, a labor of life, how is it continuously exhausting itself, dragging every breath toward death? Is this resource so exploited, as media theorist McKenzie Wark points to, that capitalism has morphed into something more deadly than capitalism: *thanaticism*, a suicidal labor of collective self-extinction? Under the threat of death, the labor of Being is design infiltrating every sphere of existence and every hour of life. Every plasmatic movement, every moment of attentiveness or sleep, every metabolic process: designers compete to make all being labor, every moment a process of accumulative-extraction-toward-death. Like ancient magic or Calvinist salvation, capital corresponds to a more desired life, allowing those with assets to live upward along the chain-of-being, closer to the life of angels, gods, celebrities. Yet accumulation never asks what is the *good life*: not for humans, and never for the snake, the bee, the water, or the mineral. *Addicted to life, designers kill in all souls the sense of justice.*

Arendt tries to push us toward action, to strive for the higher politics of praxis, to raise our visions beyond the narrow horizon of labor. Designers seem to agree, yet continuously neglect or even abolish from view the issue of labor: who does it, when, and for what purpose? Like the sweatshops, pollution, and abattoirs, the metabolisms of labor are pushed out of sight to poorer countries and regions, into surrogate bodies and closed

3   Boris Groys, "The Obligation to Self-Design," *E-flux Journal* no. 00 (November 2008): https://www.e-flux.com/journal/00/68457/the-obligation-to-self-design/.

labs. Simultaneously, designers call for more "collaboration" and "participation" while failing to see how they make all Being invisible labor, leaving little room for praxis. Without labor there can be no praxis. Instead, what we can see is how big data and the platforms on which contemporary life is enacted revert praxis into opinions, fake news, and clicktivism. Marcuse's prophesy of the one-dimensional man is rendered in real-time and high-resolution, gamified plug-n-play. *Metabolism is a process of falling apart. Labor is no one everywhere.*

As Arendt puts it, "What we are confronted with is the prospect of a society of laborers without labor, that is, without the only activity left to them. Surely, nothing could be worse."[4] Full automation, the eradication of labor, and introduction of basic income do not necessarily clash with the political dream of full and total labor, and absolute extraction. With the abolishment of labor, could everyday life become praxis, or is it simply devoid of any political possibility? Who saves us then from bare design, bare labor, and bare praxis? *Relax in labor, in un-design, to stop pursuing. You have no need to be anyone at all.*

Otto von Busch

See also
ALIENATION, *ANIMAL RATIONALE*,
MORTALITY, THOUGHTLESSNESS

---

4   Arendt, *The Human Condition*, 5.

MORTALITY

What is possibly the second blackest black paint was designed by artists in response to being blocked from using the supposed blackest black—Vanta black. The restriction was brought about by a deal between artist Amish Kapoor and Vanta patent holders for rights to its use. Ownership of the blackest black is perhaps another black hole—a void absent of light and options. Have our times become captive within an anxious addiction to black holes? A dark fantasy dance marathon on the event horizon? A precipice with foregone stakes, where an accumulation of space/time swirls like excerpts from films? A cinematic symphony of our lives, drawn inward and circling a cosmic drain at increasing velocity, sucked across the threshold toward the point of no return, a finale of flashing nonsequential memory fractals that … slow down … for just a moment, and then escape into …?

Black holes model a certain kind of dramaturgy for conceiving our mortality within late capitalism. Wile E. Coyote employs a portable black hole in an attempt to capture the Road Runner, and then, in a switch of fate, falls to what should be his own death. The ACME Corporation supplied Wile E. Coyote with 126 different items to assist in his persistent, and always failed, labor to foil the Road Runner over 43 episodes of the popular cartoon.[1] ACME goods—a box of one thousand Tornado Seeds, a Rocket-powered pogo stick, a plethora of faulty explosives, etc.—lacked reliable use value while their variety, availability, and delivery were assured. Dying doesn't count for Wile E. Coyote, as there is always another day to work and consume. Mark Fisher describes *capitalist realism* as our current condition where "capitalism seamlessly occupies the horizons of the thinkable."[2] Within the capitalist-realism-of-things, we are emancipated from immortal responsibility and relinquish

---

1   Tim Maly, "Elaborate Poster Puts All of Wile E. Coyote's ACME Purchases on Your Wall," *Wired* (December 18, 2012), https://www.wired.com/2012/12/acme-poster-kickstarter/.
2   Mark Fisher, *Capitalist Realism* (London: Zero Books, 2009), 8.

long-term logics of decision-making. Considering impacts on seven generations beyond our present time, as was observed by some indigenous communities, seems long gone.

Too many of us have been conditioned by Hollywood versions of death that are filled with packaged emotion, serene gestures of letting go, and some sense of closure as we gaze upon the dying other at a safe distance from the screen. This has become the means of reflection regarding our own mortality—a carefully mediated distancing fueled by an ephemeral collective belief of disbelief, a Lacanian Big Other.[3] The film flickers to black, and then the house lights come up illuminating not the remnants of past contributions to future well-being but rather the interpassivity of perpetual, posthumous consumption. We might imagine that, eventually, our name could appear engraved on the back of a theater chair, on the theater itself, on a building that houses several theaters, or name an entire campus for the arts if we can get really rich.

It's easier to imagine the end of the world than it is to imagine the end of capitalism ... or, beyond the end of our mortal existence.[4] *Designing in Dark Times* requires us to see and act upon the seemingly *unfathomable* in ways beyond hope and fear. Late capitalism has brought about an even deeper disillusionment with the existence of the past or the future—a post-Sisyphean exhaustion within a very noisy yet static atmosphere of political and cultural possibility. Rudolf Bahro, a German activist and iconoclast, describes this as "When the forms of an old culture are dying, the new culture is created by a few people who are not afraid to be insecure."[5]

Artist Matt Freedman, during a performance, tells a joke by Groucho Marx: "A man facing execution by hanging steps onto the platform of the gallows, and says, 'I don't think this thing is very safe.'"[6] The tension involving consciousness of our mortality

3   Slavoj Žižek, *How to Read Lacan* (New York: W.W. Norton, 2007), 8–12.
4   Fisher, *Capitalist Realism*, 2.
5   Margaret Wheatley, "The Place Beyond Fear and Hope," *Shambhala Sun* (March 2009), 81.
6   John Bruce and Pawel Wojtasik, *ACME Death Kit* (motion picture film, 2018), installation and performance, *(IM)MORTALITY*, New York: Park Place Gallery, May 2018.

and an embrace of "transcendence into a potential earthly immortality" is, according to Hannah Arendt, the opportunity space that supports the existence of politics, the common world, and the public realm.[7] This transcendence is only a possibility, not a guarantee. An overvaluation of our belief that we will die might permit us to act as though we live without affect, impact, or resonance beyond mortal life, and thus have no responsibility in the transcendence of our immortality. Similarly, Fisher, referencing Slavoj Žižek, explains capitalist ideology in regard to the overvaluing of belief as the dissociation of private subjective attitudes from the beliefs shown through externalized behaviors, thus reliant upon a structure of disavowal and benefiting from ironic distance.[8] Freedman, during his performance, tells stories referencing his own mortality. On a large pad of paper hanging around his neck, he draws upside down, illustrating anecdotes about his very real experiences with terminal illness, creating and collapsing distances of disavowal for the audience. He tears completed drawings from the pad, carelessly dropping them to the floor, posing questions around temporality, commodity, and value.

We seem to have diminished capacity for holding the tensions—the amplified and vast array of contradictions, of the human condition in the twenty-first century. In dark times, we too often: approach discourse as blood sport and call censorship safe space; disparage capitalism and covet money as holy; persecute infringements upon our personal happiness and turn a blind eye to the collateral damage caused by the loss of our empathetic acuity; and so on. Our mode is confrontational while we refuse to confront that which makes us uncomfortable. We wish only for affirmations.

Public space emerges from collaborations where people come together from a place of their humanity first, rather than from places that privilege titles, roles, expertise, or reductive competition. Designing, at its best, might be acts for creating invitations: to reckon with one's many selves, to find productivity

---

7   Hannah Arendt, *The Human Condition* (Chicago, IL: University of
    Chicago Press, [1958] 1998), 55.
8   Fisher, *Capitalist Realism*, 13.

in being uncomfortable, to abandon power that defends entrenched identity, to energize movements for identification, to exchange toward possibilities within earned trust, to *care* in the most expanded notions. These acts cannot be reduced to monetary value within our current system. Let's reverse the order of things. Perhaps we can view the last reel of the motion picture film first. Play and work, to see the end more clearly as potential rather than *The End*.

John A. Bruce

See also
ACTION, COMPREHENSION, NATALITY

NATALITY

NATALITY

> With word and deed we insert ourselves into the human
> world, and this insertion is like a second birth ... its
> impulse springs from the beginning which came into the
> world when we were born and to which we respond by
> beginning something new on our own initiative. To act, in
> its most general sense, means to take an initiative, to begin
> ... to set something into motion. This beginning is not the
> same as the beginning of the world; it is not the beginning
> of something but of somebody ... It is in the nature of
> beginning that something new is started which cannot be
> expected from whatever may have happened before. This
> character of startling unexpectedness is inherent in all
> beginnings and in all origins ... And this again is possible
> only because each man is unique, so that with each birth
> something uniquely new comes into the world ... Action
> as beginning corresponds to the fact of birth ... it is the
> actualization of the human condition of natality.
>
> Hannah Arendt, *The Human Condition*[1]

I

It is possible that no quotation from Arendt in this lexicon reads,
at least initially, as more peculiar than this one. There is much
in philosophy, more in art, on mortality. There is infinitely less
on natality. If this seems obvious it is less clear why it should
be so. We know after all how to die: and (only too well) how
to make others die for us. We know of ending. If, conversely,
birth seems obvious this is only because today its apparent
ease, and the superficial ease of beginnings in general, seems
without question, and hence to pose no problems for thought.
But if it ever was, this division is no longer true. For one thing,
beginnings, true beginnings, are proving the hardest thing. Faced

1   Hannah Arendt, *The Human Condition* (Chicago, IL: University of
     Chicago Press, [1958] 1998), 177–8.

with ending in the largest sense, with defuturing, "the negation of world futures for us, and many of our unknowing non-human others,"[2] we are demonstrating an astonishing inability (or is it a lack of confidence?) in acting, individually or collectively, in respect of what we know we should and must. In what is this staring-in-the-face of disaster rooted? To how might it be related to the historical priority given by philosophy, and especially theology, to being-toward-death? In view of the last centuries, one can all too easily make the empirical case. "'We, as civilizations, we know not only that we are mortal,' as Paul Valéry asserted after the war of 1914; we also know that we can inflict death upon ourselves … that the 'malady of death,' as Marguerite Duras might say, informs our most concealed inner recesses."[3] Given also our current unbridled extinction of other living entities, the admonition applies all too well. We could well say that, in civilizational terms, we have *reduced ourselves* to being-toward-death. Yet we have been reluctant to think about how, or even *that*, this metaphysical obsession carries through to action. Today, this disengagement looks untenable. If the glorification of mortality as the essential perspective on the meaning of human (and of nonhuman) lives has its inverse condition in our reluctance to face the actualities of our creation of death, so it disguises the fact that, rather than representing the truth of the human condition, we have *made* the theological proposition come true—and in so doing made the world over in the condition of being-toward-death. Politically anticipated in imperialism and totalitarianism—which so effectively model worlds of death and destruction—today this becomes the danger in *all* our actions. Does the fact that world-making has become, in effect, its opposite vitiate conscious action?[4] It would seem that only blind self-interest is capable of acting in

2   Tony Fry, *An Introduction to Defuturing: A New Design Philosophy* (Sydney: UNSW Press, 1999), 11.
3   Julia Kristeva, "The Malady of Grief: Duras," in *Black Sun* (New York: Columbia University Press, 1987), 221.
4   In 1947, in *Dialectic of Enlightenment*, Adorno and Horkheimer had already asked "why mankind, instead of entering into a truly human condition, is sinking into a new kind of barbarism?" Max Horkheimer and Theodor Adorno (New York: Herder and Herder, [1944, 1947] 1972), xi.

organized concert—precisely because it refuses reflection on its consequences.[5]

II

Hannah Arendt's proposition of *natality* is written against this trajectory. The concept emerges in the early 1950s, after Arendt had published the first edition of *The Origins of Totalitarianism* (1951). Arendt did not see totalitarianism as merely a historical construct. On the contrary, as she presciently observed in some concluding sentences to the first edition of *The Origins of Totalitarianism* she saw it as a model of politics no less endemic, and perhaps more so, to modern conditions of political and social life than democracy.

> The Nazis and the Bolsheviks can be sure that their factories of annihilation which demonstrate the swiftest solution to the problem of over-population, of economically superfluous and socially rootless human masses are as much an attraction as a warning. Totalitarian solutions may well survive the fall of totalitarian regimes in the form of strong temptations which will come up whenever it seems impossible to alleviate political, social, or economic misery in a manner worthy of man."[6]

But, precisely because the destructiveness and death-in-life of totalitarian political "solutions" would be a continuing and even *developing* appeal in modern life,[7] Arendt felt the necessity to attempt to think a "politics of life" that could counter the

---

5   Along with the unconscionable drive to excessive private accumulation, retrospection will identify sanctioning the refusal of reflection to action as a primary cause of disaster. See Heidegger's observations of this condition in "Overcoming Metaphysics" in Martin Heidegger, *The End of Philosophy* (Chicago, IL: University of Chicago Press, [1973] 2003), 99.

6   Hannah Arendt, *The Origins of Totalitarianism* (New York: Harvest Books, [1951] 1979), 459.

7   "The crisis of our time and its central experience have brought forth an entirely new form of government which as a potentiality and ever-present danger is only too likely to stay with us from now on … its danger is that it threatens to ravage the world as we know it … before a new beginning rising from this end has had time to assert itself." Arendt, *The Origins of Totalitarianism*, 478.

ideologies and expediency of totalitarianism.[8] Refusing the idea that it is mortality that "represents" the human she asserts instead the import of birth. In this argument it is not being-toward-death, not mortality, not ending, that is the basis of all acting and all becoming but natality. "Action as *beginning* corresponds to the fact of birth … it is the actualization of the human condition of natality." The ontological basis of persons-in-the-world is not their death but their birth. What matters is not the end but the *beginning*:

> But there remains also the truth that every end in history necessarily contains a new beginning: this beginning is the promise, the only "message" which the end can ever produce. Beginning, before it becomes a historical event, is the supreme capacity of man: politically, it is identical with man's freedom.[9]

Guaranteed by each new birth, "its impulse springs from the beginning which came into the world when we were born and to which we respond by beginning something new on our own initiative."[10]

> [But] the beginning inherent in birth can make itself felt in the world only because the newcomer possesses the capacity of beginning something anew, that is, of acting. In this sense of initiative, an element of action, and therefore of natality, is inherent in all human activities. Moreover, since action is the political activity par excellence, natality, and not mortality, may be the central category of political, as distinguished from metaphysical, thought.[11]

---

8 In a very useful extended paper on this topic by Miguel Vatter he reports that after the publication of *Origins*, Arendt felt she had not fully understood totalitarianism, since "she had not found out whether anything could be 'done' about it." Miguel Vatter, "Natality and Biopolitics in Hannah Arendt," *Revista de Ciencia Política* vol. 26, no. 2 (2006): 137–59 (see p. 150). By "done about it" she meant *at core*, in its appeal and self-justification, not merely through its ostensible military or political defeat.

9 These sentences are the last words of the second edition of *The Origins of Totalitarianism*, 479.

10 Ibid., 177.

11 Hannah Arendt, *The Human Condition* (Chicago, IL: University of Chicago Press, [1958] 1998), 8–9. Today, it is perfectly possible to argue

This is an astonishing proposition. Natality is political because it is the *ontological* condition that permits every actor to take an initiative, to begin to set something into motion.[12] Some*thing* but which is also the beginning of "somebody" (or, as politics, of *some* bodies, *some* persons). Hence it is not a moment of (preexistent) politics, but its source. Natality is the human capacity that allows and that ontologically enables every actor "to pull out of its captivation to the present circumstances."[13] Beginnings (natality) are ontologically and politically productive because natality sets in train that which opens the play of the world to "that which cannot be expected" and hence is that which opens possibility.[14] In turn, it is this capacity to open possibility that "saves" the world:

> Left to themselves, human affairs can only follow the law of mortality, which is the most certain and the only reliable law of a life spent between birth and death. It is the faculty of action that interferes with this law because it interrupts the inexorable automatic course of daily life ... The life span of man running toward death would inevitably carry everything human to ruin and destruction if it were not for the faculty of interrupting it and beginning something new, a faculty which is inherent in action like an ever-present reminder that men, though they must die, are not born in order to die but in order to begin. ... The miracle that saves the world, the realm of human affairs, from its normal, "natural" ruin is ultimately the fact of natality, in which the faculty of action is ontologically rooted. It is, in other words,

that, *for us*, natality is also a central category of the metaphysics (i.e., the basis) of what now is.

12   Or, as Arendt puts it when she is talking later in *The Human Condition*, without the capacity of "action to bring into the play of the world the new beginning of which each [person] is capable by virtue of being born, there is no new thing under the sun." Arendt, *The Human Condition*, 190.

13   Vatter, "Natality and Biopolitics in Hannah Arendt," fn. 38, 156.

14   Or, as Heidegger puts it, in a parallel conception, "a genuine beginning" is that which "contains the undisclosed abundance of the unfamiliar and extraordinary." Which also means that it necessarily therefore "contains strife with the familiar and ordinary," i.e., with that which passes itself off as the final or the inevitable or the necessary. Martin Heidegger, "The Origin of the Work of Art," in *Poetry, Language, Thought* (New York: Harper and Row, 1971), 74.

the birth of new men and the new beginning, the action they
are capable of by virtue of being born.[15]

III

Arendt's wager changes, profoundly, the structures of thought
and action. Above all, emphasis on the natalic lets us understand
again what *beginning* can be (and hence, ontologically, our view
of what humans can be). Critically against "the ever-recurring
cycle of [false] becoming" which distinguishes our times, natality
is, in effect, an attempt at revaluation of the world[16] not as
declaration as such (theologically) but via finding again the world
by insisting on the ontological value of action; not as blind acting
on the world (in indifference or even enmity to it) but in its
capacity, through beginnings, to (re)establish the "boundlessness"
of relations—and which, in more concrete terms, can lead to
the creation of public worlds ("spaces of appearance")[17] and
in which action, in Arendt's deep sense of the term, can play
itself not as death or destructiveness but as the securing of the
conditions of existence.[18] It is this that gives natality its double

---

15 Arendt, *The Origins of Totalitarianism*, 246–7.
16 Mortality, being-toward-death, devalues the world, causes us to doubt
    it and thus our abilities to act well in it and for it. Against the nihilistic
    cynicism of the reduction of the world to private interests (which now
    extends to accumulating the whole world as such) the rescue of beginning
    and therefore of action is *also* the affirmative rescue of the possibility of
    the world. As Gilles Deleuze pointed out nearly thirty years ago,

    > What we most lack is a belief in the world, we've quite lost the
    > world, it's been taken from us. If you believe in the world you
    > precipitate events, however inconspicuous, that elude control,
    > you engender new space-times, however small their surface or
    > volume. It's what you call *pietas*. Our ability to resist control,
    > or our submission to it, has to be assessed at the level of our
    > every move. We need both creativity *and* a people.

    Gilles Deleuze, "Control and Becoming: Gilles Deleuze in Conversation
    with Antonio Negri" (1990) in *Negotiations 1977–1990*, trans. Martin
    Joughin (New York: Columbia University Press, 1995), 176.
17 The spaces through which the polis occurs. See Arendt, *The Human
    Condition*, especially 198–207.
18 Kenneth Frampton, "Preface," in *Labor, Work & Architecture*
    (London: Phaidon, 2002), 7.

force, at once ontological and political—a force that is doubled today in that it is difficult, perhaps impossible, to see any other ontological basis on which it is possible to go forward addressing the colossal systemic problems that the current world system is bequeathing to the present and future.

The problem in our situation is that while we cannot stop acting as being-toward-death we cannot yet begin to act otherwise. We cannot begin to act because we possess as yet no adequate ontological model of acting outside of "blind" techno-economic impulse. Despite its fragmentary and indicative status,[19] natality is the speculative proposition that this basis already exists in the human. Certainly, from the side of design no other theoretical or ontological model, not even the early Marx, offers so consonant a model.

Seen in this light designing is a moment of the natalic capacity for beginning. In the latter is the capacity of "unexpected" or "improbable" action in relation to the conditions of life. Designing is above all a capacity for intervention and change in the relational conditions and situations of human life. It is intervention carried through as the affirmative *but always propositional* negotiation of incommensurability inherent in every human situation and condition. It is natalic in that this capacity for intervention into the conditions and relations of life ("in the background of our heritage" as Winogrand and Flores put it many years ago)[20] is a beginning that contains always the possibility of revealing the hitherto "undisclosed abundance of the unfamiliar and extraordinary" (in the realm of knowledge as much as in the realm of things), but whose real natalic work is to help preserve and explore the possibility of potentiality as part of the wider processual "dance" through which the human "structure of possibilities" are generated at any moment.

Yet there is in this concept also a warning for design that is an opportunity. Arendt is adamant that in human production

---

19 This short paper already contains many of the most developed observations Arendt made on the concept (though the category in its wider form is implicit in much of *The Human Condition*).

20 Terry Winogrand and Fernando Flores, *Understanding Computers and Cognition* (Norwood: Ablex, 1986), 163.

there is an irreplaceable relation between things, action, and speech (and, through action, on power).[21] Natality acts within, or better it encompasses, this triangle. It sets these moments in play and it is through the *negotiation* of these becoming-reciprocal moments that effective and *reflective* action in the world can happen. Designing (as sub-moment of the technological) has previously "belonged" to the realm of things. Yet what appears as natural division of labor can be seen today as the fateful shattering of a larger unity of thought and action. The natalic implies the reinversion of the domination of blind action and thus the recouping of internal relations and reciprocity between these moments. *Designing* is caught in this process. Insofar (as "Design") it continues to stay outside this wider triangle it remains essentially impotent and at the service of power. But the articulation of natalic capacity against disaster and the imposition of totalitarian "solutions"—the only "saving power" we possess—depend in no small way on the capacity to articulate the capabilities of designing *within* and in *relation to* these wider relations.

See also
CREATIVITY, FREEDOM, SPONTANEITY, SUPERFLUITY

---

21   See Arendt, *The Human Condition*, 8–9 and 200–7 (especially 204).

OBJECTIVITY

OBJECTIVITY

Everything [humans] become in contact with turns
immediately into a condition of their existence.
Hannah Arendt, *The Human Condition*[1]

I

Long before ontologically oriented design theory came to the
fore, Arendt anticipated with great prescience one of its central
dogmas: *design designs.*[2] We design the world and the world
designs us back. It is thus that we end up with "a world within
the world" of our own making, a world that is also, at the same
time, us.[3] Worlds-R-US. No pun intended (even if the human,
too, is threatening with going out of business, like the famous
corporation that recently did). "Whatever touches or enters
into a sustained relation with human life immediately assumes
the character of human existence," she goes on to say.[4] At
stake is more than an endless circularity between humans and
the tools and objects they produce; perhaps it's more akin to
the legendary serpent eating its own tail, only that this time it
wouldn't represent the endless circularity of life but humans
self-digesting their indigestible creations, while intensifying
beyond belief the socioeconomic metabolism of their lives,
wreaking havoc along the way on what we moderns refer to as
the natural world.

Rearticulating her claim once more in the same paragraph,
she asserts: "because human existence is conditioned existence,
it would be impossible without things, and things would
be a heap of unrelated articles, a non-world, if they were

1   Hannah Arendt, *The Human Condition* (Chicago, IL: University of
    Chicago Press, [1958] 1998), 9.
2   This formulation is from Australian design theorist Anne-Marie Willis,
    "Ontological Designing—Laying the Ground," *Design Philosophy Papers*
    no. 3 (1985): 80–98.
3   Tony Fry, *Becoming Human by Design* (London: Berg, 2012).
4   Arendt, *The Human Condition*, 9.

not the conditions of human existence."[5] With Foucauldian
poststructuralism, we became accustomed to understanding
power as "the conduct of conduct," in terms of impersonal
mechanisms—discourses and apparatuses—that indelibly shape
the kinds of subject we become. But Arendt's idea that there is a
force (conditioned existence) that is always acting, always busy
at work, determining who we are, points in a partially different
direction, particularly because of her emphasis on things. From
her insights, we may intuit that a Thing-form of social life has
become ensconced in our midst (different from the God-form
and the Man-form, as has been said, or the Earth-form, as it could
be hypothesized).[6] Shouldn't we also talk, then, really, about
thing-humans?

That an Earth devoid of humans would be a "nonworld,"
reveals Arendt's anthropocentrism, yet it is one from which we
can still learn, as one of the key questions of today's critical
theory is about the specificity of the human in an alleged
posthuman world. Arendt was an intellectual of her time; the
agency of things, objects, and nonhumans—from plants and
animals to microorganisms, minerals, rocks, and even spirits—
had not yet fully emerged in the scholarly domain, even if, as
we know, it was foreshadowed by some of today's intellectual
heroes (Spinoza, Bergson, Whitehead, etc. not to speak about
the multiple premodern and nonmodern ontologies for which
the entire world is alive, a universe of pan-sentience). Could
one say that hers was a sort of "analogue anthropocentrism,"
still working on the logic of representation? And that, while not
wholly appropriate to today's ever more thoroughly digitalized
worlds, her approach nevertheless bears close examination,
precisely as *homo digitalis* "fingers away" much of his existence,
making Arendtian Action nearly impossible? What rearticulations
of *the human condition* would be appropriate to the age of
the Artificial, perhaps finally enabling humanity to bypass the

5   Ibid.
6   On the God-form and the Man-form of life, see Gilles Deleuze, *Foucault*
    (Minneapolis: University of Minnesota Press, 1988), 125–8; on the
    Earth-form, Arturo Escobar, *Otro possible es possible* (Bogotá: Desde
    Abajo, 2018).

Thing-form, with which design has been enthralled? What kind of *vita activa* can design be today?

II

> When one puts objectivity in parentheses, all views, all verses in the multiverse are equally valid. Understanding this, you lose the passion for changing the other. ... [Y]ou discover that disagreements can only be solved by entering a domain of co-inspiration in which *things* are *done together* because the participants want to do them. With objectivity in parentheses, it is easy to *do things* together because one is not denying the other in the process of doing them.[7]

Arendt was writing at a time when widespread concern with the colonial other (in the post/decolonial sense) and with the nonhuman (in postdualist terms) had not yet emerged. Twisting Maturana a bit, one might arrive at a view of design as the doing/making/assembling together of things in radically relational ways, with "things" standing as humans, nonhumans, and other entities, including objects. "Things" would thus be done relationally, perhaps moving the human from a Man-form and a Thing-form of life to a much needed and desired Earth-form, within which one does not deny the other because one-self ceases to exist as such, moreover, because moderns finally figure out that the world is not made up of self-sufficient subjects confronting self-standing objects that they can manipulate at will, but of radically interdependent things, knowledges, and beings.

III

What kind of practice-action is design today? What conversations for action are most worth having? Certainly democracy is one of them.[8] It has been recently brought squarely into the

---

7   Humberto Maturana, Interview, *Oikos*, 1985; quoted in Walter Mignolo, *The Darker Side of Western Modernity* (Durham: Duke University Press, 2011), 27 (emphasis added).

8   See the plea to the design community by Ezio Manzini and Victor Margolin to rethink this relation, in DESIS Network, "Democracy and Design: What

sphere of design, as a fundamental feature of the modern human condition. Let us add an ontological dimension to this conversation. The Zapatista of Chiapas have provided us with the most succinct declaration for ontological democracy: a world where many worlds fit. Intra- and interworld democracy, radical pluriversal democracy, extended to the entire range of nonhumans: objectivity in parenthesis all the way down, restoring to humans, nonhumans, and things their full potential to cocreate worlds in which we might dwell with a modicum of content, shifting the human perhaps to an altogether different mode of conditioned existence, beyond the human (as we know it).

Arturo Escobar

See also
IN-BETWEEN, PLURALITY, PUBLIC,
TOGETHERNESS

Do You Think?" http://www.desisnetwork.org/2017/04/11/democracy-and-design-what-do-you-think/, as well as Virginia Tassinari's talks on "Regenerating Democracy," DESIS Philosophy talks, http://www.desis-philosophytalks.org/.

PARIAH
PLAY
PLURALITY
POWER
PRIVATE REALM
PUBLIC

PARIAH

Before we turn to Lessing's concept of friendship and its political relevance, we must dwell for a moment on fraternity as the eighteenth century understood it. Lessing, too, was well acquainted with it; he spoke of "philanthropic feelings," of a brotherly attachment to other human beings which springs from hatred of the world in which men are treated "inhumanly." For our purposes, however, it is important that humanity manifests itself in such brotherhood most frequently in "dark times." This kind of humanity actually becomes inevitable when the times become so extremely dark for certain groups of people that it is no longer up to them, their insight or choice, to withdraw from the world. Humanity in the form of fraternity invariably appears historically among persecuted peoples and enslaved groups; and in eighteenth-century Europe it must have been quite natural to detect it among the Jews, who then were newcomers in literary circles. This kind of humanity is the great privilege of pariah peoples; it is the advantage that the pariahs of this world always and in all circumstances can have over others. The privilege is dearly bought; it is often accompanied by so radical a loss of the world, so fearful an atrophy of all the organs with which we respond to it—starting with the common sense with which we orient ourselves in a world common to ourselves and others and going on to the sense of beauty, or taste, with which we love the world—that in extreme cases, in which pariahdom has persisted for centuries, we can speak of real worldlessness. And worldlessness, alas, is always a form of barbarism.

Hannah Arendt, *Men in Dark Times*[1]

---

[1] Hannah Arendt, *Men in Dark Times* (New York: Harcourt, Brace, [1955] 1993), 12–13.

Hanna Arendt proposes a distinction between *pariahs* and *parvenus* and this was related to the political reality she lived through: both lives a situation of exclusion, but with different attitudes. The *pariah*, and particularly the "conscious *pariah*," is "aware of himself as an outsider, aware of himself in history, or at least aware of the way in which story shaped his life." Parvenus are "social climbers who deny their historical identity and seek to 'pass' as insiders or members of the dominant culture, take the blame for their exclusion on themselves." The *parvenu* recognizes his exclusion and asks himself what he may have done wrong. The pariah knows that his outsider status "is not of his own making yet recognizes that he has some choices about and indeed some responsibility for what he does with it."[2]

The term *broken city* became shorthand for the problems of contemporary urban social life in Rio de Janeiro. Ventura makes a report,[3] sometimes personal, of the conflict situation in the city by describing two parallel worlds, that of the favela, where violence and poverty prevails, and that of the broader society, which is mobilized in marches for peace. He argued that the socioeconomic structure of the city split into two separate realities, segregating social classes, neighborhoods, and cultural groups with increasingly limited interaction among them. This radicalized the separation between "hill" and "asphalt," the shantytowns of low-income residents of *favelas* and the urbanized areas of middle and upper classes, even when "hill" and "asphalt" are geographically side by side.[4]

However, in a society in which "everybody designs,"[5] some groups in Rio de Janeiro have designed their way to reconnect this *broken city*. Two cases exemplify that:

2 Jennifer Ring, "The Pariah as Hero: Hannah Arendt's Political Actor," *Political Theory* vol. 19, no. 3 (August 1991): 441, retrieved from http://www.jstor.org/stable/191420.

3 Zuenir Ventura, *Cidade Partida* (Rio de Janeiro: Companhia das Letras, 1994).

4 Carla Cipolla et al., "Coproduced Game-Changing in Transformative Social Innovation: Reconnecting the 'Broken City' of Rio de Janeiro," *Ecology and Society* vol. 22, no. 3 (2017): 3, https://doi.org/10.5751/ES-09362-220303.

5 Ezio Manzini, *Design, When Everybody Designs* (Cambridge, MA: MIT Press, 2015).

(1) the cultural movements that take place in the Rio de Janeiro's, movements of cultural affirmation, from peripheries to centre, such as the one named *Norte Comum* (Common North); (2) the recognition of popular knowledge from peripheries in academic institutions, such as the *Universidade das Quebradas* (University of Quebradas (UQ). The next paragraphs introduce the activities of these two groups and argue that despite their status as excluded—in the broken city of Rio de Janeiro—they have acted as pariahs, following Arendt's definition, or were enabled to act as such.

Norte Comum

> *Coletivo Norte Comum (Common North Collective)* is a network of cultural producers. They live in the poorer parts of the city, yet engage in high-quality cultural production in their territories. They create local alternatives outside Rio's mainstream cultural circuit, which is concentrated in the Central-South regions.

Despite the North in their name, Norte Comum is not confined to the northern part of the city. It reaches many other areas (including the densely populated West Zone and other municipalities within the metropolitan region of Rio de Janeiro). They can be seen as acting against both physical and socio-cultural dominance of some areas of the city.

It results that, establishing new practices of co-production of cultural events, Norte Common nurtured new relations between young people of the North Zone with young people from the South and Central areas, establishing new forms of relationship in the city. The collective also makes the North Zone and the most deprived areas of the city in centres of production and consumer of high-quality culture, as there was not before them.

In this sense, the actions of the collective, scattered spatially (occurring in many neighborhoods) join different territorial areas of Rio de Janeiro around cultural activities, contributing to the transformation of the broken city.[6]

---

6   Carla Cipolla et al., "Coproduced game-changing in transformative social innovation: reconnecting the 'broken city' of Rio de Janeiro."

Universidade das Quebradas

The Universidade das Quebradas (University of Quebradas) was created in 2010 at the Federal University of Rio de Janeiro—UFRJ to promote interactions between the art and cultural producers that live in the outskirts of the city of Rio de Janeiro and the academics. The term "quebradeiros" (breakers) is an expression, or slang, to indicate those who live on the urban peripheries. The initiative creates a shared environment, to enable and promote the exchange of ideas between the students of the course—"quebradeiros" as they are called—and the teachers.

The course deals with subjects such as Philosophy, African Culture, Art and Architecture in Antiquity, Classical Epic, Greek and African Myths, Yoruba Mythology, Romanticism in Art and Literature, Black Literature and "Cordel"—a type of handmade notebook produced by lithography, of illustrated poetry, typical of northeastern Brazil. In the second part of the course, classes of Cinema, Music, Dance, Theater and elaboration of Cultural Projects are taught, as well as Language and Expression workshops.

According to the founder, Heloísa Buarque de Hollanda, professor at UFRJ, the name of the project—University of Quebradas—is because the jargon "broken" in the Northeast and São Paulo means a distant place, peripheral. It is also an allusion to the university's need to break its rigidity and open itself to the popular.

The professor also explains that the initiative aims to promote a cultural translation, a listening and recognition of the other.[7]

Pariahs and Parvenus as Two Possibilities

We celebrate participants of both initiatives—*Norte Comum* and *Universidade das Quebradas*—as *pariahs*, as one who knows

7   Iris Guardatti, Paulo Reis, and Guilherme Monteiro, "*University of Quebradas*," in Mark M. Anderson, Carla Cipolla, and Sergio Puerta (eds.), *Social Innovations Between HEI and the Broader Society: Experiences from Latin America and Europe* (Latin American Social Innovation Network perspectives, 2018).

that his outsider status is not of their own making, and take responsibility of what to do with it. *Quebradas* also emerges as a safe space to enable interactions between individuals that aim to blow up hierarchies and segregations to reconnect the city.

However, their cultural or artistic talents could also lead them to a status of *parvenus*, i.e., to live as if they would have never been excluded, by leaving behind their peers and abandoning the political practice. Projects—such as *Quebradas*—support participants to recognize their own identity, their status as *pariahs*.

They and other *pariahs* bring hope to reconnect the broken city of Rio de Janeiro that hopefully means also to overcome their current status.

Carla Cipolla

See also
CREATIVITY, DEMOCRACY, HUMANITY,
IMPERIALISM, POWER

PLAY

With two working parents, two kids, and two dogs, downtime in my family needs to be carefully scheduled into the week. Luckily, there is no shortage of lifestyle companies eager to sell me that downtime—time to relax, to play, and to "enjoy life." From tropical vacation rentals to endless streaming TV options, to lifestyle surveys in my Facebook feed—at a time when digital connectivity is eroding lines between work and play, the marketing of "play" as everything that is not work is growing increasingly sophisticated.

Hannah Arendt identifies this aggressive selling of play activities as a symptom of modernity. "All serious activities," she writes in *The Human Condition*, "irrespective of their fruits, are called labor, and every activity which is not necessary either for the life of the individual or the life process of society is subsumed under playfulness."[1] In her tripartite formulation of the human condition, which includes labor, work, and action, playfulness is placed in opposition to labor, which squeezes out work and action from the careful balance of the *vita activa*. The *vita activa*, the active life, distinct from the *vita contemplativa*, or the thinking life, is what distinguishes humans from animals, she argues, even more so than *cogito ergo sum*. It is the unique human condition wherein labor, that which is ongoing and meets our biological needs for subsistence, is put into relation with work and action; with that which has specific outcomes and meaning. For example, whittling a flute from a log, or planting and tending to a vegetable garden, or even raising children are examples of work—or labor with purposeful outcomes. Each is in relation with action, which is the means by which humans disclose themselves to each other, from a conversation with friends, to a post on social media, to a drawing or a poem. What's important about Arendt's understanding of action is that it is always open ended—it invites new beginnings. Moreover, where work and labor are harmonized with action, playfulness is also

1   Hannah Arendt, *The Human Condition* (Chicago, IL: University of Chicago Press, [1958] 1998), 127.

in the picture: it is not divided from labor, work, and action; it is the creative "tension" between the different spheres of the human condition.[2]

Arendt's critique of modern society, however, is that play, as opposed to being seen as a kind of action, functions instead as a safety valve for a modern laboring society where alienation from the outcomes of one's labor is normalized, and the *vita activa* is reduced to a simple binary between labor and play, and play becomes a surrogate for the disappearance of action. In an extended footnote in *The Human Condition*, Arendt equates this to another binary, that between necessity and freedom, wherein everything becomes either an activity to meet one's needs (i.e., we work in order to be able to live) or to be free from that necessity.

Play has unfortunately become an enabler of a laboring society, removed from the distinctly human drive of the *vita activa*. Not even the "work" of the artist is left, she says, "It is dissolved into play and has lost its worldly meaning."[3] What she means by worldly is the act of being connected to the world. When we get comfortable in our perpetual labor and release (we work in order to play) we lose sight of the world, Arendt says.[4] And this is precisely the condition that leads us to what she calls *dark times*. "Nothing in our time is more dubious than our attitude toward the world."[5] The world is all the stuff that lies

2   When this is not mutilated yet (as in modernity, where action disappears and labor and work tend to hybridize).

3   Arendt, *The Human Condition*, 128.

4   Similarities among Arendt's reflections on playfulness today and Adorno's and Horkheimer's critique of the cultural industry are striking:

> The work of art, by completely assimilating itself to need, deceitfully deprives men of precisely that liberation from the principle of utility which it should inaugurate. What might be called use value in the reception of cultural commodities is replaced by exchange value; in place of enjoyment there are gallery-visiting and factual knowledge: the prestige seeker replaces the connoisseur. The consumer becomes the ideology of the pleasure industry, whose institutions he cannot escape.

Theodor Wiesengrund Adorno and Max Horkheimer, *The Dialectic of Enlightenment* (New York: Continuum, 1999), 158.

5   Hannah Arendt, "On Humanity in Dark Times: Thoughts about Lessing," in Clara and Richard Winston (trans.), *Men in Dark Times* (New York: Harcourt, Brace, [1955] 1993), 3.

between people—in particular, the sense of public or society, the sense that one's individuality is contained within a discursive context that provides meaning. She explains: "When men [sic] are deprived of the public space—which is constituted by acting together and then fills of its own accord with the events and stories that develop into history—they retreat into their freedom of thought."[6] Dark times are the direct result of disengaging with the world, of accepting the alienation of a laboring society whose primary reward is to escape from it.

In order to retreat into our freedom of thought, we need to reject the world. We turn our backs on injustice, inequities, sometimes on blatant violence, and enjoy our freedom to think as individuals and connect with friends,[7] and we look to the world, not as something with which we have to contend, but as something we have to escape. We choose not to identify with corrupt and corrosive political leaders, because it is part of our laboring lives, not our playful lives. "Those who reject such identifications on the part of a hostile world," warns Arendt, "may feel wonderfully superior to the world, but their superiority is then truly no longer of this world; it is the superiority of a more or less well-equipped cloud-cuckoo land."[8]

We retreat into a cloud-cuckoo land, where our reality is exactly as we expect it to be—a shift from the world and its public space to an interior life, or else simply to ignore that world in favor of an imaginary world "as it ought to be" or "as it once upon a time had been."[9] What's more, this imaginary world is *well-equipped*, meaning that the structures of our society are reinforcing the appropriateness of retreat, where currently "fake" news is more popular than legitimate news; confirmation bias compels us to click on what we think we already know, and

6   Arendt, "On Humanity in Dark Times," 5.
7   When this "connection" does not lead to a politics, then it is not in Arendt's words a real connection, but rather of the sum of different forms of loneliness.
8   Ibid., 7. Arendt believes that isolation is risky, as it might lead to Totalitarianisms. In this respect, also playfulness as exit strategy is to her not so innocent as it might seem.
9   Ibid., 12.

where misinformation perpetuated by the president of the United States sows doubt on science and common sense.

While popular writers have compelled us to think about games and play as a way of "repairing the world,"[10] dark times for Arendt are manifested by our growing complacency with play, our comfy couch in the well-equipped cloud-cuckoo land. Strategies like gamification or funification only reinforce this retreat, by encouraging the binary between labor and play and the disconnection of action and politics.

But while not explicit, Arendt does leave room for a politics of recuperative playfulness,[11] where playing connects us to the world through action, where it generates discourse not about one's individual sense of fun but about the "public," or the structures that comprise the space in-between individuals. This happens not through common joy, but through what play theorist Miguel Sicart would call common pleasure. "The pleasures [play] creates are not always submissive to enjoyment, happiness, or positive traits," he says. "Play can be pleasurable when it hurts, offends, challenge and teases us, and even when we are not playing. Let's not talk about play as fun but as pleasurable, opening us to immense variations of pleasure in this world."[12] Aligned with Arendt's action, this common pleasure can result in new beginnings and new forms of creativity, forcing a turn to the world and not an escape from it.

Importantly, play does not emerge from pure freedom. Play is the result of particular systems designed with the appropriate structure and room to cultivate it. Game scholar Ian Bogost explains that to play is "to take something—anything—on its own terms, to treat it as if its existence were reasonable. The power of games lies not in their capacity to deliver rewards or enjoyment, but in the structured constraint of their design, which opens abundant possible spaces for play."[13]

10   Jane McGonigal, *Superbetter: The Power of Living Gamefully* (New York: Penguin, 2016).

11   Recuperating a sense of playfulness, as belonging to a more harmonious understanding of the human condition, where work and labor are (re) connected to action.

12   Miguel Sicart, *Play Matters* (Cambridge, MA: MIT Press, 2014), 3.

13   Ian Bogost, *Play Anything: The Pleasure of Limits, the Uses of Boredom, & the Secret of Games* (New York: Basic Books, 2016), x.

While Arendt was not concerned with games, she was concerned with the structures that enable the taking of action, and she understood that new beginnings needed to emerge from social structures (and were themselves needed to reempower the political).

As a means of reclaiming the *vita activa* and its relation to the world, play needs to be reimagined as a part of action taking, removed from its function as a mere retreat from the world, and brought into the process of making the world. It is here that aspects of Arendt's Jewishness may be present. Jewish prayer is guided by two opposing principles of Keva and Kevanah. Keva are the laws (how to pray, when to pray); and Kevanah is the exuberance, the expression, the play. Prayer is not one or the other, it is in perpetual tension between these poles. While Arendt is not interested in connecting to God, she is interested in connecting to the world, in some sense, an equally ineffable concept that requires the careful interplay of human principles.

The answer is not to reject play as a harmful retreat from reality, but reimagine play as a generator of discourse, as situated in the balance between labor and work and action, such that the work of play is not the creation of a cloud-cuckoo land, but the perpetual revealing of the world to the player. While I continue to be told by advertisers that enjoyment comes from escaping the shackles of my work and home life by retreating into a fantasy, Arendt's suggestive treatment of play leads me to attend to the lag in the systems I occupy wherein possibilities abound for new beginnings in our shared world.

Eric Gordon

See also
ACTIVISM, ALIENATION, SOLITUDE,
TECHNOLOGY, *VITA CONTEMPLATIVA*

PLURALITY

The question which seems to me to appear for the first time in the texts by Kant … is the question of the present, of present reality. It is the question: What is happening today? What is happening now? What is this "now" in which we all live and which is the site, the point [from which] I am writing?

Michel Foucault, *The Government of Self and Others*[1]

Thematized powerfully by Hannah Arendt, thoughts on plurality became particularly salient after the horrors of the Second World War and the holocaust. It seems unsurprising, then, that Arendt, who herself escaped death in a concentration camp, wrote in the 1950s that plurality is "specifically the condition—not only the *conditio sine qua non*, but the *conditio per quam*—of *all political life*."[2] Plurality, in other words, creates the condition of possibility for any political act "because we are all the same, that is, human, in such a way that *nobody is ever the same* as anyone else who ever lived, lives, or will live."[3] Plurality, in this sense, is not only the *result* of political systems but indeed *causative* of political life as such.[4] But plurality as central political theme was not only taken up in the world of political theory and philosophy. Pluralistic politics also came to figure into the thought of a perhaps surprising group of practitioners. Although at Arendt's time much of the debate was dominated by technocratic optimism, in the United States, planning theorists asked how one could possibly govern a pluralistic society. In these practical questions, plurality does not just speak to a kind of fundamental irreducibility of one person to another or to an abstract ethnic,

1 Michel Foucault, *The Government of Self and Others: Lectures at the Collège de France 1982–1983* (New York: Picador, 2010), 11.
2 Hannah Arendt, *The Human Condition* (Chicago, IL: University of Chicago Press, [1958] 1998), 7 (emphasis added).
3 Arendt, *The Human Condition*, 8 (emphasis added).
4 Certainly, Arendt is not alone in diagnosing plurality as *the* political condition. Thinkers like John Rawls, Robert A. Dahl, William Connolly,

political, or religious unity, as Arendt had in mind.[5] It also points
toward plurality of governing technique, of administrative
spheres, and of the many different forms of associating together.

One could understand this approach to theorizing plurality
as a way to make sense of a world that seemed to get more
complex, more connected, and more technologized, and one
in which traditional expertise no longer appeared entirely
appropriate to solving these complex and interdependent
issues. For these planners, plurality served as a lens through
which these interdependencies and the limit of expertise
became visible.[6] Plurality also indicates the abandonment
of a homogeneous *Volkswillen* which through its unified
action legitimates a political regime and its leader. Arendt's
formulation of plurality signals an attempt at coming to grips
with both this particular for her not very distant past and a
present that remained threatened by the continuing lure of
such homogenous will of the people.[7] But if the people are
notoriously and irremediably divided, in the sense that publics

or Bonnie Honig, and many others besides them, have theorized plurality
and its implications for politics. Whereas some have taken it to mean
a diversity of interest and interest groups in modern mass society,
others construe it as the diversity of identities and ideas in multicultural
societies. As a result, the conceptions about pluralism as an appropriate
political model for complex industrial and globalized world are similarly
stratified. In modern liberal thought, like that of Dahl or Rawls, plurality
of interests required rethinking political representation and governing
institutions. Postmodern conceptions, as those of Honig, by contrast,
object that such political bodies can never fully grasp identities which
themselves are contingent upon constant exposure to and performance in
a world external to the individual and thus cannot have fixed representable
interests. This leads proponents of such theories of plurality to propose
resistance and dissensus instead of more institutionalist forms.

5   On this, see Thorsten Bonacker, "Die politische Theorie des freiheitlichen
    Republikanismus: Hannah Arendt," in André Brodocz and Gary S. Schaal
    (eds.), *Politische Theorien der Gegenwart* (Opladen: Verlag Barbara
    Budrich, 2016), 185.

6   Michel Foucault has powerfully argued that this was particularly evident in
    Kant's text "*Was ist Aufklärung*" and that precisely this kind of reflexive
    question marks the practice of critique in modernity. Michel Foucault,
    "What Is Critique," in Sylvère Lotringer (ed.), *The Politics of Truth* (South
    Pasadena: Semiotext(e), 2007), 41–81.

7   It is unsurprising that the radical democratic theorist Sheldon Wolin faults
    Arendt for exhibiting antidemocratic tendencies. Democracy as a unified
    Rousseauian will of all hardly seems appealing in a time so close to the

and political goals are always multiple, then how does one make legitimate politically binding decisions for all?[8] This was a problem also for planning theorists.

Perhaps one of the most eloquent and forceful arguments on decision-making in pluralistic societies has been advanced by Horst Rittel in his (now seminal) concept of wicked problems.[9] This text, coauthored with the urban planner Melvin Webber, still today offers a sense of how some planners took up the problem of plurality.[10] Raising plurality as *the political problem*, Rittel and Webber asked,

> In a setting in which a plurality of publics is politically pursuing a diversity of goals, how is the larger society to deal with its wicked problems in a planful way?[11]

Plurality makes acting in concert difficult at best, and it makes planning ahead for a pluralistic society a thing of impossibility, not to mention predicting how changes to the

horrors of Hitler's Germany. Sheldon Wolin, "Hannah Arendt: Democracy and The Political," *Salmagundi* no. 60 (1983): 3–19.

8 For Arendt, this question is not very central, although it might be reflected in her preference for republicanism. Not in the sense of the U.S. major party but the political theory of a mixed regime.

9 During the 1960s, the German systems scientist Horst Rittel developed the idea of wickedness of public problems, the intractability of which he described through a set of characteristics that made such problems inaccessible to conventional rational planning approaches of the time. Such "wicked problems" had no definitive formulation, no stopping rule, and their elements were not enumerable or exhaustively describable. As a result, attempts to solve them could never be right or wrong but could only be more or less adequate. Because every such problem was essentially unique and could be a symptom of another problem, any attempt to explain the problem would inevitably both determine and limit possible resolutions. Rittel contended in a seminal paper that any such wicked problem, and the idea of planning that engaged them, would by its very nature be political (Rittel and Webber 1973).

10 This text became seminal in design. See here for instance Richard Buchanan, "Wicked Problems in Design Thinking," *Design Issues* vol. 8, no. 2 (Spring 1992): 5–21; Richard Coyne and Adrian Snodgrass, "Problem Setting within Prevalent Metaphors of Design," *Design Issues* vol. 11, no. 2 (Summer 1995): 31–61; Christian Bason, *Leading Public Design: Discovering Human-Centred Governance* (Bristol: Policy Press, 2017), among others.

11 Horst W. J. Rittel and Melvin M. Webber, "Dilemmas in a General Theory of Planning," *Policy Sciences* vol. 4, no. 2 (June 1973): 168.

built environment, to products, and services will affect diverse interests and identities. And yet, once we accept plurality as an empirical fact and unless we impose a singular vision creating "One Man of gigantic dimensions,"[12] we may have few alternatives. But Rittel was skeptical of the actual realizability and stability of this Hobbesian vision of the state. "In the pluralistic social structure of modern societies," he wrote, "there is no concentrated omnipotency."[13] In contrast to Arendt, plurality for Rittel was not an ontological reality but an empirical observation limiting the knowledge of what can be predictably planned. Plurality makes a singular social and political telos impossible.

This absence of a unifying goal was just as important to Rittel as it was to Arendt. Her conception of plurality as an account of the shared world of humans is mirrored by her view of a multiplicitous inner self. This condition of nonunity precludes any complete knowledge of the world, our time, or even ourselves. There cannot be any singular answer to how we want to live because there is no singular "we."

> Man cannot rely upon himself partly because he cannot be self-knowing. Introduced as an epistemological claim, Arendt's belief that self-knowledge is unattainable has normative implications. Theories of action that postulate an agent in charge of itself … undermine the contingency of the human world by seeing in their "coherent" self a source of stability.[14]

Like Arendt's limit to knowledge of the world and oneself posits plurality as the condition that must be protected against encroachments on human rights and threats to our inherent

12 Hannah Arendt, *The Origins of Totalitarianism* (New York: Harcourt, [1951] 1968), 465.

13 Originally published in German in 1963. This translation is from Horst W. J. Rittel, "Reflections on the Scientific and Political Significance of Decision Theory," in Protzen and Harris (eds.), *The Universe of Design: Horst Rittel's Theories of Design and Planning* (London: Routledge, 2010), 38.

14 Bonnie Honig, "Arendt, Identity, and Difference," *Political Theory* vol. 16, no. 1 (February 1988), 85.

ability to act otherwise, think up, and realize different ways of life, Rittel's sense of plurality was laced with similar limits to knowledge. "In matters of the polis," Rittel insisted, "the *symmetry of ignorance* reigns: I don't know what is best for you or for all of us, but you do not know either."[15] For Rittel, of course, this limitation was one of practice, of participation in decision-making, and it pointed to the actual structures and practices necessary to make political decisions. In other words, it was a challenge to the conventional idea of governing. While arising out of different concerns, plurality, for both Rittel and Arendt, has the implication that the practice of politics—the attempt to bring about desirable futures—will necessarily be polyphonic and multivocal.

Wicked problems, today, is taken up widely in design circles—perhaps surprisingly so. And yet, the resonance of the concept to the problems of our time is inescapable. Even questions as (deceptively) simple as how we should build, what garments we should make, or which new cell phone is best cannot possibly yield a cohesive answer.[16] Certainly, the so-called man-made world evidences its own condition of plurality. Indeed, many theorists, especially new materialists and feminist thinkers, would object to drawing a sharp a priori distinction between the natural and artificial worlds.[17] Even outside of the social sciences it has become commonplace to think about the coconstitution of the material, technological,

15 Horst Rittel, "Technological Change and Urban Structure," in *The Universe* 213 (emphasis added).

16 The importance of our material worlds as part of the considerations of plurality and the questions that arise in response to it has been central to debates among architects, designers, and engineers from the mid-1950s onward, yet often without having any clear political language to go along with it.

17 See for instance Karen Barad, "Posthumanist Performativity: Toward an Understanding of How Matter Comes to Matter," *Signs* vol. 28, no. 3 (Spring 2003), 801–31; Jane Bennett, *Vibrant Matter: A Political Ecology of Things* (Durham: Duke University Press, 2010); Donna Haraway, "Situated Knowledges: The Science Question in Feminism and the

and the social.[18] In other words, we do not simply build the material world, it shapes us, too, sometimes in ways with which we are not comfortable. Our world is pluralistic not only when it comes to humans and their desires but also in the different conceptions of what constitutes social relationships (among humans and between humans and nonhumans). Plurality as a political condition may require letting go of some control, but in a political climate as divided as that in which we find ourselves today, it sometimes appears to be an enabler of discrimination and fear.[19]

But plurality as lens through which we may see our world differently also offers opportunities. If we are inescapably caught in a "symmetry of ignorance," as Rittel wrote, then our world must be partial, incomplete, and perpetually provisional insights, always in need of other perspectives that may or may not contradict our own.[20] This means that in building a future world we will have to learn to be comfortable with contradiction and paradox. The ensuing epistemological challenge to finding the *summum bonum*, the collective good, or perhaps the lack thereof—the realization that there is not one single answer or even one single form of expertise, one single practice, scientific or otherwise, that can tell us what to do, where to go or what to build—requires a sense of humility

Privilege of Partial Perspective," *Feminist Studies* vol. 14, no. 3 (Autumn 1988): 575–99.

18 See for instance Bruno Latour, "Where Are the Missing Masses? The Sociology of a Few Mundane Artifacts," in Wiebe E. Bijker and John Law (eds.), *Shaping Technology/Building Society: Studies in Sociotechnical Change* (Cambridge, MA: MIT Press, 1992), 225–58; Michel Callon, "Society in the Making: The Study of Technology as a Tool for Sociological Analysis," in Wiebe E Bijker, Thomas P. Hughes, and Trevor Pinch (eds.), *The Social Construction of Technological Systems New Directions in the Sociology and History of Technology* (Cambridge, MA: MIT Press, 1989), 83–10.

19 This is particularly evident in recent studies of media plurality and the apparent impossibility to properly control "fake news."

20 See here Donna Haraway's seminal text, "Situated Knowledges: The Science Question in Feminism and the Privilege of Partial Perspective," *Feminist Studies* vol. 14, no. 3 (Autumn 1988): 575–99.

of all those working on behalf of a community, be they activists, experts, or designers.[21]

Anke Gruendel

See also
CITIZENSHIP, COMMON GOOD, PUBLIC, SPEECH

---

21   Bruno Latour also makes this argument about design in "A Cautious Prometheus? A Few Steps Toward a Philosophy of Design with Special Attention to Peter Sloterdijk," in Willem Schinkel and Liesbeth Noordegraaf-Eelens (eds.), *In Medias Res: Peter Sloterdijk's Spherological Poetics of Being* (Amsterdam: Amsterdam University Press, 2011), 151–64.

POWER

It has been argued that "knowledge is power." This short essay in two parts will review looking at ideas about power through the lens of Hannah Arendt, we hope to offer some thoughts about how *actions* and *words* inform the way power manifests. In particular, about the way that power in reproducing knowledge can be aided by design that shapes intentions in action, choosing either to assist democracy or to erode it.

In her book *The Human Condition* Arendt suggests that power is temporary, existing only in action and speech between people in proximity. She calls this human configuration the *space of appearance*, the space within which politics, and hence power, is enacted. For Arendt, power corresponds to the human ability not just to act but to act in concert. Power is never the property of an individual; it belongs to a group and remains in existence only so long as the group keeps together. Therefore participation is a prerequisite for power:

> whoever, for whatever reasons, isolates himself and does not partake in such being together, forfeits power and becomes impotent.[1]

Power, dependent as it is on the togetherness of people, is bounded by the plurality of human beings with all their subjectivities, knowledge, and interests and also the potential for contestation. Power is ultimately bounded by agonism, a process of argument and contestation. Agonism denies omnipotence.

So, the *space of appearance* is an "agonistic space."[2] Agonism serves not to dissipate power but to distribute it. In this way, the power that Arendt defines is what Mary Parker Follet earlier described as *power-with people* (rather than power-over people). According to Parker Follet,

1 Hannah Arendt, *The Human Condition* (Chicago, IL: University of Chicago Press, [1958] 1998), 201.
2 Chantal Mouffe, "Art and Democracy," *Open: Art as a Public Issue* no. 14 (2008): 6–15.

Genuine power can only be grown, it will slip from every arbitrary hand that grasps it; for genuine power is not coercive control, but coactive control. Coercive power is the curse of the universe; coactive power, the enrichment and advancement of every human soul.[3]

For Arendt there is only coactive power, realized through the speech and action of people in proximity. The power Arendt describes is both process (power) and product (action and speech), "the product is identical with the performing act itself."

Conversely, coercive power, power-over people, which manifests politically in the subjugation of the complexity of a *political issue or problem* and the ignorance of the diversity of peoples' perspectives and denial of their articulation and argument (whether in pursuit of a "solution" or out of ideological simplification), is not power but violence. This is important because violence, Arendt writes, will ultimately destroy power:

"In a head-on clash between violence and power, the outcome is hardly in doubt." She adds, "Nowhere is the self-defeating factor in the victory of violence over power more evident than in the use of terror to maintain domination, about whose weird successes and eventual failures we know perhaps more than any generation before us."[4]

The true performance of power—agonistic debate in pursuit of resolution—according to Arendt, is literally an "end in itself." The process matters as much as the result. She suggests "in these instances of action and speech the end (*telos*) is not pursued but lies in the activity itself which therefore becomes an *entelecheia*, and the work is not what follows and extinguishes the process but is imbedded in it; the performance is the work, is *energia*." According to Rittel and Webber "societal problems

---

3   Mary Parker Follet, *Creative Experience* (New York: Longmans, Green, 1924), xiii.

4   Hannah Arendt, *On Violence* (San Diego: Harcourt, Brace, Jovanovich, 1970).

are never solved only re-solved—over and over again."[5]
According to Arendt, "Power is what keeps the public realm,
the potential *space of appearance* between acting and speaking
men, in existence." In this way power is a necessary response to
wickedness.

Totalitarianism and tyranny close the debate, eradicate the
space of appearance, and, we would argue, foreclose on wicked
problems. In presenting wicked problems as tame problems,
by eradicating the dissenting voices and arguments that define
agonistic discourse, the protagonist moves from a state of power
to one of violence.

Rittel and Webber recognize the abhorrence of this scenario.
They argue that it

> becomes morally objectionable for the planner [politician/
> tyrant] to treat a wicked problem—a problem with no clear
> definition and no clear resolution—as though it were a
> "tame" one, or to tame a wicked problem prematurely, or
> to refuse to recognise the inherent wickedness of social
> problems.[6]

The switch from power to violence aims to subjugate
dissenting voices so as to "tame" wicked problems. Power
becomes violence as the protagonist forgoes legitimate resolution
in an attempt to force a solution by subjugating human plurality.
In doing so the tyrant protagonist reaches for omnipotence
through eradication of agonism—substituting power for
violence in the process of destroying the space of appearance
and disabling participation of the dissenting voices. Across the
twentieth century, the rise of media enabled power-by-terror
to be also conducted through the apparatus of the "culture
industry." Propaganda became one of the clearest tools of
power-as-violence.

In our times, fake news is the new propaganda. It seeks
to deny the citizen the information necessary for participation
in debate and in so doing is an act of violence. It consists of

5 Horst W. J. Rittel and Melvin M. Webber "Dilemmas in a General Theory of
   Planning," *Policy Sciences* vol. 4, no. 2 (1973): 155.
6 Ibid.

deliberate misinformation (differing from satire or parody) in its intention to mislead. It also constitutes a form of violence that is damaging to belief in truth or the ability to trust and therefore undermining democracy. Fake news destroys the space of appearance by intentionally seeking to fabricate information and mislead audiences. In the case of the 2016 U.S. election, Buzzfeed, for example, found that the top twenty fake news stories leading up to the election received more engagement on Facebook than actual news.[7] While it is impossible to categorically point to the outcomes of such developments, their threat to democracy is being taken seriously and addressed in different countries in different ways. In 2017 in the UK, MPs concerned about the way voters were targeted over Brexit launched their own inquiry/responses into fake news.[8] Taiwan went further and announced media literacy education courses to help raise awareness.[9] Across the world different countries are investigating the best way to implement algorithmic changes that could prevent the spread of fake news without encroaching on democracy.

Ultimately, ethical and responsive design has a role to play in either perpetuating and/or preventing fake news. There is an opportunity to be seized for designers and technologists to be a force for change. Human-centered service design could shape the future, by providing the design of truth checking system for information to reach the audience, allowing them, through user-centered design, to clearly understand the source of the content and decide whether or not to trust what they read and watch. Design has a role to *play* in facilitating this and in

---

7   Juju Chang, Jake Lefferman, Claire Pedersen, and Geoff Martz, "When Fake News Stories Make Real News Headlines," *ABC News*, November 29, 2016, https://abcnews.go.com/Technology/fake-news-stories-make-real-news-headlines/story?id=43845383.

8   Mike Wendling, "Solutions That Can Stop Fake News Spreading," *BBC News*, January 30, 2017, https://www.bbc.co.uk/news/blogs-trending-38769996.

9   Nicola Smith, "Schoolkids in Taiwan Will Now Be Taught How to Identify Fake News," *Time*, April 7, 2017, http://time.com/4730440/taiwan-fake-news-education/.

enhancing the agonostic qualities of the space of appearance where all words and actions can have free reign without subjugation to violence. These tenets are particularly realized in the practice of participatory design. Participatory design is "a political process, giving priority to human action and people's rights to participate in the shaping of the worlds in which they act."[10] It is democratic and emancipatory; with a commitment to ensuring everyone's voice is heard in the decision-making processes that will affect them. Robertson and Simonsen describe "genuine participation" as the change in the users' role from being informants in the design process to being "legitimate and acknowledged participants" in it.[11] From news algorithms to the staging and scripts of human encounter, design, and participatory design in particular, has something to contribute to the preservation of the space of appearance and the *power* of participatory democracy.

Designers often eschew power and are unsure how to deal with it; never knowing whether to oppose it or kowtow before it. Not only practice but theories and models of participatory design are often evidence of this. But Arendt is emphatic that we need power—*in order to counter and balance violence.* As we go forward this might be a very important lesson for design. Or as Arendt puts it in *The Human Condition,*

> Power preserves the public realm and the space of appearance, and as such it is also the lifeblood of the human artifice, which, unless it is the scene of action and speech, of the web of human affairs and relationships and the stories engendered by them, lacks its ultimate raison d'etre. Without being talked about by men and without housing them, the world would not be a human artifice but a heap of unrelated things to which each isolated individual was at liberty to add one more object; without the human artifice to house them, human affairs would be ... floating, ... futile

10 Jesper Simonsen and Toni Robertson, eds., *Routledge International Handbook of Participatory Design* (New York: Routledge, 2013), 4.
11 Ibid.

and vain. …. And without power, the space of appearance
brought forth through action and speech in public will fade
away [and with it] trust in the world as a place fit for human
appearance.[12]

Adam Thorpe and Lorraine Gamman

See also
ACTIVISM, ALIENATION, CITIZENSHIP, EVIL

12   Arendt, *The Human Condition*, 204, adapted quotation. It comes from
     Arendt's discussion of "Power and the Space of Appearance," §28, 199–207.

PRIVATE REALM

Private {pri·vate / ˈprī-vət /}

a) Intended for or restricted to the use of a particular person, group, or class
b) Set apart, belonging to oneself (not to the state), peculiar, personal, used in contrast to "publicus" and "communis"

    I. In the ancient Greek tradition upon which Hannah Arendt builds, the public realm is for the few. Those who may enter it are the heads of households. Their place in the public realm is made possible by the existence of the private realm.

    II. It is governed by speech and the discursive art of persuasion. Subjects of the public realm are orators, rational beings engaged in debate. But to be subjects in the public realm, they must first be sovereigns in their own private realms.

    III. The household is a site of autocratic rule, and its sovereign speaks the inchoate language of violence.

    IV. The private realm is, by its very nature, hidden. It is the household, the hearth, the family, the site of birth, of copulation, of eating, of defecation, of sleep, of death. It is "prepolitical" inasmuch as it ensures the survival of the species.

    V. The private, life-sustaining work of "housekeeping" became a public interest with the rise of the social realm, a middle space that blurred the lines between public and private and in so doing eroded both realms. The disappearance of the private realm, Arendt tells us, presents a threat to humanity. The public realm—a high idea—depends upon the private for its existence.

    VI. What kind of politics begins here?

Private {pri·vate / ˈprī-vət /}

a) Past participle of privare "to separate, deprive,"
   from privus

   I.   The word "private," Arendt tells us, shares DNA
        with deprivation. "In ancient feeling the privative
        trait of privacy, indicated in the word itself, was all
        important; it meant literally a state of being deprived
        of something."[1]
   II. Deprivation from what, and for whom?
   III. Deprivation: not seeing and hearing others, not being
        seen and heard by others.
   IV. Those consigned to the private realm, who cannot
        enter the public realm, have no privacy themselves;
        they live in someone else's private realm. As such,
        they are deprived of speech, of freedom, of their
        humanity, of the protection of the law.

Private {pri·vate / ˈprī-vət /}

a) Privare: to separate or deprive, and the proto-Italic *prei—
   in, meaning "in front" or "before"
b) Not invested with or engaged in public office or
   employment; as, a private citizen; private life

   I.   The private realm is by its very nature set apart,
        spatially delineated. Arendt tells us that in its ancient
        Greek form the law (Nomos / νόμος) was "quite
        literally a wall, without which there might have been
        an agglomeration of houses, a town (asty) but not a
        city, a political community."[2]
   II. The law is a wall: a shelter, a prison, a detention
        center, a port of entry, a foster home, a perimeter, a
        gate, a door that we close so as not to see ordinary
        violence.

---

1   Hannah Arendt, *The Human Condition* (Chicago, IL: University of
     Chicago Press, [1958] 1998), 38.
2   Arendt, *The Human Condition*, 6.

III. Life behind walls, within the private realm, is sometimes a bare life; the household, the place where the ancient Greeks kept slaves, was a strange instantiation of Agamben's "camp," a state of exception contained within the rule. "Law constitutes community through its destitution."[3]

IV. The walls of the home separate "political beings" from "bodies."

V. Floor plans are political precisely because they construct a space beyond political being.

VI. While we abhor violence in the public realm, we tolerate it in private. It is not the existence of regimes of violence (gendered, racialized) that offends us, but their visibility, their entry into the public realm.

VII. The wall constructs some bodies as private property, as not political beings.

Private {pri·vate / ˈprī-vət /}

a) Not expressed, withheld

b) Sequestered from company or observation; appropriated to an individual; secret; secluded; lonely; solitary; as, a private room or apartment; private prayer

I. Pain, Arendt notes, is private. It seizes us and holds us within our bodies.

II. This is also a kind of strength; to hold ourselves, fully embodied, when our skin becomes a wall.

III. We attend to sexual violence in public places, to the violations and deaths that happen in open spaces and to public figures. This violence, which turns people into things, is something we don't want to see (if seeing is a demand, a call to action).

IV. The private realm might be understood as a shelter from the public realm, but it also shelters the public realm from the specter of private violence.

---

3 Roberto Esposito, *Immunitas: The Protection and Negation of Life* (Cambridge, MA: Polity Press, 2011), 22.

Private {pri·vate / ˈprī-vət /}

a) Belonging to or concerning an individual person, company or interest
b) A person of low rank in any of various organizations

I.   The public realm should not be a place that protects the interests of property owners. It should not be privatized, yet entrance into the public realm was, in the ancient Greek model where this meditation begins, contingent upon owning property. Indeed, the majority of those occupying the private realm were not citizens. They were property.

II.   While the "other" has long been established at the limit of the human, constructed as outside the wall of the law, those consigned to the private realm were not yet even others.

III. They became "others" when they laid claim to the public realm, to the right to appear, to become visible and audible.

IV.   The exemplary public realm was paid for by those consigned to the private realm. It was built upon the backs of an underclass whose role it was to sustain life itself. Freedom, the freedom of the public realm, is parasitic; it is defined by, and rests upon, unfreedom.

V.   We live the kind of politics that began here.[4]

Macushla Robinson

See also
ALIENATION, CITIZENSHIP, LABOR, SPONTANEITY

---

4   All definitions adapted from https://www.merriam-webster.com/ and https://www.etymonline.com/.

PUBLIC

The public and publics have been a topic within design for some time now. Most of the discussion of these concepts stems from the work of John Dewey[1] often through an interpretation by Bruno Latour,[2] and more recently and with more direct connection to design, through the work of scholars such as Noortje Marres[3] or Christopher Le Dantec.[4] From these perspectives the public is a form of organization, a term that labels those that are brought together by an issue, gathered around or through or by way of a matter of concern. Hannah Arendt offers us another perspective on the public that warrants attention.[5] For Arendt there are two aspects of the public. The first is that the public is that which can be "seen and heard" by everybody.[6] The second is that "the term 'public' signifies the world itself, in so far as it is common to all of us."[7] The public, for Arendt, is not specific to or oriented by problems, but rather is a designation of the communal. Design plays an important role in Arendt's conceptualization of the public, as our togetherness is ordered by "the human artefact" or what we might more broadly refer to as the artificial.[8,9] As Arendt states,

1   John Dewey, *The Public and Its Problems* (New York: Henry Holt, 1937).
2   Bruno Latour, "From Realpolitik to Dingpolitik," in Latour and Weibel (eds.), *Making Things Public: Atmospheres of Democracy* (Cambridge, MA: MIT Press, 2005), 14–44.
3   Noortje Marres, *Material Participation: Technology, the Environment and Everyday Publics* (New York: Springer, 2016).
4   Christopher Le Dantec, *Designing Publics* (Cambridge, MA: MIT Press, 2016).
5   Hannah Arendt, *The Human Condition* (Chicago, IL: University of Chicago Press, [1958] 1998).
6   Arendt, *The Human Condition*, 50.
7   Ibid., 52.
8   Herbert Simon, *The Sciences of the Artificial* (Cambridge, MA: MIT Press, 1996).
9   Tony Fry, Clive Dilnot, and Susan Stewart, *Design and the Question of History* (London: Bloomsbury, 2015).

> To live together in the world means essentially that a world of things is between those who have it in common, as a table is located between those who sit around it.[10]

This table is not just a matter of convenience, it is a presence that is constitutive; remove the table and the relations of those who sit around it are redefined, perhaps those relations even collapse.

> What are we to make of this? Or, rather, what are we to make with this?

One response is to employ design toward making things seen and heard. This is a familiar response, and one I have come to find concerning. The critical impulse has long been to reveal that which is hidden. Certainly, there can be a kind of pleasure in this—like the experience of wonder—as we discover and put onto display the workings of the state or the market and uncover relations between factors and actors in various configurations of influence that might have gone unknown. We can witness a designerly version of this impulse in the contemporary fascination with visualization. But revealing alone is not enough because there is no assuredness that transformation will follow. Awareness and transparency do not beget change. Making things seen and heard may be necessary, but it is not sufficient.

For Arendt, the private is in contrast to the public. The private is that which cannot be seen and heard by all, that which cannot be held in common. Ironically, as we make things public in contemporary media we are also making them private, providing use and value that are separated, sequestered, and hidden as affect and action become data. Privatization is not limited to the transfer of education and care to mercantile entities, it is the systematic transformation of all that we held in common into individuated resources. The privatization of the contemporary world is not happening by accident, it is happening by design. The question is, What would it mean to instead design for the public by designing counter to privatization? Here the themes and practices of the commons and commoning become

---

10   Arendt, *The Human Condition*, 52.

important to design.[11] But in addition to designing *for* the commons, one must also explicitly design *against* privatization, lest the commons become a seductive label for a mode of the private, a kind of curated or artisanal privatization such as we sometimes experience in the so-called sharing economy.

We might also take inspiration from Arendt's example of the table as an artefact that orders us together and consider what other things we might conceptualize and make that would order us together, differently. The table is a convenient example to point to as an object of design, but these considerations should include all manner of made things: communications, events, environments, systems, and so on. Designed things then serve to both mediate and bind us together, the products and services of design become those things that participate in sustaining the public by providing structures and experiences around and between and through which we relate. This endeavor of enabling and orienting should not be limited to the formal outcomes of design, it should also include the processes and practices of designing. That is, the very procedures, methods, techniques, habits, and customs of designing as a form of action (and not only as modes of work or labor) should be both public in and of themselves, and at the same time, contributing to sustaining the public.

I want to return to a difference between Dewey and Arendt, because in this difference there is an important charge for design—a responsibility for enabling persistence. For Dewey, publics exist in relation to problems; publics form and unform as problems are articulated and resolved. But following from Arendt, publics form and unform, at least in part, as the artefacts that order them come into being and use, or disappear. In addition to being a means to gather and stage the public, the stuff of design also enables the endurance of the public. It provides

11   Fabio Franz and Bianca Elzenbaumer, "Commons & Community Economies: Entry Points to Design for Eco-Social Justice?" in Proceedings of the Design Research Society 2016 conference Brighton, England, June 27–30, 2016. Published by the Design Research Society. Anna Seravalli, "Making Commons: Attempts at Composing Prospects in the Opening of Production" (PhD diss., Malmö University, 2014).

a continuity of relations, and while these relations can and do change, there remains a means of ongoing orientation. The work of design in regard to the public might be taken to be the work of crafting objects, communications, events, environments, and systems that provide capacities for both duration and durability—capacities that make it possible for the public to carry on. One of the problems of the public, then, is the problem of persistence. How, precisely, endurance manifests in the stuff of design or through the processes and practices of designing is a question for further inquiry and experimentation. Especially in dark times we should ask, In what ways can design enable the public to persist?

Carl DiSalvo

See also
DEMOCRACY, EVIL, IN-BETWEEN, LAW

REIFICATION

REIFICATION

Viewed, however, in their worldliness, action, speech, and thought have much more in common than any one of them has with work or labor. They themselves do not "produce," bring forth anything, they are as futile as life itself. In order to become worldly things, that is, deeds and facts and events and patterns of thoughts or ideas, they must first be seen, heard, and remembered and then transformed, reified as it were, into things ... The whole factual world of human affairs depends for its reality and its continued existence ... on the transformation of the intangible into the tangibility of things. Without remembrance and without the reification which remembrance needs for its own fulfillment ... the living activities of action, speech, and thought would lose their reality at the end of each process and disappear as though they never had been.

Hannah Arendt, *The Human Condition*[1]

Hannah Arendt is the philosopher of not only natalities and new births but also of the lineages of those births and beginnings. She joins the ranks of philosophers of technology through her observation of the entirely thingly nature of reification, but, I would argue, she can also be read as a philosopher of culture, in the sense that she observes the role that things play in the establishment of *genealogies of thought and experience as the basis for the continued life of a community*. For Arendt's observation that thought and action can only "remain" in the world if reified or materialized into artefacts and systems leads us to the conclusion that reification is a *necessary condition of possibility* for society and culture in general.

Anticipating the observations of the later philosopher Bernard Stiegler, in relating this to the condition of life itself,

1   Hannah Arendt, *The Human Condition* (Chicago, IL: University of Chicago Press, [1958] 1998), 95.

Arendt reveals artefactual reification as being necessarily *negentropic*, in other words, *life* constantly defers entropic change in favor of stability and continuity by writing itself into things that do not change over time.[2] Thus, the redemption of labor lies in its ability to constantly create a new *worlds* out of "the world"—the very worlds that human beings inhabit and within which continued labor, work, and action can unfold.

There is a second aspect, less well examined, to reification, for if the plurality of human action materialized through labor finds its expression in the collective worlds that humans build for themselves, then reification is a process of not only ensuring the continuity of social, political, and cultural processes but also in ensuring *the continuity of genealogies of artefactuality itself.* Technologies do not emerge ex nihilo bereft of any historicity, but are themselves the products of long lineages of thinking in particular cosmological contexts.[3] In other words, we posit that technologies reproduce their own specificities of form and function within the bounded horizons of the worlds that they are developed in. They are also informed by genealogies of thought reproduced within civilizational unities—specific worldviews, dispositifs and *cultures*, ways of interpreting, thinking, and doing. These realities held in common help reproduce specific technologies and technological systems and environments. This continuity in invention is what ensures that technical systems, much like natural systems, also evolve, retaining and discarding characteristics over time. And this second point, largely overlooked in Arendt's move-making through *The Human Condition*, is what I find to be of most interest: her tracing of a genealogy of thought in the West is also a tracing of the genealogy

2   For Stiegler, the first form of deferral happens through the inscription of biologic information into genetic code; the second, through the nervous system and its ability to retain memories; and the third, and most pertinent to us, in the form of memory externalized, through technical systems *that are also* social, cultural, political, and economic systems.

3   As Arendt's contemporary Gilbert Simondon explicated so well, specific technologies are themselves the products of "*a technical lineage (which) is the stability of an underlying system of invention that is at once concrete and controlling.*" Gilbert Simondon, *On the Mode of Existence of Technical Objects*, trans. Ninian Mellamphy, unpublished (London: University of Western Ontario, 1958), 40.

of technics that results in technological labor winning out over deliberative action.

Echoing Heidegger,[4] Arendt was concerned about the production and continued perpetuation of a culture where violence was normalized and sewn not only into the very fabric of the artificial, necessitating the rape of nature and exploitation of human labor: *"This element of violation and violence is present in all fabrication, and homo faber, the creator of the human artifice, has always been a destroyer of nature."* However, Arendt was also increasingly concerned with how, in the modern era, violence was rapidly becoming the condition for action in the realm of the political, precisely the domain where it was supposed to be deferred in favor of deliberation and negotiation.[5]

This, perhaps more so than any other aspect of reification, is illustrative of the nature of the political as embedded in thingliness today. Our modern, mechanistic technological platforms and ecosystems are both reflections and proliferators of an increasing tendency to reify fluid human values into algorithmic signifiers that gain a life of their own, independent of the organic dynamics of humans in continuously unfolding relations with each other and their environments. Indeed, culture itself is reified, both inasmuch as it finds itself expressed as monolithic and unchanging (think of "modern tourism," "ethnic food," "coffee culture," etc.), but also in the gradual sublimation of the fluidity of difference into identity politics, where fluid, hybrid pluralities of subjectivity are reduced to spectrums, as they then become far more calculable and subject to rational categorization. Think, for example, of conversations on social media organizing themselves around points on a scale between two binaries without bringing into question the

4   For Heidegger's thoughts on the direction of modern technological development, see his "The Question Concerning Technology," in William Lovitt (trans.), *The Question Concerning Technology and Other Essays* (New York: Garland, 1977), 3–35.

5   As she notes, "Only the modern age's conviction that man can know only what he makes, that his allegedly higher capacities depend upon making and that he therefore is primarily *homo faber* and not an *animal rationale*, brought forth the much older implications of violence inherent in all interpretations of the realm of human affairs as a sphere of making." Arendt, *The Human Condition*, 228.

binaries themselves. Think of how contemporary scholarship on decolonising ontologies and categories in (Eurocentric) knowledge has brought into question the binaries of man\woman, native\settler, citizen\immigrant etc. none of which accurately capture the complexity, fluidity, and contingency of 21st century identities.

But, if we go back to our reading of Arendt as a philosopher of genealogies, the possibility of salvation from a complete dissolution of the political, and therefore of the world of human action, also offers itself. If the specificities of our technologies and the specificities of the world that they are a part of are mutually constitutive, then this opens up the question of *what other technologies and technological ways of being could be disclosed through different, plural, "other" understandings of world, as a means to escape world-alienation.*

In other words, what I would argue for is that the planned proliferation and cultivation of subjectivities *other* than those shaped and molded by the mechanisms of the modern world-system is vital for the development of plural, parallel systems of technology. And, I would further argue here, Arendt gives us a hint, partly through her emphasis on contemplation and thought (the *vita contemplativa*) rather than on action as remedy,[6] and partly through her method of tracing, as we had mentioned at the beginning of this essay, a genealogy of thought down to its Greek foundations through the entirety of *The Human Condition*—one that involves a retracing of genealogies of thought other than those of the Christian West in order to imagine and speculate on the development of sociotechnical systems other than what we inhabit today.[7] Speculation is not only the domain of philosophers though—for such a speculative project could be firmly within the purview of those who call themselves designers

6   For "Thought, finally—which we, following the premodern as well as the modern tradition, omitted from our reconsideration of the vita activa—is still possible, and no doubt actual, wherever men live under the conditions of political freedom." Ibid., 329.

7   For a more detailed argument for decolonizing the philosophy of technology as a prerequisite for decolonizing design, see my essay "What Knowledge for Decolonising the Philosophy of Technology?" (David Blamey and Brad Haylock, Distributed, 2018), 186–97.

today, or rather, for those to whom design, its histories, and genealogies become the object of study. But such a project could only be undertaken by those with the capacity to translate and materialize into existence, i.e., to *reify*, the very speculations they derive from a study of genealogies of the artificial. And thus, what we really need right now is the constitution of a new form of design studies and design history that makes philosophical contemplation and speculation and decolonizing design discourse the foundation of its program.

Ahmed Ansari

See also
BOURGEOIS, INSTRUMENTALITY, OBJECTIVITY, SUPERFLUITY

SOLITUDE
SPEECH
SPONTANEITY
STORIES
SUPERFLUITY

SOLITUDE

The following is a correspondence between anthropologist Tim Ingold and artist Sophie Krier on the topic of solitude.

It all began with a lunchtime conversation in Paris on March 30, 2018. We were talking about what Hannah Arendt had to say about solitude, and about how we would respond to it …

Sophie

I really like the idea of coming up with an assignment. So not drawing a conclusion but something that could be the start of a research.

Tim

For somebody else to pick up!

Sophie

I do think we need spaces for solitude. The basket weaver is also solitary when she's weaving the basket. Because she's with the basket. We need solitary activities that are nourishing.

Tim

I always imagine that loneliness means a sense of disconnection. It's wanting to relate to the world around you but finding out that it's not working out for some reason.

Sophie

Whereas solitude can be very empowering. Being in silence together for instance can be solitary in a connected way.

Tim

But again I probably wouldn't use that word. If I'm going for a walk in the countryside or if I'm playing the cello on my own, I would say just that: I'm walking on my own.

Sophie

This is interesting. On my own could mean on your own terms.

Tim

It's something I would say without thinking, really. If someone asks
    me if I'm going for a walk by myself or if someone else is coming
    along, I'll just say I'm going on my own. It's a perfectly natural
    thing to say.

Sophie

So solitude is not part of your vocabulary.

Tim

No, because solitude might be something you deliberately seek: "I
    want to be on my own." But you can go for a walk on your own
    without seeking solitude. Quite the opposite, in fact.

Sophie

I'm interested not so much in speaking about solitude for this
    lexicon, as in engaging with solitude. That's why I'm interested
    in the assignment option.

Tim

How about you design an assignment. And send it to me. I could
    comment on it, add to it, modify it. Or it could be: if you were
    given this assignment, how would you begin to approach it?

Sophie

An assignment from me to you, and a response from you to me. It's a
    good question, what is a good assignment?

*So it was agreed. Sophie would send her assignment to
Tim, and on receiving it, Tim would write a personal response,
drawing on his experience of playing the cello, and also send
an assignment back to Sophie. But when Sophie read Tim's
assignment, she decided to pass it on to the reader of this
lexicon: namely, you. We hope that this assignment may enrich
your awareness of the company of others and your (possibly
uneasy) thoughts.*

*

Sophie's_Solitude_assignment_for_Tim.jpeg

Search for a space where your cello and you can play in solitude. Carry out the five instructions listed below as faithfully as possible. Take a one-minute pause in between. Chosen or found notes can be played as long as needed. Are we ever really on our own? Can we be in solitude together? How does a solitary moment sound?

- *Play on your own*
- *Let your cello play a selfless note*
- *Play a note that gives your cello presence*
- *Play out of sync*
- *Search for a note that allows your cello, your surroundings, and you to melt into each other*

*

Response_to_Sophie's_Solitude_Assignment.docx
    Tim Ingold
    Aberdeen, May 2018
    This is what I found:

I can only really play in solitude. If I become conscious of the presence of another person—for example, if someone walks into the room, or I realize that they are listening next door—I have immediately to banish it from my awareness, as if they were not there. For otherwise, the other's presence would trigger a resurgent sense that it is I, myself, who is playing. And when the "I" buts in and insists on placing itself *before* the action, my playing stalls.

To play in synchrony with others means retreating into one's own shell. This, I suppose, is what it feels like to be lonely. Watching the players in an orchestra—their movements and gestures perfectly synchronized so as to produce a finely tuned performance—I imagine how lonely they must be. As a onetime orchestral player, I have experienced this loneliness myself. Orchestras are the most unsociable of collectives. To socialize with others, you must be out of sync with them.

I cannot play at the same time as holding a conversation with myself. If I want to talk to myself I have to stop playing; and if I want to start playing again I have to stop talking to myself. Thus the solitude of the player is not the same as that of the philosopher. A conversation is still going on, but it is a correspondence of movements, not a dialogue of ideas. It is feeling and sound going along together and responding to one another. I am on the inside of both. I am not conversing with myself by way of the sound and feeling of my playing; rather, sound and feeling are conversing by way of me. I am the medium of thought that is thinking itself in movement.

Why should we ever have thought that thinking is silent? Only because we equate thinking with computations in the head, as opposed to the actions in the world that are supposed to deliver its results. With the cello, playing is thinking; it is the flight of thinking from the bounds of the already thought. And it can make an awesome sound.

Playing a harmonic on an open string is quite different from playing a stopped note. Harmonics are not imposed but discovered. They are like the sounds of nature. When I play a harmonic I feel that I have somehow dissolved into the surroundings. To play a stopped note, by contrast, is to present the sound, not to present oneself. It is to let the sound be, in itself. I am simply a presenter, a go-between.

When I play, I don't know how it sounds to others. I am too close to the instrument, just as I am to my own voice. I hear the sound through my own body, and with my own gestures, so it sounds differently to me.

Assignment for the reader (you)

Make a lot of copies of this assignment, printed on attractive or colorful paper. Maybe also translated in different languages (French, English, German, Italian—depending on where you are).

Find a spot on a busy street, where lots of people are passing by. Hand a copy of this sheet to anyone who accepts.

As you give out copies, do you feel:

That it comes easily or that you have to put on a brave face?
That you are awkwardly self-conscious or that you melt into the crowd?
That your attention is caught by what is going on around you or that your mind is preoccupied with other things?

That you remember the face of each recipient, or that it is
    instantly forgotten?

Say to your interlocutor:

> You are very welcome to try out this assignment yourself,
> and to draw your own conclusions, particularly regarding
> the experience of loneliness and solitude amidst a throng of
> people.

Sophie Krier and Tim Ingold

See also
EQUALITY, PRIVATE REALM, TOGETHERNESS,
VITA CONTEMPLATIVA

SPEECH

Speech is performative. Speech is forceful. Speech is associated with the loudest, most rebellious forms of revolutionary activism. And yet, speech is precarious. Our right to speak can easily be compromised, or denied. Spontaneous, hesitant, emotional, or effusive speech is implicitly associated with the feminine. Focused, fact-based, logical, and rhetorically eloquent speech is, on the contrary, deemed impactful and heavily valued. And yet, ultimately, we tend to view speech as a lightweight form of communication—the opposite of the macho style kind of thinking that has governed centuries of knowledge production in the West. When it comes to clearly organizing and communicating ideas, it is generally assumed that speech falls short in comparison to written forms of language. In the context of today's political arena, speech is often vulgar, and name-calling abounds. Words have become unaccountable—thrown around, twisted, disputed, and, at the end of the 24 hours news cycle, forgotten. Could the darkest of times be a time when one's words are completely disjointed from one's deeds?

The index to the 1958 edition of *The Human Condition* lists a total of 21 instances where the word speech can be found. Although occurrences of the term appear throughout Hannah Arendt's book, at least half of those are located, unsurprisingly, under chapter five, "Action." Already in the prologue Arendt establishes a crucial relationship between speech and action—between the spoken word and the done deed. "Whenever the relevance of speech is at stake," she claims, "matters become political by definition, for speech is what makes a political being."[1] Speech, Arendt insists, literally "makes" men (plural) into the only way of being that matters: the political way. Speech is not just a (disputable) facet of political action. Speech defines us as beings capable of such action. Political deeds begin in speech.

---

1   Hannah Arendt, *The Human Condition* (Chicago, IL: University of Chicago Press, [1958] 1998), 3.

Arendt goes further. Speech is not simply a means toward an end but represents a vital force, an actuality, a potential in motion (*entelecheia*) in the purest Aristotelian sense.[2] Speech is its own actuality. For Arendt, speech *is* action and, in that sense, speech acts are leaps of faith. In order to engage in such performative processes, I need to trust in my own ability to find the right words and, in the midst of it all, to organize those words into a coherent and eloquent whole. I need faith in the possibility of being heard and, eventually, understood. This type of speech requires courage and conviviality.

Following a different yet related trajectory, Paul Ricœur's *The Course of Recognition* investigates the relationship between our capacity to speak, to voice out an intention, to make a promise (*pouvoir dire*), and our power to act/make (*pouvoir faire*).[3] Here's an example. Remember how, as a kid, you stood with both legs firmly planted on the ground on both sides of your brand new bicycle, shouting to get your parents' attention: "Look, I can ride without the training wheels!" Carefully placing your foot on the pedal, you looked ahead and joyfully leapt forward. And even though you eventually fell over and scraped a knee, you promptly got back up and, without hesitation, gave it another go. The skillfulness (or lack thereof) of your short ride mattered very little. What mattered was your newly acquired conviction of being able to ride that bike, which you did, if only for a few seconds. Your ability to cycle lay less in the actual physical performance than in your acknowledged status as *someone who can ride a bike without the training wheels*. This understanding of yourself as a *cyclist* began with the possibility to verbally make a claim, and, concurrently, in someone being present to hear and support that claim, therefore recognizing you as *capable*. For Ricœur, our understanding of who we are and where we stand in relation to others is constantly redefined and threatened by such processes. Ultimately, we become capable of political action

2   Arendt, *The Human Condition*, 209.
3   Paul Ricœur, *The Course of Recognition* (Boston: Harvard University Press, 2007).

as we engage in processes of mutual recognition involving this very fragile forms of speech-based interaction: as we voice and acknowledge what we can do for each other.

Speech acts are also aimed at naming and, as such, they constitute or devastate. In *Excitable Speech: A Politics of the Performative*, social theorist and linguist Judith Butler examines the nuanced implications of speech acts as constitutive forces that both give shape and set our political and social bodies "in place."[4] Butler's work problematizes the relationship of speech to action by carefully revealing how processes of recognition, and abjection, remain embedded in the power dynamics of language itself. She shows how the violence inherent in the most despicable form of name-calling—the insult—not only casts the question of the performative, political dimension of speech in a new light but can, in turn, open up unchartered territories for the target of the insult to enact their political agency, occupy other spaces, forge new identities.

As designers and as heirs to the modern scientific revolution, our education and practices are tinted by decades of top-down, authoritative modes of speech and action. Concurrently, as Arendt reminds us, it has become increasingly difficult for us to "think through what we do or make."[5] We are somehow no longer proficient in finding a voice to express such thoughts: we now rely on technologically efficient, mathematical, algebraic, or data-driven means of expression. Designing, however, always begins with a verbal claim through which one's intentions and capabilities are spoken up. At the root of all design processes (which are always collective, even if we pretend otherwise) one finds rounds of reciprocated speech acts aimed at mutual recognition. These conversations alternate between the simple voicing out of an "I can"—a promise, a commitment to action, a project—and the acknowledgment, by an "other," of our capabilities as designers, as makers and inhabitants, as users, as social actors, as citizens. Switching our

4   Judith Butler, *Excitable Speech: A Politics of the Performative* (New York: Routledge, 1997).
5   Arendt, *The Human Condition*, 3.

attention away from the figure of the designer, the product, the object, or the outcome, we may want to investigate the potential embedded in such initial conversations to offer the convivial, trusting conditions for speech to turn design into informed, political action.

Caroline Dionne

See also
CITIZENSHIP, FREEDOM, HUMAN RIGHTS,
IN-BETWEEN

SPONTANEITY

> For to destroy individuality is to destroy spontaneity, man's power to begin some thing new out of his own resources, something that cannot be explained on the basis of reactions to environment and events ... Those who aspire to total domination must liquidate all spontaneity, such as the mere existence of individuality will always engender, and track it down in its most private forms, regardless of how unpolitical and harmless these may seem. Pavlov's dog, the human specimen reduced to the most elementary reactions, the bundle of reactions that can always be liquidated and replaced by other bundles of reactions that behave in exactly the same way, is the model "citizen" of a totalitarian state; and such a citizen can be produced only imperfectly outside of the camps.
>
> Hannah Arendt, *The Origins of Totalitarianism*[1]

In *The Origins of Totalitarianism* Hannah Arendt observes that the driving force of the totalitarian political system was extreme instrumentalization. It was a system that was unable to integrate freedom and the unpredictability of human spontaneity. In Arendt's analysis, totalitarian government could transform citizens into human animals by destroying their spontaneous unpredictable attributes. Arendt defines spontaneity as "man's power to begin something new out of his own resources."[2] It suggests the ability to step outside oneself and outside one's habits in order to see things otherwise than in everydayness.[3] The capacity to initiate the new and the unexpected corresponds

---

1   Hannah Arendt, *The Origins of Totalitarianism* (New York: Harvest Books, [1951] 1979), 455.

2   Arendt, *The Origins of Totalitarianism*.

3   Jennifer Gosetti-Ferencei, "Articulate Spontaneity and the Aesthetic Imagination," in Tymieniecka (ed.), *Logos of Phenomenology and Phenomenology of the Logos, Book Five* (Netherlands: Springer, 2006), 199–220.

to the human act of birth and to what she calls the "origin-al" character of man. The capacity for human action to initiate the new and the unexpected is analogous to the way every birth signifies a new life story.[4] In totalitarian regimes, politics are enacted in the mode of "making," by setting aims and finding means to reach them, leaving civilians with no space to maneuver for change.[5] Once human spontaneity is destroyed, very little can stop people from being removed from the human condition, from being extinguished by totalitarianism. Hannah Arendt's framing of spontaneity is indicative of her general critique of instrumental technical rationality and her overall rejection of the sociopolitical ideologies of control. In Arendt's conception of the human condition it is possible to outline a distinction between, on the one hand, technical, instrumental modes of thinking and action and, on the other hand, metaphorical, imaginative, and creative action.[6] Arendt emphasizes the importance of fighting against totalitarian impulses in modern society, which curtail the possibility of creative action by curtailing human spontaneity. She argues that in order for modern citizens to make a common world, they need to regain the human capacity for spontaneity that shapes the creative power of man.

Arendt's thinking serves as a critique of contemporary society that is increasingly governed by logics of instrumental technical rationality. This can be applied to the field of design where creative practices are gradually being transformed into standardized working procedures tailored to meet criteria of efficiency and replicability. Even when defined as "designerly," much of designers' accounts of their research methods still portray them as linear and highly structured procedures, with compartmentalized foundations. Research is expected to be conducted using methods in an orderly and ordered manner

4   Hannah Arendt, *The Human Condition* (Chicago, IL: University of Chicago Press, [1958] 1998).

5   Helen Kohlen, "Troubling Practices of Control: Re-Visiting Hannah Arendt's Ideas of Human Action as Praxis of the Unpredictable," *Nursing Philosophy* vol. 16, no. 3 (2015): 161–66.

6   Mihaela Czobor-Lupp, "Hannah Arendt on the Power of Creative Making in a World of Plural Cultures," *The European Legacy* vol. 13, no. 4 (2008): 445–61.

following a plan to deliver an outcome that can be evaluated. The often messy, nonvisible, abductive processes and techniques of design inquiry do not seem to feature in discussions about method. In the current corporate quest to package and codify creativity and design thinking, much of the flexibility, spontaneity, and improvisation that constitute design craft tend to be obscured. Equally, in academic contexts, we have been reluctant to embrace these as qualities of our research methods and practices. In research and practice many people treat design as a fairly generic structured process, while in practice designers and design researchers experience design as context driven, emergent, and fluent.

Today, design professionals intervene in a variety of sociocultural, economic, and political contexts. They generate ideas and solutions in domains as different as health, culture, education, business, technology, sustainability, climate change, and international development. Qualities such as adaptation, flexibility, improvisation, and inventiveness are sorely needed to understand and intervene in such complex contexts. While designers are increasingly being sought to intervene in solving problems, little do they contribute in current interdisciplinary debates about methods and ways of generating knowledge.

I suggest that Arendt's idea of spontaneity can serve as a frame for highlighting the potential of design research and practice as sites of methodological innovation. The craft of design involves a set of actions such as imagining, creating, representing, negotiating, fabricating, generating, tinkering, and iterating. I suggest that these are not only useful for designing products and services. Designers have explored the methodological playgrounds of cinema, improvisational theatre, science, anthropology, marketing, literature, and art. In this process, they have appropriated, reframed, hybridized, and embraced tools and techniques for crafting not only products and services but also fictional worlds, what-if scenarios, breaching experiments, provocations, and inspiration. These techniques illustrate how we can generate new forms of knowledge through acts of making and reflecting. They show us ways through which we can move away from the security and comfort of traditional methods of our disciplines to pursue riskier and messier modes of inquiry. We might deploy them as research techniques for "making strange" or "training for the unexpected"—developing our ability to be responsive to fleeting and emergent contexts of change.

When we try to apply Hannah Arendt's notion of spontaneity to the question of methods and ways of knowing, it urges us to reconsider how we can develop a propensity for inventiveness, curiosity, alertness, creativity, improvisation, instantaneousness, impulsivity, responsiveness, and surprise in the way we know and act in the world. Arendt always cautioned against the imposition of technical rationalities and sociopolitical ideologies of control guiding the way we live and act with each other. She warned that whenever we remove spontaneity from action we destroy that which is really human. In these *dark times*, we need more than ever to constantly invent new ways to ask questions, expose assumptions, raise awareness, provoke and inspire novel ways of knowing and relating to our worlds.[7]

Henry Mainsah

See also
EVIL, NATALITY, PLAY, REIFICATION, SPEECH

7   Acknowledgment. This project has received funding from the European Union's Horizon 2020 Framework Programme for Research and Innovation under grant agreement No: 707706.

STORIES

Stories are not to be confused with fabrications. As Hannah
Arendt observes, stories mark new beginnings, pregnant with
unpredictable consequences, just like our own beginnings at
birth. Fabrications—not the "tangible things" Arendt alludes to
elsewhere—start with endings. Stories evolve both in the writing
and in the reading. Or, to paraphrase Walter Benjamin, in the
telling and retelling. There is no retelling—no comparison of new
experiences—permitted in the self-conscious fabrications that
have invaded contemporary public discourse, just the insistent
fabrication of propaganda.

Propaganda may be an ancient dark art, but in the context
of twenty-first-century posttruth politics, it has shape-shifted.
Our wolves appear in virtual sheep's clothing instead of ink, and
they cover more territory than their predatory ancestors could
have ever conceived. Even so, the stillborn stories proffered to
citizen-consumers today are not especially unique. They are not
so different, for example, from those told in eighteenth-century
England when London's fledgling newspapers were filled with
articles cobbled together from anonymously written "paragraphs"
and financed by the powerful to sway readers to their versions
of events.[1] There was no fact-checking then, and now the very
idea of "fact" is suspect. No amount of evidence seems to make
a difference. Prevarication was, and is, expected in a climate
where public pronouncements are just new installments in a soap
opera. This would be a comic state of affairs (and we have no
shortage of satire today) except for its frighteningly malignant
effects. Fabrications are meant to shut down any thoughts
about their contents. Coming in tidal waves, fabrications make
it seem pointless to think at all, since thinking might lead to
unanticipated actions. In other words, stories.

[1] John Brewer, *A Sentimental Murder: Love and Madness in the 18th
    Century* (New York: Farrar, Straus and Giroux, 2004), 41–4.

Where florid prose was the order of the day among eighteenth-century romantics, brevity is king today. Tweets, sound bites, and ads posing as a stories-between-stories are working to obliterate contemplation, not to mention the consideration of other points of view. Such distractions make us less focused, much to the benefit of those whose ideas cannot stand scrutiny.

But this is not to confuse brevity with poetic concision. Otherwise works like Lydia Davis's "Household Observation" wouldn't be read as the stories they are. When Davis writes: "Under all this dirt / The floor is really very clean,"[2] she hints at the chore that awaits, or more likely, questions if cleaning is needed at all. She reminds us how paradoxical it is that we care for things (like floors) that have been designed to support and care for us.[3]

Given the bleakness of our moment, a poem about cleaning the floor, or clean floors, might seem trivial. Its feminist politics may be too subtle or its object-oriented perspective too surreal. Nonetheless, Davis's "observation" is a useful example of how even the shortest of stories can trigger multiple trains of thought. Still, no one can predict what actions might result, since, to paraphrase Arendt, each of us is uniquely affected by those [people and things] with which we come into contact.[4]

This is the deeply uncertain terrain in which designers act. In my experience, the most conscientious are acutely aware of this. They take steps to anticipate and prevent any conceivable harm or confusion that their work might cause. Among the most critical is the act of listening. In industry, listening is invariably a means to an end—a product, place, or message. While in practices of design for social justice, listening is part of an open-ended process of engagement without a predetermined goal. It can happen in conversations with designers, but it can also

2   Lydia Davis, "Housekeeping Observation," in *Can't and Won't* (New York: Farrar Straus & Giroux, 2015), 90.
3   Hannah Arendt, *The Human Condition* (Chicago, IL: University of Chicago Press, [1958] 1998), 184.
4   Arendt, *The Human Condition.*

happen in story writing, particularly when the designer is the reader. This need not be just an anticipatory act to galvanize a specific exploration. It can also be done after the fact, since design is never complete except in use. For example, instead of asking residents what they like or don't like about their new housing complex, they could be invited to write their own stories about a typical day at home.

Design, then, becomes not a matter of coproduction of a particular artefact or situation but of learning from stories. This is important not only for the benefit of other similar projects but also to ensure that any future changes or innovations—in this case, to housing—are not imposed but negotiated. Language—the muscle and bone of stories that live and live on in the Arendtian sense—is critical here. This is especially true of the words designers use. Case in point, words like "change" and "innovation" imply disruption, while "repair" and "reconfigure" actively build on stories while being open to new epiphanies in the process.

As important as it is to be alert to the language of the stories that we and others hear and tell, it is equally important to listen to the stories embedded in things and places. These stories are best told in fiction and poetry where they are actors in daily life. This is not to discount the knowledge of things to be found in histories, but only to point out that fiction and poetry reveal possibilities largely missing from the finite nature of the documentary form where the ending is already known. In the hands of poets and novelists, prosaic things like staircases, luggage, or chests of drawers become catalytic agents. Not only can they viscerally conjure the sense of what it means to be evicted, to be resettled, or to be at home, they can also elicit design responses, as well as a greater awareness of the (largely unacknowledged) futurity of design. And since literary resonance is not bound by the temporality of plot and setting, its epiphanies have the added virtue of reassuring us that others have been there before us. This is no small comfort as we attempt, however modestly, to design the conditions for being truly human.

You will know how salty is the taste
of another's bread, and how hard the path
to descend and come up another man's stairs.

—Dante Alighieri, *Paradiso*[5]

Susan Yelavich

See also
IMPERIALISM, POWER, TOGETHERNESS, *VITA
CONTEMPLATIVA*

5   Dante Alighieri, *Paradiso*, in Aciman, *Out of Egypt: A Memoir*
(New York: Picador, Farrar Straus and Giroux, 1994), 273.

SUPERFLUITY

I do not like crowds.

I am not sure when I first got the realization of this simple fact. Maybe it was when my entire primary school class in Moscow was taken to a mass demonstration on every big holiday. Or maybe it was in college, when our classes got cancelled whenever the heads of friendly states visited the capital, and we had to join crowds that lined the streets to greet their passing cortège. We were warned to keep our spots, and we were watched; only a few daredevils would risk taking off to a neighborhood beer joint. For the overall effect of the demonstration, it obviously made no difference. In those Soviet gatherings, the role of every individual was simply to be a cog in the crowd. The refrain of a popular marching song of the time still rings in my head:

I, You, He, She,
All together—family!
All together—our Country!
"We" contains one million "me"!

With characteristic precision, Hanna Arendt noted that for the totalitarian power, "individuality, anything indeed that distinguishes one man from another, is intolerable."[1] Not by chance, in Soviet society the very notion of "individualism" was often tagged with a derogatory label "bourgeois," and the whole thing was disparaged as a suspicious and antisocial phenomenon.

In classes of Russian literature we studied the hero of nineteenth-century poems and novels, "a superfluous man." Evgeny Onegin and Oblomov are perhaps the best-known examples. This character, usually a wealthy and educated individual, could not find meaning in his life, spending days in idle entertainment, feeling unneeded, bored, and mildly

1   Hannah Arendt, *The Origins of Totalitarianism* (New York: Harvest Books, [1951] 1979), 457.

depressed. The progressive critics of the time deemed this character "superfluous" because he could not advance the cause of social reforms and, eventually, would not help the revolution. No wonder that the Bolshevik revolution of 1917 soon got rid of these upper-class intellectuals: they were needed for the new regime even less than for the old one. The self-reflective superfluous man could not survive because the totalitarian power deemed *all people* superfluous, in other words redundant, dispensable, devoid of special human value. "Precisely because man's resources are so great, he can be fully dominated only when he becomes a specimen of the animal-species man,"[2] wrote Hanna Arendt. One of the earliest and bleakest dystopian novels *We*, written by Yevgeny Zamyatin in 1921,[3] provided a sinister premonition to Arendt's vision. (It has a distinction of being the very first book banned by the fledgling Soviet regime.)

It comes as no surprise that the idea of *mass* production did not sit well with my sensibility when I became an industrial designer. In the admirable Eames's motto: "The best for the most for the least," I heard a note of disregard for individual people's tastes, peculiarities, and personal histories. From the early years of my design career, I became infatuated with keepsakes, mementoes, and souvenirs. Keepsakes hold people's unique histories and personal memories; they are a stand against anonymous crowd mentality. W. G. Sebald, one of my favorite writers, wrote that "memories lie slumbering within us for months and years, quietly proliferating, until they are woken by some trifle and in some strange way blind us to life."[4] These "trifles" are designed and manufactured in order to connect with the owner through a dense web of emotional links. Much of my studio's creative output has been devoted to rethinking the genre

---

2   Arendt, *The Origins of Totalitarian*, 457.
3   Yevgeny Zamyatin, *We*, trans. Clarence Brown (London: Penguin Twentieth Century Classics, 1993).
4   W. G. Sebald, *Rings of Saturn*, trans. Michael Hulse (London: Harvill Press, 1998), 255.
    The writings of Sebald, imbued with an incomparable blend of melancholy and humanism, provide a strongest possible antidote to every aspect of totalitarian mentality.

of souvenir by bringing it closer to the complex reality of the twenty-first century.

Souvenirs are closely related to the notions of irony and humor. "The free zone of humour," in the words of critic Adam Gopnik, has always been a fertile ground for daring creative experimentation. For that reason, irony and laughter in general have been sworn enemies of the totalitarian state. Irony invites doubt; doubt begets discontent; discontent provokes action. It is hard to think of comedians in Stalin's or Hitler's regimes, even though there must have been some. In the Soviet Union of my youth, the irony vacuum was filled with so-called anecdotes—an endless array of Russian jokes, created anonymously and passed from one mouth to another on a daily basis. The anecdotes appeared as a response to every major social event, or they offered a wry comment on existential conditions of the entire political system:

> "What is the difference between the freedoms in the USA and the USSR?"—"Simple: in USSR, there is freedom of speech. In the USA, there is also freedom *after* speech."
>
> (Recently, this old joke resurfaced with a new answer: "We have exactly the same freedom of speech. In America, one can walk on the street with a placard 'Down with Trump!' and not get arrested. In Russia, one can *also* go out with a placard 'Down with Trump!' and not get arrested.")

If the goal of totalitarian state, says Hanna Arendt, is to create "marionettes without the slightest trace of spontaneity,"[5] the tacit response of the Russian people was to affirm their humble and instinctive individualism. Whether expressed in their collections of keepsakes, or in their self-deprecating jokes, or in their privately shared personal memories, this proved to be a feat that no state power could ever take away.

Constantin Boym

See also
COURAGE, EVIL, PARIAH, TOTALITARIANISM

5   Arendt, *The Origins of Totalitarianism*, 457.

TECHNOLOGY
THOUGHT
THOUGHTLESSNESS
TOGETHERNESS
TOTALITARIANISM

TECHNOLOGY

To learn to speak about technology is to learn to speak about ourselves.

We must seek to deeply understand and vividly describe the ways in which "we make machines," "they remake us,"[1] and we make up lives and worlds together with things and with each other. In making up worlds, we imagine, dream, and encounter infinite possibilities. These dreams come in many forms: meanings and metaphors, images and imaginaries, as well as visualizations and visions of alternative futures. Whose dreams are enacted in these worlds? Whose visions shape the realities of these dark times? Whose lives are made possible? And, whose are made impossible, irrelevant, or, even, entirely eliminated?

From Mary Shelley's Frankenstein in 1818 to the German Bauhaus school in 1919 and early cybernetics, humans have questioned the nature of our own relationship to our inventions, materials, and machines.[2] Writing sixty years ago, in 1958, Hannah Arendt stated that the "problem of technology, that is, of the transformation of life and world through the introduction of the machine" lay in our overemphasis on the instrumentality of machines as tools in the service of humans.[3] Such a focus is evident (and, even, accelerated) today with our constant attempts to predict, measure, quantify, surveil, and calculate all manner

1   This is a reference to a seminar at the University of Chicago by Peter Galison, "Building Crashing Thinking: We Make Machines, They Remake Us," accessed on May 2, 2018, http://english.uchicago.edu/courses/building-crashing-thinking-we-make-machines-they-remake-us.

2   David H. Guston, Ed Finn, and Jason Scott Robert, eds., *Frankenstein: Annotated for Scientists, Engineers, and Creators of All Kinds* (Cambridge, MA: MIT Press, 2017); Gropius, "Bauhaus Manifesto and Program," *Weimar: The administration of the Staatliche Bauhaus* (1919); Norbert Wiener, *The Human Use of Human Beings: Cybernetics and Society* (New York: Perseus Books Group, 1988); Fred Turner, *The Democratic Surround: Multimedia and American Liberalism from World War II to the Psychedelic Sixties* (Chicago, IL: University of Chicago Press, 2013).

3   Hannah Arendt, *The Human Condition* (Chicago, IL: University of Chicago Press, [1958] 1998), 151.

of human and nonhuman processes at the planetary, global, national, regional, urban, organizational, and individual scales. At the center of these efforts to capture and control data is an unshakable belief in rational, universal, and scientific knowledge gained through the analysis of data (and, in particular, "big data") in order to find solutions to problems.

Our obsession with instrumentality along with the ways in which technologies are embedded in neoliberal capitalist socioeconomic forms reinforces values of efficiency, convenience, and individualism.[4] These values often reappear in design criteria and engineering requirements that specify the need for flexibility, adaptability, modularity, resilience, seamlessness, agility, smartness, openness, and, yes, even (and perhaps especially) participation.

Participation invites us all to contribute our labor (as well as that of the natural environment) freely to sustaining an unsustainable system. These priorities are demonstrated through our federal spending on autonomous vehicles, our urban efforts to deploy sensors and cameras throughout cities, our corporate evangelism of artificial intelligence and robots, and, even, in our own adoption of voice-activated in-home assistants and self-tracking technologies. In accepting these prescribed relations with technology rather than resisting, reshaping, and questioning them, we foreclose other ways of living and world-making. Yes, we often appropriate and use technologies in unexpected ways, but to what degree can we truly counter the politics inherent in their design?

With regard to these shifting agencies between humans and machines, Arendt asks whether "machines still serve the world and its things, or if, to the contrary, they and the automatic motion of their processes have begun to rule and even destroy the world and things," pointing out that the end not only justifies the means but it also "produces and organizes them."[5] Today, while many of these same concerns are present in our debates about the implications of technology, the size, scale, and reach

4   Hamid R. Ekbia and Bonnie Nardi, *Heteromation, and Other Stories of Computing and Capitalism* (Cambridge, MA: MIT Press, 2017).
5   Arendt, *The Human Condition*, 151–3.

of technology (and, specifically, computational technology) have transformed significantly over the past sixty years—from huge machines the size of entire rooms to small portable mobile devices to tiny embedded sensors.[6] In addition, our definitions of technology (and scientific advancements) have moved beyond the computation and toward the biological. Drawing on Werner Heisenberg who referred to technology as "a biological development of mankind," Arendt's text foreshadowed these developments, stating that "future technology may yet consist of channeling the universal forces of the cosmos around us into the nature of the earth," and that "[it] remains to be seen whether these future techniques will transform the household of nature as we have known it since the beginning of our world to the same extent or even more than the present technology has changed the very worldliness of the human artifice."[7]

We now have a richer set of philosophical concepts, vocabularies, and literacies to theorize the relationships between humans and machines. Rather than talking of a discrete, functional notion of "technology," it is more useful to consider the nature of the sociotechnical. To encounter technology is to encounter society (and its politics) quite literally in material form.[8] With this framing, technologies can be understood not merely as tools but, rather, as rituals and cultures that inscribe norms, values, and politics.[9] These concepts serve as guiding lights for designing in dark times, for posing critical questions about alternative possible futures rather than merely pursuing solutionism.

Technology, then, is neither a problem nor a solution but is rather an intimate becoming in which we can see ourselves in systems and systems in ourselves.[10] Following feminist

6   Mark Weiser, "The Computer for the Twenty-First Century," *Scientific American* vol. 265, no. 3 (1991): 94–104

7   Arendt, *The Human Condition*, 150.

8   Langdon Winner, "Do Artifacts Have Politics?" in Winner (ed.), *The Whale and the Reactor: A Search for Limits in an Age of High Technology* (Chicago, IL: University of Chicago Press, 1986).

9   James Carey, *Communication as Culture: Essays on Media and Society*, Media and Popular Culture: I (New York: Unwin Hyman, 1988).

10   Laura Forlano, "Data Rituals in Intimate Infrastructures: Crip Time and the Disabled Cyborg Body as an Epistemic Site of Feminist Science," *Catalyst: Feminism, Theory, Technoscience* vol. 3, no. 2 (2017).

technoscience, we are (and always were) cyborg, posthuman, and more-than-human.[11] These notions emphasize the local, situated, embodied, partial, and affective knowledges that have been long ignored and devalued by scientific rationalism and universalism. In decentering the human condition in the field of design, such concepts make space not only for the consideration of our complex relations, networks, and assemblages with technology and things but also for the ways in which we coexist with natural environment.[12] In coexisting with technologies as well as with the natural environment, it is beneficial to think of how, instead of focusing exclusively on the creation of novel technologies, we might draw on practices of maintenance, repair, and care for making and remaking lives and worlds.[13]

Rather than the instrumentalism and solutionism that Arendt rightly identifies as problematic, we must make space for the speculative[14] and imaginative, the accidental and experimental, and, ultimately, the generous and poetic possibilities of technology in order to design "a world where many worlds fit," as Arturo Escobar writes, quoting the Zapatistas in Chiapas, Mexico, in *Designs for the Pluriverse*.[15] These multiple worlds

11   Donna Haraway, "A Cyborg Manifesto: Science, Technology, and Socialist-Feminism in the Late Twentieth Century," in *Simians, Cyborgs and Women: The Reinvention of Nature* (New York: Routledge, 1991).
12   Laura Forlano, "Decentering the Human in the Design of Collaborative Cities," *Design Issues* vol. 32, no. 3 (2016); "Posthumanism and Design," *She Ji: The Journal of Design, Economics, and Innovation* vol. 3, no. 1 (2017); Nancy Smith, Shaowen Bardzell, and Jeffrey Bardzell, "Designing for Cohabitation: Naturecultures, Hybrids, and Decentering the Human in Design" (paper presented at the Proceedings of the 2017 CHI Conference on Human Factors in Computing Systems, 2017).
13   Daniela Rosner and Morgan Ames, "Designing for Repair?: Infrastructures and Materialities of Breakdown" (paper presented at the Proceedings of the 17th ACM conference on Computer supported cooperative work & social computing, 2014); Steven Jackson, "Rethinking Repair," in Gillespie, Boczkowski, and Foot (ed.), *Media Technologies: Essays on Communication, Materiality, and Society* (Cambridge, MA: MIT Press, 2014).
14   Anthony Dunne and Fiona Raby, *Speculative Everything: Design, Fiction, and Social Dreaming* (Cambridge, MA: MIT Press, 2013).
15   Arturo Escobar, *Designs for the Pluriverse: Radical Interdependence, Autonomy, and the Making of Worlds* (Durham: Duke University Press, 2018).

must be linked through principles of design justice, drawing on our creative abilities to create and imagine new relations, with each other, with technologies, and with the natural environment.[16]

When technology fails us, we fail ourselves.

Laura Forlano

See also
IN-BETWEEN, POWER, PUBLIC, REIFICATION,
THOUGHTLESSNESS

16   Walidah Imarisha and Adrienne Maree Brown, eds., *Octavia's Brood: Science Fiction Stories from Social Justice Movements* (Oakland, CA: AK Press, 2015); Sasha Costanza-Chock, ed., *Design Justice in Action*, vol. 3, Design Justice (Design Justice Network, 2017).

THOUGHT

> The only thing that can help us, I think, is réfléchir. And
> to think always means to think critically. And to think
> is always hostile. Every thought actually undermines
> whatever there is of rigid rules, general conviction, etcetera.
> Everything which happens in thinking is subject to a critical
> examination of whatever there is. That is, there are no
> dangerous thoughts for the simple reason that thinking is
> such a dangerous enterprise.
>
> Hannah Arendt, *The Last Interview and Other Conversations*[1]

The first time I looked at the quote opening this text, I faced a
moment of suspension of judgment, a moment in which I was
forced to pause and think. The strength and content of the quote
made me question my assumptions on my own work, theoretical
apparatus, and research practices. I read the invitation in
the quotation to enter the space of a *critical examination of
whatever there is* and to *undermine whatever there is of rigid
rules, general conviction, etc.*[2]

To do this, I have been thrown into compulsory rereadings of
Arendt's work and commentaries on her thinking, combined with
the moments of solitude and reflection that are the necessary
steps to get to what she considered "proper thinking," the
capacity of one's own consciousness to question the existing
and to bring about something new. Thinking, in such moments,
becomes a way of stepping back from the usual, from the
common sense shared by the political or professional collectives
we inhabit, and opens up to imagination, the capacity to judge
things and events, trying to liberate ourselves from universal
concepts to evaluate the particular situation in which, as a

1   Hannah Arendt, *Hannah Arendt: The Last Interview and Other
    Conversations* (Brooklyn: Melville House, 2013).
2   Arendt, *Hannah Arendt.*

person, one is immersed.[3] Thinking, or *réfléchir*—what Arendt called in *Men in Dark Times*, the "ability of thought"—is a discussion with oneself. It is therefore a situated activity focusing on the particular and, from the specificity of the particular, being able to generate novelty in thought, novelties so dangerous to even affect general concepts, the universal.

My situated particular in design lies at the crossroads among sociology, human–computer interaction, and the participatory design of digital technologies.[4] This common world is constituted by all the institutions and practices that constitute academic disciplines, conferences, and journals and the like, as well as theories and methods against which claims of validity and novelty are advanced. What I do in my practice can probably be referred to as community-based participatory design of digital technologies[5] where theories deal with the relations among groups of people and where the "community-based participatory design" revolves around the participation of people to/in shaping the technologies themselves as "design things."[6] Both theories and methods refer to a specific tradition that was once called Scandinavian Design,[7] at least in the form of seeking to engage

3   Maurizio Passerin d'Entrèves, "Hannah Arendt," in Zalta (ed.), *The Stanford Encyclopedia of Philosophy* (Summer 2018), https://plato.stanford.edu/archives/sum2018/entries/arendt/.

4   With Participatory Design of Digital Technologies, I refer to an academic and practical tradition that originated in Scandinavia in the 1970s. This tradition has seen the method and techniques of participatory design as a way for the workers to influence the digital technologies to be implemented in the workplace. At the moment, the Participatory Design Conference, the main venue for gatherings of scholars, practitioners, and activists in the field, exceeds the focus on the workplace and on digital technologies. For more information, see www.pdc2018.org and www.pdcproceedings.org.

5   Carl DiSalvo, Andrew Clement, and Volkmar Pipek, "Participatory Design for, with, and by Communities," in Simonsen and Robertson (eds.), *International Handbook of Participatory Design* (Oxford: Routledge, 2012), 182–209.

6   Pelle Ehn, "Participation in Design Things," in *Proceedings of the Tenth Anniversary Conference on Participatory Design 2008* (Indianapolis: Indiana University, 2008), 92–101, http://dl.acm.org/citation.cfm?id=1795234.1795248.

7   Pelle Ehn, "Scandinavian Design: On Participation and Skill," in Paul S. Adler and Terry A. Winograd (eds.), *Usability* (Oxford: Oxford University Press, 1992), 96–132.

the trade unions into the design of digital technologies in order to help foster an agenda of industrial democracy.[8] Over the years, despite the presence of a strong commitment on industrial relations and political economy in the initial efforts of participatory design, the commitment to political economy has decreased significantly.[9] Although recent efforts to revive the political angle are present,[10] in the last decade or so participatory design has been read by some as co-opted by neoliberal practices.[11]

The "dangerous path" stimulated by Arendt's quote causes me to question why that happened, why such a potentially fruitful approach to the understanding and construction of digital technologies, actions intended immediately as political is now seen as losing its goals of building emancipatory capacity. Why are practitioners and scholars in the field losing the ambition of supporting others—the members of the *polis* they inhabit—to be empowered, articulate demands, and enforce them?

One answer Arendt helped me to formulate stems from her understanding of the character of political judgment.[12] Arendt sees this as involving two elements: the capacity of thinking representatively, that is, from the standpoint of others; and the capacity of orienting oneself in the common world. The practice of community-based participatory design is, in fact, both an act

---

8   UTOPIA Project Group, "The UTOPIA Project: On Training, Technology and Products Viewed from the Quality of Work Perspective," Arbetlivscentrum, 1981.

9   Kim Halskov and Nicolai Brodersen Hansen, "The Diversity of Participatory Design Research Practice at PDC 2002–2012," *International Journal of Human-Computer Studies* 74 (February 2015): 81–92.

10 Kim Halskov and Nicolai Brodersen Hansen, "The Diversity of Participatory Design Research Practice Participatory Design Today," in *Proceedings of the 14th Participatory Design Conference* (New York: ACM, 2016), 1–10.

11 Liam Bannon and Pelle Ehn, "Design Matters in Participatory Design," in *Routledge Handbook of Participatory Design* (London: Routledge, 2012), 37–63; Pelle Ehn, "Utopias Lost and Futures-in-the-Making: Marginal Notes on Innovation, Design and Democracy," in *Proceedings of the 13th Participatory Design Conference: Short Papers, Industry Cases, Workshop Descriptions, Doctoral Consortium Papers, and Keynote Abstracts – Volume 2* (New York: ACM, 2014), 191–3.

12 Hannah Arendt, *Between Past and Future*, ed. Jerome Kohn (New York: Penguin, 2006).

of thinking and translating the standpoint of others, through methods and techniques, and the capacity of drifting the design project after having understood the different stands, through analysis and continuous engagement. Nevertheless, the abilities of "represent" and "orient" make sense, for Arendt, only when in relation with the common world. *Réfléchir* is what made me understand that this is the issue for practices losing their emancipatory capacity: focusing on the common world of the designers and the participants—often existing only during the design process—without focusing on the world that is common among the designers, the participants, and other human beings. How does the world we inhabit, as designers and people, look like? is a question that is missing more and more. *Réfléchir*, in Arendt's terms, can force us to recognize our belonging to a common world that extends beyond our own practices and that our own practices translate, reproducing parts of it while transforming others.

It is this recognition that pushes to understand the changing political–economic conditions and how a mutated political judgment relates to participatory design. Scandinavia in the late 1970s–early 1980s—where participatory design of information technologies originated as Scandinavia Design, in which designers were working closely with the trade unions[13]—is very different from the current conditions of capitalism.

In fact, the changing political–economic landscape has transformed production, consumption, and social relations, drifting away from mass production to post-Fordism and now "platform capitalism"[14]—which itself has important consequences for the practice of participatory design[15]—and

13 Pelle Ehn, "Scandinavian Design: On Participation and Skill," 96–132.
14 Nick Srnicek, *Platform Capitalism* (Cambridge, MA: Polity Press, 2016).
15 Joan Greenbaum, "Post Modern Times: Participation Beyond the Workplace," in Blomberg, Kensing, and Erickson (eds.), *PDC'96 Proceedings of the Participatory Design Conference* (Cambridge: Computer Professionals for Social Responsibility, November 1996). Gabriela Avram, Jaz Hee-jeong Choi, Stefano De Paoli, Ann Light, Peter Lyle and Maurizio Teli, "Repositioning CoDesign in the Age of Platform Capitalism: From Sharing to Caring," *CoDesign*, vol. 15, no. 3 (2019): 185-91, DOI: 10.1080/15710882.2019.1638063.

these changes have affected our role as designers, academics, and practitioners. We are now more precarious in our labor conditions.[16] But we are also part of a systemic investment of resource into the design and development of new technologies aimed at supporting contemporary processes extracting value from human life as a whole and not only from the time spent at the workplace.[17] Borrowing from a different tradition from Arendt's one, professionals in participatory design can be considered as contributing to the *general intellect* as Marx called it in "Fragments on the machines."[18] Therefore, it's not only a matter of recognizing the knowledge and creativity part of the design process; it is also a matter of recognizing how the specific skills of designers and academics are a crucial part of the wider socioeconomic transformations.

When life is put to work, what if we, as professionals, start to *réfléchir* not only about theories, practices, and methods but also about ourselves as workers? What if, other than working with the trade unions as at the origin of participatory design, we think about ourselves as economic and political collective actors? What can *réfléchir*, in these conditions, help us to unveil?

Maurizio Teli

See also
COMPREHENSION, METABOLISM, PLURALITY

16 Bianca Elzenbaumer and Caterina Giuliani, "Designers' Inquiry: Mapping the Socio-Economic Conditions of Designers in Italy," *Ephemera: Theory & Politics in Organization* vol. 14, no. 3 (2014): 451–9.
17 Cristina Morini and Andrea Fumagalli, "Life Put to Work: Towards a Life Theory of Value," *Ephemera: Theory & Politics in Organization* vol. 10, nos 3/4 (2010): 234–52.
18 Karl Marx, *Grundrisse, Foundations of the Critique of Political Economy by Karl Marx* (London: Penguin Classics, 1993).

THOUGHTLESSNESS

Acting without thinking, due consideration, reflection upon consequences: thoughtlessness. Over half a century ago Hannah Arendt characterized it as a consequence of life lived in an everyday world that robs the subject of time to think.[1] Yet, she also realized that the unending worldly demand to express thought is met by outpourings of words, unthinkingly drawn from other moments, minds, and mouths. From Arendt's observations of over sixty years ago, has anything changed? Yes, the world of the human material condition has. But what of continuity—has anything remained the same? Again, yes: thoughtlessness.

In thinking about the relation between thinking and the negation of thought, as the essence of thoughtlessness, what is it that actually has remained the same with the passing of time? Here we stumble. There is clearly no universal answer to this question. Thinking is always situated in a world of cultural difference that Eurocentrism, for instance, strives to cover over. Which means "thinking on thinking" follows, by default, thought situated and grounded epistemologically in (my) time and place.

One needs to recognize that Arendt, as a favored student of Martin Heidegger, understood thinking in a way that critically engaged his (rather than just mirroring it). So said, Heidegger viewed thinking as a condition that exists beyond casual modes of thinking or philosophy.[2] It is lived, and thus can be viewed as existing beyond institutional circumscription and disciplinary strictures. For him, thinking in modern times had placed thinking itself in danger. Arendt's comments on thoughtlessness echo his concern.

Looked at from the present, understood as "the future of the past" (an understanding that takes us toward Walter Benjamin's notion of the "everlasting now"), thoughtlessness, as thought-less-thought, thinking without thinking, has taken on a

---

1 Hannah Arendt, *Men in Dark Times* (New York: Harcourt, Brace, [1955] 1993).
2 See Martin Heidegger, *What Is Called Thinking*, trans. J. Glenn Gray (New York: Harper and Row, 1968); Arendt, *Men in Dark Times*.

hyperinflated form that transforms the same into difference. It goes like this:

Our species has always been technological. Early *Homo sapiens* arrived in a world where numerous stone, wood, and bone tools were in use. These tools ontologically increasingly changed the world in which we hominoids inhabited, while also "acting back" to change our species' biomechanical and cognitive capabilities. The instrument, the tool, directly enhanced our species' ability to act and think instrumentally—a thinking that thinks how to, not why, with limited cognizance of consequence: thinking less sufficient thought! The form and operation of the world of contemporary human habitation evidences the amplification of the creative and destructive dialectical character of this process of mind.

Thoughtlessly, in making a world we destroy a world—so the futural nature of our instrumentalism was/is defuturing. Brought to thinking, instrumental thought is equally, indivisibly, and deeply implicated in the creation and destruction of the mind.

Moving on: as Heidegger pointed out, technology is the destiny of metaphysics. Contemporary instrumentalism, with its inherent colonizing propensity, is a marker of metaphysics becoming technology in a reified form (artificial intelligence [AI]). As such, for all the claims, elevation, promotion, adoption, and operational thought invested in "intelligent technologies" (as a "thinking for"), AI is yet a domain of absolute humanlessness, of which thoughtlessness is one characteristic.

A threshold has been crossed, as implied by the emergence of the discussion of the "posthuman." And while historically instrumental thought has had the ability to bring wondrous things into being—things that exceed the seemingly impossible—it has a fundamental flaw. In its functional propensity it is unable to comprehend the consequences of, and take responsibility for, what is created: consider no matter their difference, cigarettes, atomic weapons, computers, nanotechnology, the Internet, etc., all share the unthought of future effects. This flaw is now beyond measure, an irony in an age increasingly governed by the rule of metrics.

Now we are wondering if there is a difference between unthinkingly thinking and thoughtlessness. Another yes.

A forceful reiteration: myopia and the unthinking inherent to structural instrumentalism has led, and continues to lead, our species to a series of overlapping triangular defuturing dynamics. Consider:

- The unsustainable (as powered by capital, design, and technology) producing impacts that reduce the finitude of life as "we" know it leading to > an anthropocentrically driven planetary sixth extinction event evident in a huge loss of biodiversity > linked to hegemonic technology, and the beginning of the end of the human condition as an exchange between our species being and technology. At the extreme, the body lives on but the mind is deindividuated >

- That life lived in a state of teleological illusion has produced a sense of there being progress toward species development and civilization. Yet as instrumental thinkers "we" remain the same (as an (un)thinking animal whose animality was/is repressed). The now dominant mode of education is (how to) instrumental (get a job). At almost every level hegemonic instrumentalism is creating, at an unprecedented scale, systems and management structures that displace critical knowledge and emplace functional "thinking" (Nietzsche understood this as nihilism, the death of all value) > so in the inequity and unevenness of global change, created by thoughtlessness unthinking being posed as thinking, fragmentation, and abandonment, conflict escalates.

To think and know the momentum and defuturing force that absolute thoughtlessness (anthropocentric being) has unleashed upon our planet is to become alienated and to despair. Understandably one may withdraw from the world, as others do and have done in times past. But is it not better to share the company of Lessing who, as Arendt tells, "never felt at home in the world as it then existed and probably never wanted to, and still after his own fashion he always remained committed to it." In the hyperconsumerist defuturing world of the *hard times* in which one now lives, one trembles as the thoughtlessness of "clichés, stock phrases, adherence to conventional, standardized codes of expression and conduct" wash over us. These tropes of thoughtlessness fold into "the banality of evil" of, as we have seen, the still unchecked operative instrumental system that was liberated by fascism as a normative regime of absolute compliance that Arendt and Zygmunt Bauman exposed as remaining unchecked.[3]

Neither hope, idealistic, nor utopianism will get "us" to a viable future. But rather it will be courage, the will to survive, and somehow the fashioning of the resilient in a created age of sustainment, this from an economy and culture of modesty. So in critical difference "we" stand facing the impossible, but knowing the history of our species is a history of new knowledge attaining it.

Tony Fry

See also
ANTHROPOCENTRISM, COMPREHENSION,
PARIAH, VIOLENCE

---

3   Zygmunt Bauman, *Modernity and the Holocaust* (New York: Cornell University Press, 1989); Arendt, *Men in Dark Times*.

TOGETHERNESS

> In acting and speaking, men show who they are, reveal
> actively their unique personal identities and thus make their
> appearance in the human world … This revelatory quality of
> speech and action comes to the fore where people are with
> others and neither for nor against them—that is, in sheer
> human togetherness.
>
> Hanna Arendt, The Human Condition[1]

Always attentive to the relation between speech and action,
Arendt wrote elsewhere that "for the Greeks the essence of
friendship consisted of discourse"[2] and explained that *philia*
(friendship among citizens) becomes possible by a constant
interchange of talk that unites citizens in a *polis*. The political
importance of friendship resides in discourse, since the talking
about the "common world" among human beings makes the
world more humane:

> Whatever cannot become the object of discourse—the
> truly sublime, the truly horrible or the uncanny—may find
> a human voice through which to sound into the world, but
> it is not exactly human. We humanize what is going on in
> the world and in ourselves only by speaking of it, and in the
> course of speaking of it we learn to be human.[3]

If we consider design a discourse, one that is enacted and
materialized in multiple ways, and taking the more specific
example of the design of three-dimensional artefacts, could
we say that most of the things we have designed are neither
for nor against anyone? Arendt warns us that togetherness is
lost once we are for or against someone, once we engage in an

---

1   Hannah Arendt, *The Human Condition* (Chicago, IL: University of
    Chicago Press, [1958] 1998), 180.
2   Hannah Arendt, *Men in Dark Times* (New York: Harcourt, Brace,
    1955), 24.
3   Ibid., 25.

action plan and cease to perceive the immediacy of what is.[4] Design, however, is a future-oriented activity and thus based on an "action plan" of some kind, even when open or spontaneous. There is a "gathering" performed by design. Design *devises*, which implies creating divisions, arranging partitions, material and sensible, including some and excluding others.[5] Thus, a form of togetherness is inscribed in, by, and through things that tend to maintain us in our relating to (some) others. The norm of the devising through design has been human—done by humans and *for* humans. If, in the best case, there is a togetherness enacted through design, it is most clearly *for* humans and no other being: devising *for* some of "us," the privileged minority that consumes most, in the so-called global north. Today, this norm is (rightly) under challenge: the demand is that the dialogue of design should include more and other humans (all humans) but also other-than-human agents. This calls on us to become much more aware how the "togetherness" enacted through design occurs—and how, equally, it sometimes fails.

To think of togetherness from a design "perspective" it is necessary to conceive a "how." Things are not just *with* one another, but they are *with* one another *in particular ways*, there is always a "how": I am at home, sitting on a chair, writing on a table, listening to my daughter play, and my mother work in another room. This is a basic description of a sense of togetherness that I feel right now; being together with my daughter and mother, but it happens in this particular way and mediated through these things. I can be more inclusive in my description and relate to even more material arrangements, and others, both near and far; and I, and them, *and* … the always present "and" of which William James, Gilles Deleuze, and many others have reminded us. "And" *relates*, and it prefigures that "how," which will become a specific form of "with." This is the potential dimension of design, the gathering that things facilitate. To take one example from the list above, this chair that I am sitting on, from the 1970s and made of wood, was not conceived,

4 Arendt, *The Human Condition*, 180.
5 Martín Ávila, *Devices: On Hospitality, Hostility and Design* (Gothenburg: ArtMonitor, 2012).

devised, designed, by thinking the human *and* the tree. Even less, the human *and* the tree *and* the birds that disperse its seeds *and* the soil that maintain this ecosystem's capacity to grow trees *and*... to practice togetherness through design one should ask: how many *ands* are inscribed in our designs? So far, and without a doubt, one can confirm that the *ands* are too few for long-term cohabitation, even if we would only consider the *ands* inscribed *for* humans—let alone those for other-than-human beings.

Arendt starts chapter five of *The Human Condition*, which is about "action," with the following quote by Isaak Dinesen: "All sorrows can be borne if you put them into a story or tell a story about them." With Dinesen in mind, we can continue to elaborate upon design as a discursive *response*, that is, as "action." We can thus speak of the cathartic capacity of materialization, engaging in making something; whether that is through the sensuality of inscribing words on a screen or crafting a model in wood. This concept of design as discursive *response*, as "action" relates to the wider human capacity to speculate through design, and its potential for reimagining and reconfiguring the places we inhabit. What stories do we tell through things? Traces of all kind reveal the lack of ecological understanding of "our" culture. It is clear that design cannot continue to reinstantiate the destructive patterns of behavior imposed by anthropocentric industries. There is a need for an ethical commitment to create designs that acknowledge other beings and to create a culture that devises disruptions of anthropocentric spatialities and temporalities. *Responding ecologically, in working to increase life-affirming response-abilities;*[6] *design action can include, across scales, what might be called "pluralities" of address, when we inscribe the "hows" in and through the things that we use. The particular ways in which things are with one another, inscribing as many ands as we can possibly engage.* "Our" abilities-to-respond must come to terms with responsibility by explicitly working for and with accountability. Devising in response to what? Where? When? For whom? Imagine, for

6   Donna Haraway, *Staying with the Trouble. Making Kin in the Chthulucene* (Durham: Duke University Press, 2016).

example, devising an artefact for medicinal purposes, which is designed not only for the person that will benefit from it but also for the plant that produces the chemical components for the medicine, as well as some of the plant's main visitors, for example, its pollinators.[7] The more inclusive the thought, the more caring the conceptions.

We are capable of this, and this difficult task becomes joyful when we understand and feel another sense of togetherness through an extended sense of friendship, of *philia*, which some have expressed as *biophilia*, designing *for* what lives, *through* what lives (while embracing transience and death) by a sense of ecological belonging. Many of our sorrows could be borne if put into things, with others, with care. Other voices, not exactly human, may find a thing through which to sound into the world.

Martín Ávila

See also
ANTHROPOCENTRISM, HUMANITY, PLURALITY

---

7   Martín Ávila, "Ecologizing, Decolonizing: An Artefactual Perspective," DESIGN+POWER, no. 7 (Oslo: Nordes, 2017), www.nordes.org.

TOTALITARIANISM

It is in the very nature of totalitarian regimes to demand unlimited power. Such power can only be secured if literally all men, without a single exception, are reliably dominated in every aspect of their life. ...Totalitarianism strives not toward despotic rule over men, but towards a system in which men are superfluous. Total power can be achieved and safeguarded only in a world of conditioned reflexes, of marionettes without the slightest trace of spontaneity. Precisely because man's resources are so great, he can be fully dominated only when he becomes a specimen of the animal-species man. Therefore ... individuality, anything indeed that distinguishes one man from another, is intolerable. As long as all men have not been made equally superfluous ... the ideal of totalitarian domination has not been achieved ... The danger ... is that today with populations and homelessness everywhere on the increase, masses of people are continuously rendered superfluous if we continue to think at our world in utilitarian terms. Political, social, and economical events everywhere are in silent conspiracy with totalitarian instruments devised for making men superfluous. The implied temptation is well understood by the utilitarian common sense of the masses, who in most countries are too desperate to retain much fear of death ... Totalitarian solutions may well survive the fall of totalitarian regimes in the form of strong temptations which will come whenever it seems impossible to alleviate political, social or economic misery in a manner worthy of man.

Hannah Arendt, *The Origins of Totalitarianism*[1]

---

1   Hannah Arendt, *The Origins of Totalitarianism* (New York: Harvest Books, [1951] 1979), 456–8.

I

As an analytic term, "Totalitarianism" has had a short life. Originating in the 1920s in the political theory of Carl Schmitt, it came to prominence immediately after the Second World War as a means of describing—and in large part equating—the structural similarities of Hitler's and Stalin's regimes. The opening of China and the fall of the Soviet Union between 1989 and 1991 effectively eroded both its rhetorical and analytical force. What immediately replaced it was, in effect, the proposition of the victor: *Pax Americana*, formulated, in Francis Fukuyama's famous model, as the "end of history": the emergence, globally and conterminously, of market forces and universal democracy: the latter as the "natural" political form of the former.

In this model there was no room for totalitarian regimes.[2] The surviving fragments of communism (Cuba, Cambodia) appeared as anachronistic in that moment as did outbursts of seemingly petty nationalisms (Yugoslavia after 1991) or the rise of fundamentalisms (Islamic, Jewish, Hindu, Christian, etc.), which even then were disfiguring Fukuyama's idealized model.

Twenty-five years on, the political, economic, and cultural landscape is very different. Under the pressures of the increasingly fragile economic system the always illusory model of a politically beneficent, "democratic" neoliberalism has evaporated. Democracy is under threat not only from once thought relatively "backward" regimes (Poland, Hungary, Turkey) or from regimes historically and structurally hostile to any forms of democratic politics (Russia, China) but in its supposed core. Donald Trump in the United States is only the most visible (and in many ways the accidental) expression of the wider aspiration (which has its increasingly less discreet European parallels)[3] to

---

2   See, *The End of History and the Last Man*, published first as an essay in *The National Interest* (1989) and then in book form by the Free Press, New York, 1992.

3   And not only in authoritarianism and the petty fascisms, consider the EU bureaucracy's all but contempt for European political processes—a contempt that is now bringing forth its own reactions that are leading, seemingly paradoxically, to greater public support for authoritarian "answers" to political and social problems.

secure permanent control of every aspect of at least political and social as well as, most obviously, economic decision-making.

But this statement perhaps gives too much to politics. For what is really evident across the last forty years or so is that we are living through the global victory of economic interests *over* politics—what Alain Badiou tellingly characterized as "the revenge of all that is most blind and objective in the economic appropriation of technics over all that is most subjective and voluntary in politics."[4] The conjunction of global supply chains, finance capitalism, and digital technologies has made possible historically unprecedented levels of private accumulation. Yet the parallel sense that sooner or later this "glorious party" must come to an end produces a situation not of calm but of stress. The paradoxical felt precarity of wealth accumulation creates a political demand for what is left of the nation-state to take on despotic and totalitarian forms. What began (at least in theory) as the beneficence of the victory of capitalism over every competing model translates, thirty years on, into a defensiveness that manifests in ever colder and ever harder reactions to challenge.

In the 1940s Adorno said at one point that Fascism could well come to America, only it would not be called Fascism. There is something today of the same thing with regard to Totalitarianism. As a structural construct in its historical sense the parallel can easily be overdone. But in an age not only of tendencies to petty despotism but also and perhaps in the long run more seriously, such developments as China's increasing march toward "information totalitarianism," not only is Orwell's *1984* taking on new resonance, so too is Arendt's at once subtler—but also bolder—understanding of "Totalitarianism." When Arendt notes that total systems strive "toward despotic rule over men, but [also] towards a system in which men are superfluous," she

---

4   Alain Badiou, *The Century* (Cambridge, MA: Polity Press, 2006), 9. "Blind" here should be read not literally—private wealth knows very well what it is doing, but as the deliberate blindness to cost and above all to consequences (meaning, consequences for others). Technics has yielded, without exception, to appropriation by private economic interest. Today, the term "public good" is almost an oxymoron. In the United States *every* initiative for new schemes of public transport meets financed opposition. It is perfectly possible that, within a decade, in the UK, the public sector will have all but disappeared.

is grasping and articulating the underlying form to which the global economic system is already moving. Despotic rule is a global political tendency today, but the deep *economic* impulse is likewise toward the totalitarian. Orbán in Hungary, Erdogan in Turkey, and so on may stand as the figureheads of would-be despotic power, but it is Google (and the like) that ultimately demands the greater control. Google must safeguard itself— in terms of *its* power—precisely as Arendt (allowing for the language of 1951) described, that in regard to the ends which it pursues, "all men, without a single exception" must be "*reliably* dominated in every aspect of their life." To do this there must be created "a world of conditioned reflexes," of persons "without the slightest trace of spontaneity."[5]

It is difficult to see the rise of artificial intelligence, the totalization of data, the invasion of the subject "in their most secret innervations"[6] as *other* than the aspiration, conscious and unconscious, to create, maintain, and extend this condition. Today, this means essentially, for us today and the immediate future, the reduction of persons to nothing *other than* data, to becoming subjects *for* consumption.[7] But those who are

---

5   As Donald Norman put it presciently a few years ago,

> Most people would say [of Google] 'we're the users, and the product is advertising … But in fact, the advertisers are the users and you are the product. They say their goal is to gather all the knowledge in the world in one place, but really their goal is to gather all of the people in the world and sell them.

Quoted in Johnson, "Don Norman: Google doesn't get people it sells them," *Tech News and Analysis*, September 5, 2011.

6   The phrase is Theodor Adorno's. It appears in his paragraph on technology ("Do not knock") in Theodor Wiesengrund Adorno, *Minima Moralia* (London: NLB, 1974), 40. What was mechanical in Adorno is today organized through the merger of infotech and biotech, both, needless to say, organized by and for private interest.

7   A remarkable example of the latter is given in a recent article in The Guardian (UK) concerning a smartphone app for birth control. Approved by the Swedish Health Ministry, but now under investigation, the app (called "Natural cycles") works on registering the precise temperature of the vagina on a daily basis. It turns out, however, that the algorithms on which the app is based work successfully *only* to the extent that the woman's biological cycle is stable, that she is, as it were, "programmable." To the extent she manifests human variance in behavior or biology, it has the potential to fail. See Olivia Sudjic, " 'I Felt Colossally Naive': The Backlash against the Birth Control App," *The Guardian*, July 21, 2018.

reduced in this way are superfluous, either as subjects in any active sense—subjects without what Kant would have called "autonomy" or what today we would say was the capacity to act toward self-configuring the world (rather than accepting the given configurations "forced" on us)—or, what will become increasingly evident in the next decades, superfluous per se, which means expendable, those whose lives, as "victims" cannot be allowed economically or politically—*even ethically*—to be of account. The global population can then be divided into those who are superfluous as persons in Arendt's sense (but who are tolerated as units of data, for consumption, or for that labor that cannot be mechanized) and those who are superfluous per se (those whose levels of consumption are too low to matter; "refugees," of which there will be increasingly large numbers as the century progresses, and not only from the global south; indeed "refugees" will be all those who are refugees from the breakdown, *for them*, of the economic system which once, at least, had a demand for property-less labor).

The conjunction that Arendt saw incipient in 1951 is today beginning to become the new global reality:

> The danger … is that today with populations and homelessness everywhere on the increase, masses of people are continuously rendered superfluous if we continue to think at our world in utilitarian terms. Political, social, and economical events everywhere are in silent conspiracy with totalitarian instruments devised for making men superfluous.[8]

Where the political sphere is not captured in lies it serves the ends of economics. The latter gives guidance to the former—it employs it, often literally.[9] What emerges in this conjunction is a particularly twenty-first-century form of totalitarianism.

8   Arendt, *The Origins of Totalitarianism*, 456–8.
9   A sadly typical instance of this was the recent attempt to block a United Nations World Health Assembly resolution in support of breast-feeding. There was nothing moral in this opposition (how could there be?). It was simply made at the behest of the U.S. babyfood industry. The attempts included blackmail and threats to smaller nations. See Ed Pilkington, "Administration's Opposition to Breastfeeding Resolution Sparks Outrage," *The Guardian*, July 8, 2018.

It does not (yet) feel like the C20th models[10]—nonetheless, the underlying conjunction, in both West and East, between economic interest and forms of the denial of any real democratic politics, is becoming increasingly evident. Its major consequence—the one it most desires to achieve—is the forcing of a closure of any possibility of qualitative change. In effect, stasis is enshrined. In these circumstances obsessions over despotic individuals or nuances of identity politics are irrelevant. The real erasure is that of the possibility of transformation (at least without the precondition of catastrophe).

II

Where, if anywhere, does this leave designing? Or, what is "design" to do in this situation? The first demand might be that we lose the last vestiges of naivety concerning the situation as a whole.

The second might be to take seriously Arendt's insight that it is the tendency of all absolute regimes to sooner or later declare *persons as such* (and all other living things) superfluous[11]. This requires not simply opposition but *affirmative* opposition. The human subject—and, to repeat, all other living species—must be seen not as a "victim(s)" or "cost" but as a resource, that is, affirmatively. The designer and design thinker John Chris Jones understood this many years ago. In one of the sharpest essays he wrote in the 1970s he says, in conclusion,

> There are now several billion of us and soon more and I for one rejoice in that. I cannot see that the presence of people is a problem if it is allowed that each of us is really human, whatever role it is the system has recently been forcing us to play. We are numerous: that is the challenge, the new

10 Though actions in 2018 by the current U.S. administration in removing the children of would-be migrants to the United States reenact procedures all too familiar from the 1930s and 1940s.

11 The subject is indivisible from the wider context of all other living things. This is why the erosion of nonhuman species is so significant. Current rates of mass extinction, running at roughly 100 times the background rate, presage our own.

excitement of life as it never was before. It's time to change our aims. To see ourselves collectively as different, able to respond to the new conditions of human life.[12]

The refusal of superfluity, the affirmation of capability, goes along in this proposition with reassertion of idea of *designing* (the lower case is deliberate) as the exploration of the capability of dealing, well, with problems—Rittel's "wicked problems," of which today we have legion, not the least of which is that the purported "solutions" to problems so often take essentially totalitarian forms. Design has a bad history of acquiescence to the total in whatever form it has manifested in history. Today is no different. Against this, however, the affirmation of possibilities *other* than totalitarian for engaging with the deep steering problems of our times depends, in part, on the modeled articulation of the subject's capabilities (meaning here *all* subjects, *all* living things) for dealing with both problems and possibilities in ways that contest and exceed totalitarian "solutions." In many ways, Arendt's most chilling line in the quotation above is the last one—that "Totalitarian solutions may well survive the fall of totalitarian regimes in the form of strong temptations which will come whenever it seems impossible to alleviate political, social or economic misery in a manner worthy of man."

See also
BUREAUCRACY, EVIL, NATALITY, VIOLENCE

12   John Chris Jones, *Essays in Design* (London: Wiley, 1984), 33–4.

VIOLENCE
VITA ACTIVA
VITA CONTEMPLATIVA

VIOLENCE

How dark are these times? The gathering storm clouds on the horizon—the emergence of ultranationalist and separatist movements; the spike in hate crimes; the rise of authoritarian strongmen—seem to have darkened the skies and blotted out hope that the near future might foretell greater freedoms. The neoliberal shibboleth that globalization was a rising tide to lift all boats is running headlong into born-again isolationism and the fracturing of hard-won alliances. If, throughout the modern era, the pendulum has swung back and forth between blinkered optimism and doomsday pessimism, in what direction can we say it is swinging today?

Steven Pinker, in *The Better Angels of Our Nature*, an encyclopedic accounting of rates of violence throughout history (albeit primarily in the West), makes the counterintuitive claim that, despite all appearances, we are living in progressively more peaceful times:

> The problem I have set out to understand is the reduction in violence at many scales—in the family, in the neighbourhood, between tribes and other factions, and among major nations and states. If the history of violence at each level of granularity had an idiosyncratic trajectory, each would belong in a separate book. But to my repeated astonishment, the global trends in almost all of them, viewed from the vantage point of the present, point downward.[1]

Armed with reams of statistics, Pinker argues that these trend lines are, indeed, consistently arcing downward. Even more

---

1 Steven Pinker, *The Better Angels of our Nature* (New York: Viking, 2011), xxii. Pinker's argument is sweeping, and not all agree with his premise or the means by which he substantiates it. For critical responses to his argument, see John Gray, "Steven Pinker is Wrong about Violence and War," in *The Guardian*, March 13, 2015 and John Arquilla, "The Big Kill: Sorry, Steven Pinker, the World isn't Getting Less Violent," in *FP*, December 3, 2012.

unsettling than that conclusion, perhaps, is the audacity of the argument itself.

The grim meta-narrative that drives so much of our cultural and political analysis, that we are going to "hell in a handbasket," feels so self-evidently true that we rarely pause to question it. Is it possible that the sustained critique that intellectuals and academics have made—helping us to understand the genealogies of power, inequality, and violence—is its own form of blinkered skepticism? As Pinker points out, "a large swath of our intellectual culture is loath to admit that there could be anything good about civilization, modernity, and Western society."[2] Pinker is not dismissive of the violence that does persist, and he insists that any form of violence demands vigilant efforts to vanquish it. Still, he contends that without taking the long view we overinflate the dangers of the present, falling victim to the overhyped individual incidences that the modern media circus assaults us with. As a prophylaxis against the infectious heat of that media torrent, Pinker draws us in through the cooler channels of data and statistics.

Could it be, though, that Pinker's eye for data might also reveal its own blind spot? Statistical data analysis can be a powerful, analytical tool. But are there forms of violence that resist measurement—that don't easily yield to becoming data? Behaviors that become crime statistics in a predominantly Black or Hispanic neighborhood (horsing around, doing drugs, hanging out on the street) are often tacitly ignored by authorities in white neighborhoods. Gender-based violence is routinely underreported. What matters is not just what is counted but also what is not counted. And when these presuppositions get baked into algorithms that determine things such as parole, loan, or job eligibility, the blind spots aggregate into invisible, systemic forms of discrimination or racism. They may not leave an immediate mark on the skin, but their capacity to limit freedom and opportunity is no less punishing.[3]

2   Pinker, *Better Angels*, xxii.
3   Angwin, Larson, Mattu and Kirchner, "Machine Bias: There's Software Used across the Country to Predict Future Criminals. And It's Biased against Blacks," in *ProPublica*, May 23, 2016, https://www.propublica.org/article/machine-bias-risk-assessments-in-criminal-sentencing.

In her discussion of violence—in relation to strength, power, authority, and force—Hannah Arendt focuses on "implements" as the distinguishing characteristic of violence. She writes:

> Violence … does not depend on numbers or opinions, but on implements, and the implements of violence, as I mentioned before, like all other tools, increase and multiply human strength. Those who opposed violence with mere power will soon find that they are confronted not by men but by men's artifacts, whose inhumanity and destructive effectiveness increase in proportion to the distance separating the opponents.[4]

Writing, by and large, in the shadow of bureaucratized genocide as well as the atomic bomb, Arendt ties her notion of violence to those designed artefacts that amplify its effects. Arendt understood the insidious impact of bureaucratic systems of public management, or what she called "the rule of Nobody." She revealed a subtle and chilling form of oppression inherent in these anonymous systems:

> If, in accord with traditional political thought, we identify tyranny as government that is not held to give account of itself, rule by Nobody is clearly the most tyrannical of all.[5]

If statistical data is to become the basis upon which the modern bureaucratic state operates—and it has already seeped deeply into the decision-making apparatus within criminal justice (predictive policing), the judiciary (bail amounts and sentence length), education (standardized tests), and financial services (credit scoring)—it risks carrying with it, like a virus, all of the subtle biases and blind spots that infect the original data. Arendt suggests that "violence … does not depend on numbers and opinions," and yet what we are precipitously plunging toward is precisely the weaponization of both. Data scientist Cathy O'Neill terms these algorithmic time bombs "weapons of math destruction," though her clever pun belies their brutal efficacy

4   Hannah Arendt, *On Violence* (Orlando: Harcourt, 1969), 53.
5   Arendt, *On Violence*, 38.

(as she demonstrates).[6] These new forms of violence are indeed strengthened in their distance from the perpetrators; ruthless, inscrutable, and anonymous, they inflict new forms of violence upon their already disempowered victims. The effects of these implements may not be immediately written on the body, but they work their violence more indirectly. These black box algorithms are accountable to few, understood by few, and felt by many. There is Nobody to point to, which may make them "the most tyrannical of all." Violence, as we knew it, may be in decline. What is more alarming is how effortlessly it cloaks itself in the implements of the new.

Jamer Hunt

See also
BUREAUCRACY, EVIL, TOTALITARIANISM

6   Cathy O'Neill, *Weapons of Math Destruction: How Big Data Increases Inequality and Threatens Democracy* (New York: Broadway Books, 2016), 3.

VITA ACTIVA

Hannah Arendt's conception of an "active life"[1] is that of a life "devoted to public-political matters." Her vision of an active life envisions individuals who do not give up acting in public space and place themselves in relation with others to take care of the general interest (i.e., political action).

This conceptualization of an active life and the model of active subject sharply contrast with the dominant model of the economic agent, the *homo economicus*. According to mainstream economic doctrine, the infrastructure of the *homo economicus* represents the best instrument for achieving social well-being because it ensures, through decentralized decisions and exchanges based on the evaluation of maximization of individual interest, it is possible to achieve an optimal allocation of costs and benefits in society. But the theory of the commons teaches us that there are resources that are not subject to those rules, and the phenomena of collective action in cities, for social innovation, collaborative economy, and the commons seem to question the traditional economic approach and entail the emergence of a new model of economic agent, the *mulier activa*.[2] The *mulier activa* offers an enlarged sphere of motivation for individual and collective action and a different approach to acting. It envisages a model of an individual not guided by the perpetual quest to maximize its own material interests, an individual unwilling to act alone. The economic and sociologic literature already proposed definitions of *homo civicus*,[3]

1   Hannah Arendt, *The Human Condition* (Chicago, IL: University of Chicago Press, [1958] 1998).
2   This approach was already proposed in the *Opinion of the European Committee of the Regions, The Local and Regional Dimension of the Sharing Economy*, approved by the Committee of the Regions of the European Union (CoR) on December 4, 2015. Available at: http://www.labgov.it/2016/06/30/the-local-and-regional-dimensions-of-the-sharing-economy-by-christian-iaione/. See also Christian Iaione, "Poolism" *LabGov.city*, http://www.labgov.it/2015/08/20/poolism/.
3   Franco Cassano, *Homo civicus. La ragionevole follia dei beni comuni* (Bari: Dedalo, 2004).

homo collaborans,[4] *homo reciprocans*,[5] *homo cooperans*.[6] The hypothesis generated by the research efforts spent in the urban commons and the city as a common envisages the fact that, if the context is designed in different ways, the rise of the economic agent of a *mulier activa* could be stimulated and cultivated. The definition of *mulier activa* is heavily rooted in the concept of individuals entailed by Hannah Arendt's conception of *vita activa*.

The emergence of new models of economic agents such as the *mulier activa* is not to be interpreted as a substitution of the traditional economic agent. The two agent models are not wholly incompatible, it is indeed to be expected that the model of the individual as a self-interested agent aimed at maximizing a short-term profit can be accompanied[7] by a model of the individual willing to cooperate to achieve purposes of general interest following rules based on reciprocity and trust. The prominent scholars of the commons Elinor Ostrom and Marco Janssen already warned researchers of the risk of thinking that the paradigm of *homo economicus* does not find application anymore.[8] On the contrary, in formulating research hypotheses, it is always advisable to take into account the fact that many behaviors are modeled by the imprint of the traditional economic agent, although they are able to respect reciprocity norms.[9]

Within the logic of the traditional market, consumers tend to be conceived as passive subjects, also because the products purchased are never produced by those who purchase them. There is never a direct collaboration, a circular and collaborative dynamic. The same applies to the forms of government of urban infrastructures and services, where the prevailing dynamic is

4   Harald Heinrichs, Im Zeitalter des homo collaborans: sharing economy," *Politische Okologie* vol. 135 (2013): 99.
5   Samuel Bowles and Herbert Gintis, "Behavioural science: homo reciprocans," *Nature* no. 415 (2002): 125–8.
6   Tine De Moor, *Homo Cooperans: Institutions for Collective Action and the Compassionate Society* (Utrecht: Universiteit Utrecht, 2013).
7   Marco A. Janssen and Elinor Ostrom, "Empirically Based, Agent-Based Models," *Ecology and Society* vol. 11, no. 2 (2006): 39.
8   Ibid.
9   Elinor Ostrom, "A Behavioral Approach to the Rational Choice Theory of Collective Action," *American Political Science Review* vol. 92, no. 1 (1998): 1–22; Elinor Ostrom, *Understanding Institutional Diversity* (Princeton, NJ: Princeton University Press, 2005).

that of providing a service. This situation can change through the enabling of a principle of collaboration close to competition. Applied to the City, this structure would provide the basis for a model of a collaborative city or Co-city,[10] which stimulates the construction of public–private–people partnerships, involving the actors of the institutional ecosystem to quintuple helix model of governance of urban innovation. This model would involve five categories of actors: civic entrepreneurs or the unorganized public, public authorities, businesses, NGOs, and knowledge institutions. These urban cogovernance arrangements would have the aim of fostering social innovation, facilitating the emergence of pooling economies as drivers of community-led local economic development, and promoting inclusive urban regeneration processes. The concept of the urban commons[11] and of the transitions toward City as a commons,[12] or Co-City contributes to sketch some lines of reasoning for a legal reconstruction of the phenomenon of the collective action on urban commons, infrastructures, and collaborative economy from both the theoretical and applied standpoint. To build a robust theoretical and empirically grounded paradigm based on the foundations of theory of the commons, it is necessary, however, to acquire a new key to understanding the implications in terms of legal and economic models. The starting point can be an evolution of the conceptualization of the economic agent based on the model of *homo economicus*[13] as a self-interested profit or utility maximizing individual, toward a *mulier activa*

---

10   Christian Iaione, "The Co-City," *American Journal of Economics and Sociology* (2016): 415.

11   Sheila R. Foster, "Collective Action and the Urban Commons," *Notre Dame Law Review* vol. 87, no. 57 (2011); Iaione, "Governing the Urban Commons," *Italian Journal of Public Law* vol. 7, no. 1 (2015): 170.

12   Sheila R. Foster and Christian Iaione, "The City as a Commons," *Yale Law and Policy Review* vol. 34, no. 2 (2016). See also Sheila R. Foster and Christian Iaione, "Ostrom in the City: Design Principles and Practices for the Urban Commons," forthcoming in *Routledge Handbook of the Study of the Commons*, eds. Dan Cole, Blake Hudson, and Jonathan Rosenbloom (New York: Routledge, 2018).

13   Elinor Ostrom, "A Behavioral Approach to the Rational Choice Theory of Collective Action," *American Political Science Review* vol. 92, no. 1 (1998), 1–22; See also Elinor Ostrom, *Understanding Institutional Diversity* (Princeton, NJ: Princeton University Press, 2005).

as a concept of individual action within the urban public sphere that builds on Arendt's concept of *vita activa*. A key observation point is offered by the emergence of urban innovations and evolutions that are reshaping urban (and periurban) development and land use, urban and local economic patterns, urban welfare systems and democratic and political processes, as well as governmental decision-making and organization. In some cases, networks of urban commons or a certain degree of polycentricism in the governance of urban resources can be observed so that a transformation of the city into a commons—a collaborative space—supported and enabled by the state can be identified.[14] Cities such as Barcelona, Naples, Ghent are implementing policies enabling civic uses and civic management of city resources, assets, services. Communities such as West Harlem in New York City are exploring cooperatively owned microgrids as a means to help vulnerable populations cope with climate change impacts and reduce energy costs in the transition from a fossil fuel to a renewable energy economy.

Christian Iaione and Elena De Nictolis

See also
COMMON WORLD, DEMOCRACY, *HOMO FABER*

---

14 Sheila R. Foster and Christian Iaione, "Ostrom in the City: Design Principles for the Urban Commons," *Nature of Cities* (2017), https://www.thenatureofcities.com/2017/08/20/ostrom-city-design-principles-urban-commons/.

VITA CONTEMPLATIVA

I

As many commentators have pointed out, Arendt's entire philosophical oeuvre is rife with distinctions, and the most important distinction is between *vita activa* and *vita contemplativa*. The latter is, above all, the philosopher's way of life, the prerogative for armchair adherence to eternal truths and "speechless wonder"[1] before and above opinion and, as such, removed from the messiness of worldly concerns.

The disengaged nature of *vita contemplativa* indeed makes one wonder about the relevance of thinking through design as politics and, even more so, of designing in dark times. What does seeking exile in unabated contemplation really have to offer us, we might ask, when "staying with trouble," to paraphrase feminist philosopher Donna Haraway,[2] ought to be our *designerly* knee-jerk response. The better option, then, might be to respectfully advise you, dear reader, to return to *vita activa* or any other entry in this lexicon that has caught your attention. But then again, if staying with the trouble should apply everywhere, as we have just proclaimed, stay with us just a little longer.

In Arendt's close reading,[3] it was the untimely death of Socrates, following his failure to persuade the Athenian judges, that led Plato to instigate a reversal of the roles of *vita activa* and *vita contemplativa* as the governing principle of political life in the Greek *polis*, in favor of the latter.[4] Arendt points to this pivotal shift in Western thought as the moment of inception of

1 Hannah Arendt, "Philosophy and Politics," *Social Research* vol. 71, no. 3 (2004): 449.
2 Donna Haraway, *Staying with the Trouble: Making Kin in the Chthulucene* (Durham: Duke University Press, 2016).
3 Hannah Arendt, *The Human Condition* (Chicago, IL: University of Chicago Press, [1958] 1998); Arendt, "Philosophy and Politics," 427–54.
4 Maurizio Passerin D'Entrèves, *The Political Philosophy of Hannah Arendt* (Taylor & Francis e-Library, 2001).

political philosophy. For Plato this meant the elevation of eternal truth at the expense of both persuasion (*peithein*) and opinion (*doxa*)—the main activities of political intercourse in the public realm. Tellingly, Arendt refers to this as the "tyranny of truth"[5] as it represses what is temporally considered good according to opinions among the people of the *polis* for the eternal truth of a philosopher king. With the advent of Modernity the hierarchy transformed once again. Contemplation, or the pondering of truths in silence, has given way to *homo faber*, or the fabrication of knowledge as thought. What began as *vita contemplativa* had at this point changed into a preoccupation with processes and labor.

Arendt's analysis of the modern age foregrounds the rise of process, labor, and progress as constituents of the public realm. Under the conditions of Modernity, contemplation as withdrawal had lost its direct political relevance. However, for Arendt, in this process *vita contemplativa* is not relegated to the history of political philosophy. It is rekindled as a precondition for understanding Judgement, which for Arendt is a faculty ascribed to the "non-participating spectator."[6] Unlike philosophers who withdraw, the spectator only retires temporarily from active participation and hence "is not independent of the view of others."[7] This dissimilarity is significant because contemplation, thus construed, takes place *within* "intersubjective and public dimensions,"[8] i.e., as an extension of the world, but in a space in which the spectator is free because he or she, at the same time, is disengaged and hence able to satisfy curiosity; to experience strong, even dangerous emotions; to consider even heretical ideas.

---

5   Arendt, "Philosophy and Politics," 431.
6   Hannah Arendt, *The Life of the Mind: Volume Two, Willing*
      (New York: Harcourt Brace Jovanovich, 1979).
7   Arendt, *The Life of the Mind*, 94.
8   D'Entrèves, *The Political Philosophy of Hannah Arendt*, 131.

II

If we now turn to look at design, it might appear, at first sight, that it is thoroughly contained in *vita activa*. As "it collaborates actively and proactively in the social construction of meaning,"[9] there does not seem to be much need for detached contemplation. On closer inspection, however, specific traditions within design and design research such as speculative design and design fiction do produce artefacts, often in the form of prototypes that challenge existing assumptions and cause a sense of curiosity and wonder in its audience. This, to be sure, is not the articulation of wonder as the underlying principle of philosophy before Descartes,[10] but rather the result of techné: carefully crafted materials and signs, designed specifically to produce a jolt of wonder[11] and "prompt speculation in the viewer about the world these objects belong to."[12] Even if this affective state is only local and passing, it may still have a shimmer of light to offer the world. Arendt understood the world as that which lies between people, previously illuminated by the powers of the public realm and now in perpetual decline.[13]

But contemplation in design need not only have relevance as detached wondering. Echoing Donald Schön's notion of reflection-in-action,[14] it may as well be seen as a productive *judgment-in-action*, emphasizing the performative conditions under which contemplation happens as a momentary shift of attention within action that, in turn, enables a reconception of

9   Victor Margolin quoted in Ezio Manzini, *Design, When Everybody Designs: An Introduction to Design for Social Innovation* (Cambridge, MA: MIT Press, 2015), 35.
10   Arendt, *The Human Condition*, 276.
11   While the allure of designed objects differs in kind from philosophical wonder, it can also open up new possibilities of thought.
12   Anthony Dunne and Fiona Raby, *Speculative Everything: Design, Fiction, and Social Dreaming* (Cambridge, MA: MIT Press, 2013), 92.
13   Hannah Arendt, "On Humanity in Dark Times: Thoughts about Lessing," in *Men in Dark Times* (New York: Harcourt, Brace, [1955] 1993), 3–31.
14   Schön defines a reflection-*in*-action contrary to reflection-*on*-action, as that which takes place in the midst of—and thus not separated from—action. Donald Schön, *The Reflective Practitioner: How Professionals Think in Action* (New York: Basic Books, 1983).

the unfolding events. The following case shows what such a judgment-in-action might entail.

As part of a design project, entitled Social Games Against Crime, a board game prototype was designed and played to help build a better understanding of a group of teenagers' experiences with visiting their incarcerated fathers. The game layout depicts a city with familiar locations and the possibility of conscribing friends, families, and notabilities to help each player overcome a number of real-life obstacles to fulfill a dream. The game was played with family therapists who had intimate knowledge of the player's life situation. One of the players was a 14-year-old girl, Mira. As her dream, she articulated a wish to visit her father less often, and acknowledged as her main obstacle to fulfill this dream a lack of courage to tell him and bear the consequences. In the course of playing and interacting with the other teenagers and the therapists, Mira brought a helper into the game, modeled on one of her father's friends, Jake, as the only person that could make her father listen and accept her wishes. In trying to resolve her predicament through previous counseling, the therapists had never heard of Jake as a possible future go-between.

This case shows that contemplation activated through design can afford a momentary stepping-out of the real, without leaving the social context. What this transient switch from action to contemplation offsets in Mira is a sudden power to pass judgment and retrospectively change her perception of past actions. Moreover, it is from this reconceptualization of the past that she could be able to alter the future in a more positive direction. The effect may be infinitely small in the great scheme of political things, but it is nevertheless testimony to the fact that "staying with the trouble" and "making-with"[15] do not exclude—may in fact be encouraged by—a moderate dose of Arendtian contemplation. In this respect, the application of *vita contemplativa* to the practice of design, as suggested here, entails a doing away with the notion's original dialectical

---

15   Haraway, *Staying with the Trouble: Making Kin in the Chthulucene.*

relationship to *vita activa*. But we will argue, that it is precisely this composition with action that makes contemplation relevant in dark times, as a means of *selbstdanken*—the ability of thinking for oneself—which for Arendt[16] is inherently linked to humanity and freedom.

Tau U. Lenskjold, Thomas Markussen, and Eva Knutz

See also
IN-BETWEEN, SOLITUDE, SPONTANEITY

---

16   Arendt's notion of "Selbstdenken" is an appraisal of German writer Gottfried Lessing who, she contends, never quite felt at home in the world but at the same time refused to seek refuge in thought and philosophy. See Hannah Arendt, *Men in Dark Times* (New York: Harcourt, Brace, [1955] 1993).

AFTERWORD: THE ILLUMINATIONS OF HANNAH ARENDT

Richard J. Bernstein

In the preface to her 1968 collection of essays, *Men in Dark Times*, Hannah Arendt wrote: "Even in the darkest of times we have the right to expect some illumination." Today, in our own dark time, Arendt's work is being read with a new urgency, precisely because it provides such illumination.

Born in Germany in 1906, Arendt studied with prominent philosophers of her time, but fled the country in 1933, living for a time in Paris and later in the United States. She is best known for her major works, including "The Human Condition," "On Violence," "Truth and Politics," "The Origins of Totalitarianism," and especially "Eichmann in Jerusalem: A Report on the Banality of Evil," which grew out of her coverage of the trial of the Nazi Adolf Eichmann for The New Yorker.

She was remarkably perceptive about some of the deepest problems, perplexities, and dangerous tendencies in modern political life, many of them still with us today. When she speaks of "dark times" and warns of the "exhortations, moral and otherwise, that under the pretext of upholding old truths degrade all truth in meaningless triviality" we can hear not only a critique of the horrors of twentieth-century totalitarianism but also a warning about forces pervading the politics of the United States and Europe today.

Arendt was one of the first major political thinkers to warn that the ever-increasing numbers of stateless persons and refugees would continue to be an intractable problem. One of Arendt's early articles, the 1943 essay "We Refugees," based on her personal experiences of statelessness, raises fundamental questions. In it, she graphically describes what it means to lose one's home, one's language, and one's occupation and concludes with a more general claim about the political consequences of the new mass phenomenon—the "creation" of masses of people forced to leave their homes and their country: "Refugees driven from country to county represent the new vanguard of their peoples ... The comity of European peoples went to pieces when, and because, it allowed its weakest member to be excluded and persecuted."

When Arendt wrote this she could scarcely have realized how relevant her observations would be in 2018. Almost every significant political event during the past 100 years has resulted in the multiplication of new categories of refugees, and there appears to be no end in sight. There are now millions of people in refugee camps with little hope that they will be able to return to their homes or ever find a new one.

In her 1951 work, "The Origins of Totalitarianism," Arendt wrote of refugees: "The calamity of the rightless is not that they are deprived of life, liberty and the pursuit of happiness, or of equality before the law and freedom of opinion, but that they no longer belonged to any community whatsoever." The loss of community has the consequence of expelling a people from humanity itself. Appeals to abstract human rights are meaningless unless there are effective institutions to guarantee these rights. The most fundamental right is the "right to have rights."

By dwelling on the horrors of totalitarianism and grasping that the aim of total domination is to destroy human spontaneity, individuality, and plurality, Arendt probed what it means fully to live a human life in a political community and begin something new—what she called natality. She also sought to probe the threats to the dignity of politics—the type of politics in which individuals confront each other as political equals, deliberate, and act together—a politics in which empowerment can grow and public freedom can thrive without violence.

Her essay "Truth and Politics," published in 1967, might have been written yesterday. Her analysis of systematic lying and the danger it presents to factual truths is urgently relevant. Because factual truths are contingent and consequently might have been otherwise, it is all too easy to destroy factual truth and substitute "alternative facts."

In "Truth and Politics," she wrote: "Freedom of opinion is a farce unless factual information is guaranteed and the facts themselves are not in dispute." Unfortunately one of the most successful techniques for blurring the distinction between factual truth and falsehood is to claim that any so-called factual truth is just another opinion—something we hear almost every day from the current administration. What happened so blatantly in totalitarian regimes is being practiced today by leading politicians with great success—creating a fictional world of "alternative facts."

According to Arendt, there is an even greater danger:

> The result of a consistent and total substitution of lies for factual truth is not that the lies will now be accepted as truth, and the truth defamed as lies, but that the sense by which we take our bearings in the real world—and the category of truth vs. falsehood is among the mental means to this end—is being destroyed.

The possibilities for lying become boundless and frequently meet with little resistance.

Many liberals are perplexed that when their fact-checking clearly and definitively shows that a lie is a lie, people seem unconcerned and indifferent. But Arendt understood how propaganda really works. "What convinces masses are not facts, not even invented facts, but only the consistency of the system of which they are presumably a part."

People who feel that they have been neglected and forgotten yearn for a narrative—even an invented fictional one—that will make sense of the anxiety they are experiencing, and promises some sort of redemption. An authoritarian leader has enormous advantages by exploiting anxieties and creating a fiction that people want to believe. A fictional story that promises to solve one's problems is much more appealing than facts and "reasonable" arguments.

Arendt was not a doomsayer. To counter her warnings about political dangers, she elaborated a detailed conception of the dignity of politics. Because of our natality, our capacity to act, we can always begin something new. The deepest theme in Arendt is the need to take responsibility for our political lives.

She warned against being seduced by nihilism, cynicism, or indifference. She was bold in her description of the lying, deception, self-deception, image-making, and the attempt of those in power to destroy the very distinction between truth and falsehood.

Her defense of the dignity of politics provides a critical standard for judging the situation many of us find ourselves in today, where the opportunity to participate, to act in concert, and to engage in genuine debate with our peers is being diminished. We must resist the temptation to opt out of politics and to assume that nothing can be done in the face of all the current ugliness, deception, and corruption. Arendt's lifelong project was to honestly confront and comprehend the darkness of our times, without losing sight of the possibility of transcendence and illumination. It should be our project, too.

CONTRIBUTORS

Mariana Amatullo is associate professor of Strategic Design and Management at Parsons School of Design, The New School and the cofounder of Designmatters at Art Center College of Design. Her scholarship and teaching engage broadly with questions about the agency of design in organizational culture and social innovation contexts. *See* HUMAN RIGHTS.

Ahmed Ansari is assistant professor in the department of Technology, Culture and Society at NYU Tandon. His research interests intersect between design studies, cultural theory, and the philosophy and history of technology in the Indian subcontinent. He is also a founding member of the *Decolonizing Design* platform. *See* REIFICATION.

Simone Ashby is assistant professor in Communication and Cognition at Tilburg University, where she teaches New Media Design. Her research brings together approaches from ethnography, human-centered design, speech science, and computational linguistics for transforming data into media and helping people become more connected and empowered in their communities. *See* COMMON WORLD.

James Auger is enseignant-chercheur at the École normale supérieure Paris-Saclay and associate professor at RMIT Europe. His practice-based design research examines the social, cultural, and personal impacts of technology and the products that exist as a result of its development and application. *See* COMMON WORLD.

Martín Ávila is a designer, researcher, and professor of Design at Konstfack in Stockholm, Sweden. His postdoctoral project *Symbiotic Tactics* (2013–16) has been the first of its kind to be financed by the Swedish Research Council. Martín's research is design-driven and addresses forms of interspecies cohabitation. See also www.martinavila.com. *See* TOGETHERNESS.

Nik Baerten was trained as a knowledge engineer (artificial intelligence). For several years he was active as a multidisciplinary researcher at the Digital Culture Department of Maastricht McLuhan Institute (NL). In 2004 he cofounded Pantopicon, a foresight and design studio based in Antwerp (Belgium). The studio crafts provocative futures in order to stimulate debate regarding tomorrow's challenges and opportunities. *See* BEGINNINGS.

Jocelyn Bailey is a designer and researcher with particular expertise in social design and policy. She is currently undertaking an AHRC-supported PhD at the University of Brighton, critically examining the growth of design practices within and for government. She has worked for Westminster think tank Policy Connect, cultural consultancy BOP, and design agency Uscreates. She originally trained as an architect at Cambridge University. *See* LAW.

Massimo Bianchini (designer, PhD in design) is assistant professor at the Design Department of Politecnico di Milano. He is cofounder and lab manager of Polifactory (www.polifactory.polimi.it), the makerspace of Politecnico di Milano, a multidisciplinary research lab that investigates the relationship between design and the change of production models. From 2014 he has codeveloped pilot projects with public bodies and institutions exploring the creation of innovation ecosystems based on openP2P collaboration between designers, makers, and makerspaces, user innovators, and enterprises (www.nextdesigninnovation.it, www.fabric-action.org,distributeddesign.eu). *See HOMO FABER*.

Thomas Binder is professor in codesign at the Royal Danish Academy of Fine Arts Schools of Architecture, Design and Conservation. He is a founding member of the codesign research center, CODE. His research includes contributions to methods and tools for experimental design research and open innovation processes. *See* FREEDOM.

Andrea Botero is researcher at the School of Arts, Design and Architecture of Aalto University and conspirator at the design studio Suo&Co. Her design and research work explores the possibilities and contradictions inherent in the design of environments, tools, and media that afford more relational and caring interactions among and between people and their environment. *See* HUMANITY.

Constantin Boym founded his design studio in New York in 1986, together with his partner Laurene Leon. In 2009 Boym Partners were winners of the National Design Award. Their work is included in the permanent collection of the Museum of Modern Art in New York. Presently, Constantin serves as Chair of Industrial Design at Pratt Institute. His most recent book is *Keepsakes: A Design Memoir* (2015). *See* SUPERFLUITY.

Jamie Brassett is reader in Philosophy, Design and Innovation at University of the Arts London and Programme Research Director at Central Saint Martins. He has a PhD in Philosophy from University of Warwick (1993). Jamie co-edited (with Betti Marenko) *Deleuze and Design* (EUP 2015) and is currently editing two collections: on anticipation (with John O'Reilly) and superheroes (with Richard Reynolds), both forthcoming 2021. *See* CREATIVITY.

John A. Bruce is a design strategist and filmmaker. His work involves ethnography for addressing complexity. He is assistant professor of Strategic Design at Parsons School of Design. He was a 2015/16 fellow at the Graduate Institute for Design Ethnography and Social Thought at The New School. *See* MORTALITY.

Pablo Calderón Salazar is a designer, educator, and researcher. He works as an associate professor at the Product Design School of the Jorge Tadeo Lozano University (Bogotá, Colombia). He produces texts, installations, graphics, videos, interventions, and objects that provoke reflection around relevant issues in society, while attempting to hint at better ways of living together. *See* BOURGEOIS.

Carla Cipolla is associate professor of the Universidade Federal do Rio de Janeiro—UFRJ/Coppe, where she runs a DESIS Lab. Her research activities are developed in the intersection between design for social innovation and service design and are focused on the importance of interpersonal relationships in services, particularly on those that aim to deliver positive social change. *See* PARIAH.

Elena De Nictolis is post-doc researcher at LUISS Guido Carli University, Italy, and a research associate at LabGov—LABoratory for the GOVernance of the City as Commons (www.labgov.city) since 2012. Under the supervision of Sheila Foster and Christian Iaione, she is currently engaged with a groundbreaking international applied research project, the "Co-Cities Project." *See VITA ACTIVA*.

Chiara Del Gaudio is assistant professor at the School of Industrial Design of Carleton University (Canada). Her main research interests are: strategic design for social innovation, design as a political process, participatory and collaborative design approaches, power and conflict within the design process, and the limits of current design practices for more democratic futures. *See* HUMANITY.

Clive Dilnot Until 2017, he was professor of Design Studies at the Parsons School of Design, New York. Recent work includes *Design and the Question of History* (2015); *A John Heskett Reader: Design History Economics* (ed.) (2016); *Design and the Creation of Value* (ed.) (2017). *See* ANTHROPOCENTRISM.

Caroline Dionne is assistant professor in the History & Theory of Design Practice at Parsons School of Design, The New School. Sitting at the intersection of literature, language theories, architecture, and social movements, her research examines the relationship between language processes and place-making in collective design practices. Some of her recent essays can be found in *Reading Architecture: Literary Imagination and Architectural Experience* (2018), *OASE 96 Social Poetics: The Architecture of Use and Appropriation* (NAI, 2016), *Architecture's Appeal* (2015). *See* SPEECH.

Carl DiSalvo is associate professor at the Georgia Institute of Technology. His research explores the political qualities of contemporary design, in both theory and practice. He is also an editor of the journal *Design Issues. See* PUBLIC.

Arturo Escobar is professor of Anthropology, emeritus at the University of North Carolina, Chapel Hill. His main interests are: political ecology, ontological design, and the anthropology of globalization, social movements, and technoscience. He is engaged in transition design in the Colombian Cauca valley region. He recently published *Designs for the Pluriverse: Radical Interdependence, Autonomy, and the Making of Worlds*. *See* OBJECTIVITY.

Laura Forlano, a Fulbright award-winning and National Science Foundation-funded scholar, is a writer, social scientist, and design researcher. She is associate professor at the Institute of Design at Illinois Institute of Technology. She received her PhD in communications from Columbia University. She is coeditor of *Bauhaus Futures*. *See* TECHNOLOGY.

Tony Fry is principal, The Studio at the Edge of the World, Launceston, Tasmania; adjunct professor, University of Tasmania; and visiting professor at Universidad de Ibague, Colombia. Tony has held academic positions in Australia and internationally and is the author of fourteen books—his latest is *Unstaging War: Confronting Conflict and Peace* (2019). *See* THOUGHTLESSNESS.

Alastair Fuad-Luke is a design facilitator, educator, writer, and activist. His books include *Agents of Alternatives*, *Design Activism*, and *The Eco-design Handbook*. He is a full professor at the Faculty of Design & Art, the Free University of Bozen-Bolzano, Italy, and previously professor of Emerging Design Practices, School of Arts, Design and Architecture, Aalto University, Finland. *See* ACTIVISM.

Lorraine Gamman is professor of Design at Central Saint Martins where in 1999 she founded the Design Against Crime Research Centre that she continues to direct. She is currently PI on several collaborative design research projects working with prisoners and staff in UK prisons, writes on design, and is coeditor of *Tricky Design—The Ethics of Things* (2019). *See* POWER.

Claudia Garduño García is associate professor at the Postgraduate Unit on Industrial Design, Universidad Nacional

Autónoma de México. She is the founder of Aalto LAB Mexico and the research director of the Design Your Action. *See* IMPERIALISM.

Eric Gordon is professor of Civic Media and the director of the Engagement Lab at Emerson College in Boston. His research focuses on building better interfaces between publics and civic organizations in a context of diminishing trust. He has codesigned interventions for large and small organizations around the world, with a special emphasis on play, delight, and deliberation. His book (with Gabriel Mugar), *Meaningful Inefficiencies: Civic Design in an Age of Digital Expediency* (Oxford University Press, 2020), further explores the role of play in civic life. *See* PLAY.

Anke Gruendel is part-time assistant professor at Parsons, The New School for Design and a PhD candidate in Politics at the New School for Social Research. She holds an MA in Design Studies from Parsons and has a background in biology and liberal arts. Her research enquires into public sector design and its relationship to the changing debates that shaped ideas of governance, knowledge production, and decision-making in post-Second World War technical democracy in the United States and Europe. *See* PLURALITY.

Joachim Halse, PhD, is a design anthropologist deploying learning technologies for improving lifesaving medical care as Design Manager at Laerdal Medical. Previously Joachim codirected the Center for Codesign Research and was head of the MA codesign program at the Royal Danish Academy of Fine Arts—School of Design. *See* ACTION.

Julian Hanna is assistant professor in Culture Studies at Tilburg University. His research focuses on critical intersections between culture, politics, and technology. In 2017 he received the CCCB Cultural Innovation International Prize with James Auger and Laura Watts for The Newton Machine. His latest book is *The Manifesto Handbook: 95 Theses on an Incendiary Form* (2020). *See* COMMON WORLD.

Jamer Hunt is the vice provost for transdisciplinary initiatives at The New School and founding director (2009–15) of the graduate program in Transdisciplinary Design at Parsons. With Paola Antonelli at the MoMA he was cocreator of the award-winning curatorial experiment and book *Design and Violence* (2013–15). *See* VIOLENCE.

Liesbeth Huybrechts (1979, Belgium) is associate professor in the Faculty of Architecture, UHasselt. She is involved in research and teaching in the areas of participatory design, public (urban) space, interaction design, and design anthropology. She is involved in the Living Lab De Andere Markt, focused on the future of work. *See* COMMON INTERESTS.

Christian Iaione is associate professor of Urban Law and Policy, Regulatory Innovation and Land Use at LUISS University, Italy, and codirector of LabGov—LABoratory for the GOVernance of the City as Commons (www.labgov.city). He is a member of the Sharing Economy International Advisory Board of the Seoul Metropolitan Government. He is an Urban Innovative Actions expert appointed by the European Commission for the Co-City project of Turin, Italy; lead expert of the EU Urbact program; and a member of the Urban Partnership on Innovative and Responsible Procurement within the Urban Agenda for the EU. *See VITA ACTIVA*.

Tim Ingold is emeritus professor of Social Anthropology at the University of Aberdeen, where he directed the EU-funded interdisciplinary research project "Knowing from the Inside: Anthropology, Art, Architecture and Design" (2013–18). Recent publications include *Lines* (2007), *Being Alive* (2011), *Making* (2013), *The Life of Lines* (2015), *Anthropology and/as education* (2018). *See* SOLITUDE.

Michael Kaethler is a researcher, educator, and curator with a particular interest in how knowledge works in moments of creative production and collaboration. He is a research fellow at the Department of Architecture at KU Leuven and teaches theory and writing for the Social Design masters at Design Academy Eindhoven. *See* BOURGEOIS.

Mahmoud Keshavarz is a postdoctoral researcher at the Engaging Vulnerability Research Program, Uppsala University. He is the author of *The Design Politics of the Passport: Materiality, Immobility and Dissent* (Bloomsbury), cofounder of *Decolonizing Design* group, and coeditor of *Design and Culture* journal. *See* CITIZENSHIP.

Eva Knutz is associate professor at the Department for Design & Communication, University of Southern Denmark. Eva works with social design, speculative design, and citizen participation in relation to crime and healthcare—and she has developed a number of prototypes and tools to support vulnerable groups in society. *See VITA CONTEMPLATIVA.*

Sophie Krier is an artist and researcher affiliated to EnsadLab-PSL Research University Paris. She founded the publication series *Field Essays* channeled by Onomatopee to explore forms of knowing embedded in artistic processes, and directs *Art & Design Practice*, an experimental Liberal Arts & Sciences track at University College Roosevelt (NL). *See* SOLITUDE.

Outi Kuittinen is executive at the Nordic think tank Demos Helsinki. Her work concentrates on creating collective transition. Her expertise is in bringing together actors—organizations, groups, individuals—across sectors to find a common goal and ways of acting together to achieve desired change. She holds M.Soc.Sci (political science) from the University of Helsinki and has been a visiting Fulbright scholar in the New School and Harvard University. *See* FABRICATION.

Tau U. Lenskjold is associate professor at the University of Southern Denmark. His work investigates design collaborations with disadvantaged groups and collective engagements around ecological issues. Drawing on participatory and experimental practices from codesign, speculative prototyping, and activism, the research explores design as an inquiring approach toward social and environmental sustainability. *See VITA CONTEMPLATIVA.*

Stefano Maffei (architect and PhD in Design) is full professor at the School of Design, Politecnico di Milano. He's the director of Polifactory, the Makerspace of Politecnico di Milano and also of the Service Design Master POLIdesign, Politecnico di Milano. He received the XXII° Compasso D'Oro Prize for Design Research with Design Research Maps (2011). *See HOMO FABER*.

Henry Mainsah is senior researcher at the Norwegian Institute for Consumer Research, Oslo Metropolitan University. He was previously a Marie Curie fellow at the Centre for Interdisciplinary Methodologies, University of Warwick, and an associate professor at the Oslo School of Architecture and Design. He holds a PhD in Media and Communication from the University of Oslo. His research interests include interdisciplinary research methods, digital and social media, design, literacies, and youth culture. *See* SPONTANEITY.

Ezio Manzini works on design for social innovation. He started DESIS Network. Presently, he collaborates with Elisava (Barcelona), Politecnico (Milano), Tongji (Shanghai), Jiangnan (Wuxi). Recent books: *Design, When Everybody Designs*, MIT Press 2015; *Politics of the Everyday*, Bloomsbury 2019. *See* DEMOCRACY.

Victor Margolin was professor emeritus of Design History at the University of Illinois, Chicago. He was a founding editor and coeditor of the academic design journal *Design Issues*. Books that he has written, edited, or coedited include *The Struggle for Utopia: Rodchenko, Lissitzky, Moholy-Nagy, 1917–1936*; *Design Discourse*; *Discovering Design*; *The Idea of Design*; *The Designed World: Images, Objects, Environments*; and *The Politics of the Artificial: Essays on Design and Design Studies*. The first two volumes of his three-volume *World History of Design* were published in April 2015. *See* HISTORY.

Thomas Markussen is associate professor and cofounder of the Social Design Research Unit, at the University of Southern Denmark. In his work, Markussen focuses on how design can be used as a political and critical aesthetic practice, notably in the fields of social design, design activism, and design fiction. *See VITA CONTEMPLATIVA*.

Sónia Matos is associate research faculty at ITI-LARSyS as well as a lecturer at the School of Design, University of Edinburgh.

Using ethnographic and participatory research methods, she partakes in the creation of interventions designed to safeguard cultural and natural heritage. *See* COMMON WORLD.

Shannon Mattern is professor of anthropology at The New School. Her writing and teaching focus on media architectures and infrastructures and spatial epistemologies. She has written books about libraries, maps, and the history of urban intelligence, and she writes a column for *Places* journal. You can find her at wordsinspace.net. *See* BUREAUCRACY.

Andrew Morrison is the director of the Centre for Design Research at the Oslo School of Architecture and Design. Working within and across design, urbanism, and landscape through design and cultural perspectives, his current work focuses on anticipation studies with attention to narrative, poetics, and practices. Andrew was chair of the 3rd International Conference on Anticipation held at AHO in October 2019. *See* COURAGE.

Aleksi Neuvonen is the cofounder of the Nordic think tank Demos Helsinki. He is a futures researcher and an expert on urban development and lifestyle changes. Currently Aleksi Neuvonen is in charge of Demos Helsinki's The Next Era initiative on fair and sustainable transition to postindustrial society. He holds MA (philosophy) from University of Helsinki and is currently preparing his PhD in planning theory in Tampere University of Technology and Radboud University Nijmegen. *See* FABRICATION.

Dimeji Onafuwa's work seeks to understand commons-based approaches to user experience on platforms. He holds a PhD in Transition Design from Carnegie Mellon University and an MBA in management from The University of North Carolina at Charlotte. Dimeji is currently a senior researcher at Microsoft. *See* COMMON GOOD.

Macushla Robinson is a curator based in New York City. Formerly assistant curator of Contemporary International Art at the Art Gallery of New South Wales, she has published in Art & Australia, Art Monthly and ArtAsiaPacific, as well as several exhibition catalogues. Her research sits at the intersection of art and politics, feminism and race. Her doctoral dissertation examines practices of inheritance and intergenerational wealth through art objects. *See* PRIVATE REALM.

Søren Rosenbak is a PhD candidate at Umeå Institute of Design in Sweden. His research concerns the prototyping of a pataphysically infused design practice, and the making of the science of imagining solutions, a theory for a design becoming conscious of itself. *See* ALIENATION.

Martha Rosler is an American artist. She works in photography, text, installation, sculpture, and performance. Rosler's work is centered on everyday life and the public sphere, often with an eye to women's experience. Recurrent concerns are the media and war, as well as architecture and the built environment, from housing and homelessness to places of passage and systems of transport. *See* READING HANNAH ARENDT.

Andrew Shea is founder and principal of MANY Design and assistant professor of Integrated Design at Parsons School of Design. His design writing includes the book *Designing for Social Change: Strategies for Community-Based Design* and serving as an editor of *LEAP Dialogues: Career Pathways in Design for Social Innovation*, among others. *See* HUMAN RIGHTS.

Nidhi Srinivas is associate professor of Management at the New School and also teaches at Parsons School of Design. His research focuses on critical theory and approaches to enhancing the capacity of managers and designers to generate socially responsive organizations. He has published widely and been awarded several fellowships. *See* EVIL.

Eduardo Staszowski is associate professor of Design Strategies at Parsons School of Design, and director/cofounder of the Parsons DESIS Lab. He studies design as a method and language, and its role as an intermediary, creating and orienting processes of social innovation and sustainability. He seeks ways to enhance participation in policy development and civic design. Founding editor, *Designing in Dark Times* and *Radical Thinkers in Design*.

Radhika Subramaniam is associate professor of Visual Culture at Parsons School of Design, The New School where she was the first director/chief curator of the Sheila C. Johnson Design Center (SJDC) from 2009 to 2017. Her interdisciplinary practice explores the poetics and politics of crises and surprises through urban crowds, walking, cultures of catastrophe, art, and human–animal relationships. *See ANIMAL LABORANS.*

Virginia Tassinari is a postdoctoral fellow at Politecnico di Milano (It), visiting professor at LUCA School of Arts (Be), and design researcher for Pantopicon (Be), an Antwerp-based foresight and design studio. Her research in design and philosophy has a specific focus on design for social innovation, participatory design, and design activism.

Maurizio Teli is associate professor in Techno-Anthropology and Participation at Aalborg University, Denmark. He works in interdisciplinary contexts focusing on the political dimensions of digital technologies through participatory design. His current interests include design practices aware of socio-ecological inequalities and aiming at counteracting them through social cooperation. *See* THOUGHT.

Mathilda Tham's work constitutes an agile metadesign dance across products, systems, and paradigms to seed change in a broad context of sustainable futures. Current sites include fashion, housing for permaculture, and age creativity. She is a professor of Design, Linnaeus University, Sweden, and metadesign researcher, Goldsmiths, University of London. *See* EQUALITY.

Adam Thorpe is professor of Socially Responsive Design at Central Saint Martins College, University of the Arts London (UAL). He is codirector of the Design Against Crime Research Centre and coordinator of the UAL DESIS Lab (Design for Social Innovation and Sustainability). He is principal investigator of the Public Collaboration Lab delivered in partnership with London Borough of Camden, focused on participatory design for service, social and policy innovation at a local level. Adam's research focus is collaborative design for social impact. *See* POWER.

Cameron Tonkinwise is the professor and director of Design Studies at the University of Technology Sydney. He is also the research director of the Design Innovation Research Centre. Cameron's research and teaching concerns Transition Design—the role human-scale design can play in enabling social system change toward more equitable futures. *See ANIMAL RATIONALE*.

Otto von Busch is associate professor of Integrated Design at Parsons School of Design. In his research he explores how the powers of fashion can be bent to achieve a positive personal and social condition with which the Everyperson is free to grow to their full potential. *See* METABOLISM.

Anne-Marie Willis is visiting professor in the School of Architecture and Built Environment at the University of Adelaide, and former professor of Design Theory at the German University in Cairo. She is the author and editor of several books, the most recent being *The Design Philosophy Reader* (2019). *See* LABOR.

Susan Yelavich is associate professor of Design Studies program at Parsons School of Design. She is a fellow of the American Academy of Rome and the Bogliasco Foundation. Her most recent book is *Design as Future-Making* (2014). Her next book is entitled *Thinking Design through Literature* (2019). *See* STORIES.

Francesco Zurlo (PhD in industrial design) is full professor of Industrial Design at Politecnico di Milano, in the courses of Integrated Product Design and Management Engineering. He is deputy dean of the Design School and head of the Courses in Product Design (BA+MAs) of Politecnico di Milano. *See* INSTRUMENTALITY.